The Wirele
Ala

C000182558

Alan Palmer is the sole author of 35 works, which have been translated into 18 languages and published in 22 countries. He has also worked as a co-author on seven books, five in collaboration with his late wife, Veronica. In 1980 Alan was elected a Fellow of the Royal Society of Literature.

He was born in 1926 at Ilford in metropolitan Essex. His schooling was at Bancroft's, Woodford Green from where he won a scholarship to Oriel College, Oxford. After serving in the navy at the end of the war Alan read history at Oxford getting a First in 1950. He stayed another year at Oriel, completing work for an M.Litt. thesis on diplomatic history, and in September 1951 was appointed Head of History at Highgate School.

Much though Alan enjoyed teaching, he retired in 1969 to become a freelance writer living for 42 years at Woodstock, Oxfordshire. During the original series of the BBC's Mastermind Alan supplied over 3,000 specialist questions, mainly on European history or on London's past. For relaxation he enjoys watching cricket, plays and ballet. Alan has travelled widely, especially in central Europe and the Balkans.

Other titles by Alan Palmer:

The Gardeners of Salonika.
The Macedonian Campaign 1915-1918.
Victory 1918
The Decline and Fall of the Ottoman Empire
An Encyclopaedia of Napoleon's Europe
The Salient. Ypres, 1914-1918
The East End: Four Centuries of London Life
Northern Shores (The Baltic). A history of the Baltic Sea and its peoples
The Twilight of the Habsburgs
Napoleon in Russia
Napoleon and Marie Louise, The Second Empress
The Penguin Dictionary of Twentieth-Century History
Bismarck
Life and Times of George IV (Kings & Queens)
Crowned cousins: the Anglo-German Royal Connection
Banner of Battle: The Story of the Crimean War
Metternich Councillor of Europe
Alexander I Tsar of War and Peace
The Chancelleries of Europe. The working of diplomacy 1815-1918
Bernadotte: Napoleon's Marshal, Sweden's King
Dictionary of British Empire and Commonwealth
The Kaiser: Warlord of the Second Reich.
The Lands Between. A History of East-Central Europe 1815-1965

And with Veronica Palmer:
Chronology of British History
Royal England: A Historical Gazetteer
Who's Who in Bloomsbury
Who's Who in Shakespeare's England
A Dictionary of Historical Quotations

The Wireless in the Corner

A boy's eye view of London in peace and war

Alan Palmer

Matador
9 Priory Business Park,
Wistow Road, Kibworth Beauchamp,
Leicestershire. LE8 0RX
Tel: 0116 279 2299
Email: books@troubador.co.uk
Web: www.troubador.co.uk/matador
Twitter: @matadorbooks

ISBN 978 1788036 320

British Library Cataloguing in Publication Data.
A catalogue record for this book is available from the British Library.

Printed and bound by CPI Group (UK) Ltd, Croydon, CR0 4YY
Typeset in 11pt Aldine401 BT by Troubador Publishing Ltd, Leicester, UK

Matador is an imprint of Troubador Publishing Ltd

MIX
Paper from
responsible sources
FSC
www.fsc.org
FSC® C013604

I dedicate this to Clare and Robert Brown.
With love and gratitude for so many days of pleasure
over the last 30 years.

CONTENTS

PREFACE

This book is the personal account of a boy brought up in London's eastern suburbia during the second quarter of the twentieth century, the years Asa Briggs has called 'The Golden Age of Broadcasting'. It is based upon occasional diary entries, family letters, photograph albums and newspaper cuttings. Above all, it relies on a sharp visual and aural memory.

I am the only child of elderly parents, living at Gants Hill in unfashionable Ilford, eight miles east of the City. Discovering a wider world kept me inquisitive. Among my earliest toys was an enamelled tin globe which I would spin, stop with a finger, and ask: 'What's this place?' One afternoon I surreptitiously opened a drawer in my parents' bedroom and found medals and a crumpled piece of aluminium which my mother said came from a Zeppelin my father saw shot down at Salonika. That led to a series of questions, and I heard about the Great War and the battle fronts where he and my uncles had fought only a few years previously. When I was six we went to Belgium on the first of seven visits to the Continent before war confined us to home shores. I felt so gripped by all that was happening in Europe that observing international affairs became as much a hobby as collecting stamps. I listened to the wireless news bulletins every evening. Any record of my boyhood must therefore be as much personalised political, social and military history as reminiscence.

In writing *The Wireless in the Corner* I have taken care never to invent thoughts based on present assumptions and always to distinguish between what we knew then and what we know now. I give precise dates where possible: chronology brings discipline to historical record and helps a reader relate a particular event to what was happening elsewhere. The strain of the Blitz, and later of flying bombs and rockets, was relieved by moments of peace and contentment so dear to me that I try to recapture them in these pages alongside the days and nights of drama that surround them. Matters that particularly interested me at the time receive fuller treatment than other topics of equal, or arguably greater, importance. I have tried to hold nostalgia in check but I include some light-hearted incidents, for I am convinced that Clio, the Muse who records the Past, possesses a sense of ironic humour which I am happy to respect.

Alan Palmer
Oxford 2017

ACKNOWLEDGEMENTS

My deepest gratitude must be to my mother and father who gave me so many opportunities to indulge my hobbies and took me to places that stimulated a sense of the past which enriched my boyhood.

I could not have completed this book without the practical assistance of Christopher Johnson and the wise counsel of his wife, Charmian Hearne. I also profited greatly from the professional skills and experience of Linden Lawson and Rebecca Fraser.

Among other friends to whom I am heavily indebted are my ex-pupils at Highgate, Tony Lawdham and Lewis Rudd. I welcomed constructive comments from friends who read sections of the book, including David and Jan Bolton, John and Jill Griffin, Miranda Jones, and my niece Catherine Kelsall. Alessandra Bassarovska, Katherine Palmer, Elizabeth Crowley, Elizabeth Maylor and Eleanor Williamson kindly helped me in various ways.

I also benefitted greatly from reminiscences of contemporaries. Chief among them is my oldest friend Derek Tatnall, the 'boy next door' in Ilford. My cousin Madeline Lawson had vivid memories of the London Blitz. So too had Denis and Mary Kendal; Arthur Wallis remembered Essex in the 1930s. Both Mary Cumming and my sister-in-law Anne Connelly shared with me their memories of wartime girlhood.

Sadly many friends with whom I discussed the book have died before I could thank them in print. They include Sir Martin Gilbert, my cousin Joyce Gillatt, my school friend Ted Ellis, and my companion at Oxford and in naval training John Locke.

The custodian of the Cricket Society Library kindly verified details of the 1939 Ilford Cricket Week. I am especially grateful for the assistance I received from the Trustees of the London Library's Carlyle Fund and also for help from staff of the library, of which I was a member for more than 60 years.

The Wireless in the Corner is dedicated to Clare and Robert Brown, who have heartened and encouraged me so often during these last 30 years and who read and discussed much of this book with me as it was being written.

ONE

What's in a Name?

A clammy afternoon at Westminster: the hands of Big Ben, veiled in autumn haze, show the time as 2.25. Off St Thomas's Hospital, moored river steamers are packed with spectators. Office workers linger on Victoria Embankment, their lunch hour long over. Women's cloches sit firmly on shingled hair. Almost every man wears a hat: a bowler, a trilby or on the open top of buses a cloth cap, like the delivery boys and draymen. River and road traffic – petrol driven, horse drawn, electric powered – is at a standstill. An air of expectancy prevails.

Eagle eyes peer downstream into the murk above the East End docks. A speck sharpens into the outline of a biplane with floats. 'There he is!' someone shouts. The pilot passes behind St Paul's, dips wings to salute friends in Fleet Street and veers towards the Thames, the marking G-EBFO standing out clearly on the fuselage. He eases gently down over the Houses of Parliament, turns back to have the flow of the river behind him and lets the seaplane skim as gracefully as a swan to a mooring off the Members' terrace. Cheers ring out; hats wave in greeting. A goggled figure muffled in a flying suit clambers down from the open cockpit. It is 1 October 1926, and Alan Cobham – a 32-year-old Londoner from Camberwell who spent four years on the Western Front – completes the first flight ever made to Australia and back. My father was in Holborn that Friday as G-EBFO flew over the City, my mother's youngest sister among the crowd in Whitehall. Neither could remember a burst of enthusiasm to match this welcome home since the victory parade after the Great War. Sir Alan Cobham – the knighthood followed a few weeks later – had shot to fame with the speed of a comet in orbit. He burst into the papers in 1921 as director of an air-taxi service hired to city-hop a mysterious American 5,000 miles around Europe for purposes unknown. Over the next five years more distant ventures, 'to open up airways of the Empire', made exciting reading in the morning papers. It was however the challenge of Australia and back that caught the public's imagination. In 1919 two Australians, the brothers Keith and Ross Macpherson Smith, returned home from the war by flying from Hounslow to Darwin in 28 days, but no one had as yet completed the round trip.

Cobham never intended to make the journey alone; he sought help for his flight from an expert mechanic, Alfred Elliott. As G-EBFO followed the Euphrates down from Baghdad an Arab sharpshooter, suspicious of British markings four years after RAF bombs quelled an incipient Iraqi revolt, loosed off his rifle at the intruder and hit the rear cockpit. Poor Elliott was dead when the plane reached Basra. The tragedy left Cobham with the triple task of piloting, navigating and maintaining his seaplane for the remaining 25,000 miles of the flight. As he started back from Sydney public sentiment willed him to succeed. Press coverage kept excitement on the boil. Even before Cobham reached Italy he was accepted by Londoners as Man of the Year. 'Alan' had been a not uncommon name since the turn of the century; now there was a rush to bestow it on the autumn's babies. I was one of them, an 'Alan' born in suburban Ilford on 28 September 1926 as the people's hero flew the last lap of his epic adventure. He went on to lift the lid off darkest Africa for Imperial Airways and supervise a 'circus' of skilled pilots who staged air shows across the country, awakening thousands of people to the reality of aviation.

I remain proud to carry the Christian name of the first Englishman to pluck triumph from the skies in time of peace. Yet I am surprised my parents followed the fashion that autumn. Neither was air-minded; Mother never flew in her 68-year life, and when in 1937 Dad and I took what was for both of us a first flight, she watched anxiously until the pilot taxied down again after a mere half-hour circuit over Zeebrugge and the Belgian coast.

They did, however, have a remote romantic association with the conquest of the air. In July 1909 Warwick Palmer and Edie Perriam went on a well-chaperoned holiday to Folkestone a few days after Louis Blériot made the first flight across the Channel, from Sangatte to Dover. They walked by themselves along the cliffs to inspect gashes in the field left by his crash landing. In the relative privacy of their stroll back to Folkestone, Edie accepted

Warwick's proposal of marriage. Perhaps, consciously or subconsciously, this near acquaintance with historic aviation determined the name of their only child, born 17 years later.

Like most youngsters in my age group, I followed reports of pioneer flights by Amelia Earhart, Amy Johnson, Jim Mollison, and Jean Batten, and one of my earliest memories is of Dad twiddling the dial of his wireless set to pick up a commentary from a Schneider Trophy Air Race. But ships and the sea were of greater interest to me. Had I lived in Croydon or Hendon or Hounslow no doubt I should have looked more to the skies but our house at Ilford was only five miles from the sweep of the Thames through Gallions Reach. I grew up to the sound of muffled trumpeting at night from river craft and the sight on journeys to town of coloured funnels and company pennons on ships berthed at the quays of London's lively dockland.

For lively it remained in those years, despite deepening shadows of trade recession. Only think for a moment of the variety of shipping beneath G-EBFO's wings as Cobham flew up the Thames on the Friday he returned from Australia. The Peninsular and Oriental's liner *Kaiser-i-Hind* was heading downriver for Bombay; the Union Castle's *Sandgate Castle* was outward bound for Cape Town; and the British India Line's *Madara* was sailing for East Africa via Suez and Port Sudan. In the King George V Dock the P&O's *Nagoya* was loading ahead of Saturday's departure for Colombo and Calcutta. At Tilbury yet another ship in the P&O fleet was making ready for Fremantle and Sydney. Then there were the merchantmen: vessels from Canada in the Millwall Docks unloading grain by conveyor belt, and timber for stacking in huge sheds on the Isle of Dogs; barrels of tobacco along the quays of the London Dock; a 'banana boat' at Canary Wharf; a ship newly in from Bordeaux with casks of wine at a wharf east of Tower Bridge. Elsewhere the Port of London Authority (PLA) provided for imports of sugar, coffee, tea and rice as well as exports of manufactured goods, electrical appliances, machinery, clothing and many other commodities too.

The banks of the Thames from London Bridge down to Tilbury ensured that London kept its primacy among ports of the world.

Many families in Ilford had work dependent on the docks or on shipping companies. My mother's father Henry Perriam (who lived near us) and his brother Bill (who lodged with us) came up from Devon in 1872 to take desk jobs at wharves in London; both had only recently retired when I was born. Dad's work, however, had nothing to do with the river; he was managing clerk at Martineau and Reid, solicitors in Raymond Buildings, Gray's Inn. It was a sound, secure job which he had held since 1906 and for which he was thankful during the Great Depression.

He needed a pastime for mental relaxation, however. As a young man he played lowly local cricket on Saturday afternoons, but he was 41 by 1926 and rather stiff in the right leg. His interests were necessarily sedentary; he had become a wireless enthusiast. Not as a technician, for he was no scientist. His approach to radio was that of a grown-up youngster playing with a favourite toy. He would knob-twiddle until the right sound came through, then sit back listening contentedly with an air of mission accomplished. If he picked up Hilversum, Paris, distant Vienna or Barcelona he was delighted, even though he could not understand a word he heard; it was, he felt, a good return for the ten-shilling licence fee 'wireless receiver' owners paid the Postmaster General each year.

The Times on the day that I was born advertised a Pelican set, 'complete with loud speaker in cabinet' and 'no aerial required', at a price 'from £19-5 shillings', well over £1,500 by 2016 values. That sum would have been far beyond Dad's means. He made do at first with a crystal set but by the time I was old enough to notice such matters he had acquired at second hand a Pelican, though one long past its prime. Mother mistrusted the set; she insisted that the batteries leaked. I was kept well away from it, just as I was from the gas cooker in the kitchen.

Rather strangely in 1930–31, a time when the Depression dug deepest into people's lives, the sale of wireless sets in the London area steadily rose. There seem to have been two main reasons for the boom: the price of sets fell sharply with the coming of materials other than wood for outer casings; and purchase by instalments, already an American practice for furniture, had arrived in Britain. Perhaps, too, possession of a wireless set raised social standing by a few inches, though not so high as owning a smart and shiny motor-car. Light industry actually expanded, with small firms finding nearby markets in suburbia. By 1931 a company in Kent was mass producing 'the people's set' for five guineas (£5 five shillings). Dad waited another year and then disposed of the Pelican in favour of an eight-guinea 'Ekco' wireless from an Essex factory, inland from Southend. The set was compact and so well made that it was still in service in his bedroom 34 years later. Never once do I recall it needing repair.

At first Mother was no happier with the Ekco than with the Pelican. The wireless was cased in Bakelite, a synthetic resin named after its Dutch inventor, L. Baekeland, and popular in the 1930's. Shiny brown Bakelite did not suit the restful décor of the front room, she insisted, and the newcomer was banished to the top of a small table at the back of the dining room.

Mother was a voracious reader; I suspect she was prejudiced against radio because the noise distracted her from the book on her lap but, if so, the fare the British Broadcasting Corporation offered soon won her over. Sir John Reith, the BBC's director-general, may have seemed to many who served him an arrogant dictator but his mission to spread knowledge of 'endeavour and achievement' possessed an educational purpose of which Mother was bound to approve. She recognised that the BBC's carefully balanced fare – plays, concerts, talks, 'clean' music-hall – enhanced the enjoyment of family life rather than diminished it. Within a month or so the table was brought a few feet forward across the corner of the room and chairs rearranged to give the Ekco pride of place; it is odd that families were in the habit of facing their wireless set long before they had to look from necessity at a television screen. In 1941, when persistent air raids led to many changes about the house, Mother promoted the Ekco to an alcove corner in the front sitting room, with a framed photograph of Churchill smiling from the wall above it. There would be moments in those years when we gathered round the set waiting apprehensively for news but more often, like thousands of other families across London suburbia, we were content to settle back for fun, enlightenment and entertainment. We were rarely disappointed. The eight-guinea Ekco was the best bargain my father ever bought.

TWO

Across the Roding

A visitor to Ilford in my earliest years, coming down from Liverpool Street, would have caught a first glimpse of the town as the train crossed a small river and dismissed it as a place of little interest. To the north a gently sloping hill of Edwardian terraced houses was dominated by St Andrew's, a large red-brick church recently completed. To the south, older buildings on a steeper hill up from the River Roding looked commonplace. Outside the station, the place bustled with metropolitan hustle. Maroon private 'pirate' buses competed for passengers with the more familiar red 'General' buses. Green and ochre tramcars ran down to Barking or up to Barkingside. Taxi-drivers waited, alert for those in too much of a hurry to take bus or tram.

A cinema, the Super, faced the station; a theatre, the Hippodrome, was south of it, above Ilford Broadway. Rival banks – National Provincial, Lloyds, Barclays – seemed to glower at each other from opposite corners of the street. There was a cluster of department stores, different in architectural design and commercial appeal: Wests, with a classical stone façade, was proudly up-market; Bodgers' arcade was cheaper, compact and friendlier; Moultons displayed efficiency, with a network of overhead wires catapulting payments and receipts to and from a cashier, to the fascination of any boy or girl out shopping with Mummy.

In all this activity there was nothing unusual. Many fringe suburbs north and south of the Thames had similar centres. Yet Ilford was not simply a dormitory to accommodate London wage-earners. It had roots deep in the past. Those buildings on the hill up from the River Roding included an eighteenth-century inn and the thirteenth-century brick wall of a hospice that was once a refuge for lepers. Moreover, although the Roding never formed a county boundary – that ran closer to the City, along the banks of the Lea – the river had long marked a social frontier. Once across the Roding, a traveller to Colchester or beyond in the seventeenth century could feel that London was behind him. Here was a small town of character indisputably in Essex, a good place for riders and horses to take a rest. Ilford acquired a *raison d'être*. By the end of the Napoleonic Wars it was reckoned a lively 'respectable roadside town', with about 3,000 inhabitants. Ilford remained a staging post for coaches trundling eastwards well into Queen Victoria's reign. The coming of railways, and in particular the introduction in 1863 of a two penny 'working men's ticket' by the GER (Great Eastern Railway), encouraged families to move out from the East End, a trend that continued into the twentieth century. In 1911 the last census before the Great War recorded that the population had risen to 78,188 men, women and children.

In that year my parents bought their first house, not however in Ilford but in neighbouring East Ham. Mother remained there while Dad was serving overseas but after the war they began, rather slowly, to consider a move. It was a time when around London generally new arterial roads met social needs previously offered by railways. In 1924 work started on the first section of Eastern Avenue, the A11, covering nine miles from Wanstead to Romford. Astute developers quickly bought up land close to the route. Small building firms offered homes more compact in style than their Edwardian predecessors and at an affordable price; they found a ready market. One autumn afternoon in 1924 Mother and Dad took a bus over to north Ilford to see houses on a gently rising slope known on the map as Gants Hill. They liked what they saw, found a bargain house for under £350, and shortly before Christmas moved into no. 38 Clarence Avenue.

The house was small. Upstairs were a bathroom and three bedrooms – I was born in the front one. Downstairs we had a dining room, sitting room, kitchen and an outdoor lavatory, protected from the rain by a small conservatory, no garage, no side entrance, not even a telephone line until after Hitler's war. My bedroom window gave an unbroken view over a triangle of gardens in which roses entwined wooden arches and there was a proliferation of young fruit trees, our contribution being a cherry. Some 50 yards to the left I could see the back of houses in The Crescent, while Blenheim Avenue was to the right, with a bungalow on the corner, breaking the look-alike monotony common to many suburban streets. Treetops in Valentine's Park, less than a quarter of a mile away, formed a greyish-green backcloth to the red roofs of the two roads. Sometimes in clear evening light I spotted rooks wheeling above the last surviving elms of the park's eighteenth-century landscaped garden.

I loved that scene. My den became a playroom, a sickroom and a study. There I dreamt of achievements never attempted and ambitions never fulfilled. The last night I slept there was 31 August 1951, the eve of my marriage to Veronic Cotdell, elder daughter of a vicar in Forest Gate.

Clarence Avenue had more character than roads around it. Half the northern side flanked private tennis courts, with a club's mock-rural pavilion in the centre. No. 38 looked out on these courts. I doubt if the standard of tennis was high. As I grew up, no Joan Hunter Dunn caught the eye and I cannot recall a Perry-esque running forehand or the dainty ground strokes of a budding Bunny Austin. At weekends, balls occasionally shot over the wire fencing and bounced into the privet of our front garden. Until war closed the courts down, I never ran short of all that was needed to practise high catches or play soft-ball cricket with friends in the park.

In those years neighbours remained on surname terms, however close their friendship might be: thus Mr and Mrs Tatnall at no. 40 never addressed my parents as 'Warwick' and 'Edie'. Their son, Derek, was born five months after me and we became natural playmates. Both of us were only children; more unusually, we were only grandchildren, on the distaff side. Derek's grandparents, Mr and Mrs Lloyd, lived at no. 42 and he saw them every day. My family links were almost as tight, for Grandfather Perriam purchased 339 Eastern Avenue, five minutes' walk away; his unmarried daughters Amy (aged 30) and Elsie (26) moved in with their parents. Their married sister Margaret Hubbard and her elderly husband bought 189 Eastern Avenue, opposite the end of The Drive. Uncle Bill, my grandfather's bachelor brother, who was born before the Crimean War, lodged with us, his room next to mine.

This surfeit of loving relatives might have made me a pampered pet. That misfortune was (I hope) avoided, thanks largely to my father's good sense and experience: he was the eldest in a family of nine. My aunts Margaret and Amy were both college-trained no-nonsense school teachers and though Grandfather Perriam was generous by nature he retained a Victorian assumption that the head of a family could expect to have his needs met promptly and his word obeyed. Mother, who was 40 when I was born, was firm, though she may have been over-protective; her anxious 'Do be careful, Alan' sometimes seems to echo down seven decades. I do not think I was spoilt but in the absence of brothers and sisters Mother and Dad inevitably became close companions. Undoubtedly I was a lucky boy, able to enjoy a secure existence and develop interests of my own at a time of insecurity for many less fortunate youngsters.

The distinguished novelist Nina Bawden, who was

born in Ilford a year before me, remembered it in her autobiography as 'ugly and featureless'. Yet I recall Gants Hill in the 30's with affection; it was a good suburb in which to grow up. Traffic was steady along Eastern Avenue but London's arterial tentacles did not yet grip the place. There were few cars in Clarence Avenue. Milk would be delivered each morning on a horse float from United Dairies; the laundry was collected by a horse-drawn London Cooperative Society van on Monday afternoon, and on Saturday I liked to give a lump of sugar to the greengrocer's horse while Mother selected potatoes and vegetables fresh from his owner's farm, a few miles to the east. A rag and bone man, with a sadly skinny horse, would come down the road every few weeks. A knife-grinder, with a lathe, used pedal power. So too, until 1938, did the butcher's boy, cycling round with meat Mother had selected at Mr Martin's shop in Redbridge Lane. Fresh bread and cakes we bought over the counter at a bakery across Cranbrook Road.

On Friday afternoon Mr Polly from Walthamstow arrived with a large, walk-in grocery van. The only other regular internal combustion intruders, Black and White coaches, also came from Walthamstow. They made the top of Clarence Avenue a boarding point for excursions to the coast on summer Saturdays and Bank Holidays. Some neighbours tut-tutted at their presence but I recall with contented nostalgia an outing in August 1935 when Whitstable looked exotic and Herne Bay was not yet Suburbia-on-Sea. I also remember how the journey home brought a first encounter with gridlocked traffic as we approached Blackwall Tunnel.

Locally, Valentine's Park was the great attraction. The gate nearest us opened on to formal gardens laid out by Robert Surman in the reign of George I. There was an artificial canal, with clusters of rhododendron on one bank, a grotto and cascades. North of Valentine's mansion – also early eighteenth century – came a walled garden with a dovecot and neatly trimmed paths bordered by box. From June onwards there was a rich fragrance of roses and wallflowers.

As a youngster I tended to take these delights for granted and hurry on to the open spaces of public parkland; sloping down to a brook, the park remained gloriously Edwardian with a bandstand, bowling greens for ladies and gentlemen, a refreshment room and a lake on which you could either hire a rowing boat or pup-pup-pup around on a tuppenny circuit in a motor launch. Between the bowling greens and Cranbrook Road was the cricket ground, where from 1935 onwards Essex played two county championship matches each May. The Cranbrook fed water to a small pool on which by the age of seven I was happy to sail a toy yacht.

If we wanted fields and farmland, open country was ours in 20 minutes, with a short bus ride to Barkingside and then heading off towards Fairlop. Here there was a cluster of farms on land which a hundred years back in time formed the southern fringe of Hainault Forest, and the plain remained a quiet enclave of rural Essex. We could stroll uphill along a little used road to the fields of Chigwell Row, where the air was good and you looked down on the dome of St Paul's, 12 miles away. There were no high buildings around it. One Sunday afternoon in 1932 we saw an unexpected intruder: the slim leaded pencil outline of the airship *Graf Zeppelin* hovered over the City on a goodwill flight during an interlude of Anglo-German friendship. But normally Chigwell Row trips were uneventful, good for picnics or blackberrying. A bus from The Chequers Inn took us home in half an hour.

Buses played a major role in daily life; I liked to clamber to the upper deck of any we boarded. Our local ones were covered but in several outer suburbs buses remained topless as late as 1932. If caught by a sudden shower, as Grandfather and I were once at Loughton, you protected legs and trousers under a rainproof coverlet fastened to the seat in front. It was assumed you would be wearing a hat or a cap. A few brave souls would nestle under umbrellas and, if the day was windy, hope the driver kept his speed down.

To visit the City we generally took a train to Liverpool Street or Fenchurch Street from Ilford station on the

LNER (London and North Eastern Railway). But my favourite way was by bus from Gants Hill right through to Victoria. In the centre of town all London lay at my feet. Nadezhda Krupskaya, Lenin's wife, describes how, when they were in exile, 'Vladimir Ilyich loved going on long rides about the town on top of an omnibus' because it was possible 'to view the life of the people'. What pleased Lenin in Edwardian London delighted me 30 years later. If the bus could only move forward at a snail's pace so much the better, for it let me follow bowler-hatted City ants hurrying to the Tube: 'Star, Noos, Standurt' came the call from evening paper vendors. Would an ant pause to buy a copy? If so, which of the three? Dad would bring home the *Evening Standard*, but I spotted that *The Star* seemed to be selling well. 'Best for racing tips', I was told years later.

Like most children from suburbia I was taken to the zoo, the main museums, Madame Tussaud's, Westminster Abbey, the Tower of London and St Paul's. Only the National Gallery bored me. I particularly liked the London Museum, then in Lancaster House, where dioramas brought to life the past of the great city through the ages.

One outing took me well away from London. Derek Tatnall's grandfather, Mr Lloyd, who had river connections, once took the two of us down the Thames on the *Crested Eagle* paddle steamer to Chatham Navy Day, the first time I boarded a cruiser and saw the cramped conditions in a submarine. One afternoon Grandfather Perriam took me to the British and Foreign Wharf, where he was a clerk for 50 years and I was content to stand on the quay and count wine casks unloaded off a ship newly in from Bordeaux.

In 1936 a family friend invited Dad, Mother and me to Mount Pleasant Sorting Office, where I was amazed to discover an underground Post Office railway in operation. It linked half a dozen sorting offices and enabled letters and parcels to be carried speedily in electrically operated trains for six and a half miles under some of the busiest roads of the capital, from Whitechapel to Paddington. The train's carriages were small; they reminded me of the seating section on a big dipper. I doubt if a train carried more than a dozen bags of letters or half a dozen bags of parcels but, in the half hour we were there, five or six train loads went through. It was a good way to beat traffic congestion. Small wonder the postal service was so good. Stick a penny stamp on a letter in Westminster at midday and the evening postman would deliver it in Ilford, ten miles away, six hours later. I well remember my grandparents getting cards from 'the girls' (my aunts) saying: 'We've got tickets for a show tonight. Will be home late. Don't wait up.'

Many happenings I cannot date precisely but one event stamped vividly in memory can be verified, for it was covered by all London's papers. On 13 October 1929 I was playing in the back garden when Mother called out from the kitchen, 'Alan, look up in the sky!' From above the trees of the park, majestically and almost noiselessly, a grey airship was heading our way; I could read the figure 'R101' on the fuselage. At first I stood puzzled at the sight, for there was no sound of engines as from an aeroplane, only a low buzz. Then I dashed through the house to see the airship disappear over the tennis courts as it flew back to the especially constructed hangar at Cardington in Bedfordshire. The *Daily Express* records that the flight was the R101's maiden trip, a publicity venture in which 'guest passengers enjoyed a four-course lunch in a five-hour voyage over London and the south-eastern suburbs'.

I was fascinated by what I had seen. For 12 months the family cut out pictures of the R101, inside and outside, for me. Dad would tell me about flights planned to Canada and India. Suddenly, soon after my next birthday, the cuttings stopped coming in and so did all talk of the airship. Then one day I saw for myself a picture of people standing around a model of the R101. Dad explained they were trying to discover why the airship had hit a hill near Paris on its first flight to India and been destroyed. I was wretchedly miserable, as if I had lost a favourite pet. The full extent of the tragedy at Beauvais on 7 October 1930, when 48 people perished in a ball of fire, was kept from me.

Within a week of the R101's 1929 publicity flight came news of the Wall Street Crash, when leading American financial institutions panicked over the fragility of an artificial boom and the New York stock exchange downloaded 13 million shares in a single day's trading. The subsequent withdrawal of American funds to Europe marked the start of a world slump which struck Britain hardest in 1931 and the pound was devalued by 25 per cent.

Such economic problems meant nothing to a five-year-old. The slump did not impinge on our way of life to any great extent; the South-East escaped the blight that fell on the North, the Midlands and much of Wales and Scotland. But trade suffered; there was unemployment in the docks. From Southend Pier I saw lines of ships laid up in the Thames Estuary, and there was another silent line in the River Fal when next we went to Cornwall. Friends in north London were shocked by the destitution of hunger marchers as they passed through prosperous suburbs with a petition for Parliament; but we saw no marchers from East Anglia crossing the Roding. I was however puzzled when Dad said to Mother, 'Poor old Smithy has lost his car.' Presumably Mr Smith was a 'representative' for a firm in difficulties. Lose a car? Surely he knew where he had put something that big?

By 1936 I had become politically conscious and followed the misfortunes of the Jarrow Marchers sympathetically from reports in Uncle Bill's *News Chronicle*, the most liberal-inclined London daily. In 1931, however, I was still a chick pecking the eggshell of political reality. But when a visitor kindly treated me to a copy of *Chick's Own* I brushed the children's weekly aside. 'Soppy,' I scoffed. Very properly I was spanked for not saying 'Thank you'.

Chick or not, it was at this time I sensed something being hidden from me. Mother's lifelong friend, Bessie Skinner, who lived in Osborne Road, Forest Gate, was 'At Home' on Monday afternoons and Mother often took me with her when she looked in upon the gathering. 'Auntie Bessie', as I called her, was invariably kind, taking care I was happy. Generally I 'helped' the maid, Molly, in the kitchen while the guests talked on and on in the sitting room. Molly – young, pretty and very Irish – would recall life in Cork during 'The Troubles'. I did not follow tales she told; I simply liked the music of her words. But one Monday in 1931 Molly was not there. I stayed in the drawing room, fingering picture books. Soon I became bored and I looked around me. Most guests I knew by sight. They came from Auntie Bessie's church. This time, however, I spotted a new face, younger and more expressive than the others. I have no idea what topics they discussed. As with Molly, I tuned in to the newcomer; no lilting brogue this time, though; a gentle voice, occasionally rising in tone. She seemed flustered as I stared intently at her. Who could blame her?

'Who was that funny lady next to Miss Donovan?' I asked Mother on the way home. She knew that by 'funny' I meant 'different' and glanced at me with surprise, simply saying 'She's had a dreadful life', and hastily changed the subject.

The 'funny lady' was not at any more 'At Homes' to which I was taken but by the time I was ten I had ferreted out much about her 'dreadful life'. She was Avis Graydon, only sister of Edith Thompson, a young woman whose folly and fate continue to be associated with Ilford's twentieth-century past.

Shortly after midnight on 4 October 1922 Percy Thompson and his petite, auburn-haired 34-year-old wife Edith were walking back from Ilford station to their home in Kensington Gardens after an evening at a West

End farce. A man leapt out from bushes near their house and plunged a knife several times into Percy's neck before running off. Hysterical screams awoke neighbours who sought to comfort Edith and sent for Percy's brother who lived locally. He told the police he suspected Edith of having an affair with Frederick Bywaters, a P&O line assistant purser seven years her junior, who rented a flat at Upper Norwood.

The police went to Bywaters' flat, where they found passionate letters in which Edith said she was trying to kill her husband, either by poison or by putting powdered glass in his porridge; the letters left no doubt she wanted to spend the rest of her days with Bywaters. He was arrested and taken to Ilford police station, where detectives were already questioning Edith. After further interrogation Bywaters was charged with murder, and Edith Thompson was arrested as his accomplice.

The couple stood trial at the Old Bailey nine weeks after the murder. The only evidence against Edith was the cache of letters, for two eminent pathologists confirmed there were no traces of glass or poisin in Thompson's stomach. Edith's defence counsel showed that Percy Thompson was a bully who had been seen to ill-treat his wife. Against counsel's advice Edith insisted on taking the stand herself and made a bad impression on the jury. Both Bywaters and Edith were found guilty and sentenced to death.

No woman had been hanged in England for 15 years

and there seemed good grounds for a reprieve. Yet, despite widespread sympathy for Edith as a victim of domestic violence she was hanged in Holloway on 9 January 1923, a mere 97 days after the murder. Bywaters died in neighbouring Pentonville a few minutes earlier. At Edith's execution something appalling happened. Almost certainly as the trap of the gallows opened she suffered a miscarriage.

Avis, who was 18 months younger than Edith, had known deep sorrow: the love of her life was killed in 1917 at Passchendaele. Bywaters was a classmate of the sisters' youngest brother and Avis was his close friend until he became fatally infatuated with Edith. She was a defence witness at the trial, pouring scorn on the fantasising letters as 'pure imagination on my sister's part'. As the year ended, she wrote to Bonar Law, the Prime Minister, pleading for mercy on the grounds that the jury had only seen 'the foolish letters of an over-wrought, unhappy woman'.

Most people in East Ham and much of Ilford sympathised with Avis, as did my parents. They were convinced Edith was a victim of social prejudice, guilty of revelling in the sin of adultery rather than incitement to murder. But knife crime in respectable London suburbs was extremely rare. During the Second World War I knew a family in Buckhurst Hill who thought the affair so sordid that it irreparably tarnished Ilford's reputation. By their reckoning I came from the suburb that's 'not quite right', and they made no attempt to hide their sense of superiority over Ilford and everything connected with the town, apart from Wests department store.

It was, however, to north Ilford that Avis and her father retired in 1938. They were living in Roll Gardens when war broke out. Auntie Bessie visited them and noticed a prie-dieu in an alcove with pictures of the sisters together on the wall above it. I recognised Avis shopping with her father at Gants Hill in the spring of 1940, for I had never forgotten her appearance or her voice. Soon afterwards she had a narrow escape when a German plane was brought down and fell on empty shops close to her home, but she survived the war and persisted with her mission to clear her sister's name.

One evening in 1973 I switched on the radio in my study at Woodstock and heard once again that persuasive voice insisting to a sympathetic Audrey Russell that Edith was no murderer. Four years later she died aged 81, to the end an indomitable crusader for justice as she saw it. Her friends succeeded in securing a Christian burial for Edith in 1997 at Brookwood Cemetery.

Mother was right in not attempting to enlighten me about the 'funny lady' to whom I offered a plate of sandwiches at Osborne Road that Monday so many years before. I was too young to understand the concept of murder, let alone the complexities of a *crime passionnel*. But I am glad I met Avis Graydon and am proud that, at such an early age, her personality left a deep impression on me.

THREE

Willingly to School

Valentine's School in Beehive Lane was no show place. It had been built as a church school some 60 years previously and the single storey stone building retained the grime of time. Daylight in the classrooms came from a window set so high it prevented anything outside interfering with the three Rs.

Beyond an asphalt playground were more classrooms in surplus army huts, hurriedly acquired to meet the post-war baby boom. The school's days were numbered and in 1937 it was replaced by a new primary school off Redbridge Lane. Yet when, on my fifth birthday, Mother walked me the half mile to begin my schooling I hopped along the pavement as if I was off to a beach; a school at last; I could hardly believe it .

I was not disappointed. Both years at Valentine's were happy; I liked teachers and classmates. Several youngsters from Clarence Avenue were already there and Derek Tatnall came the following February, as soon as he was five. Teachers were single in those days, though a married ex-teacher might come briefly on supply in an emergency.

Derek and I think we were taught by a Miss Whisker, though she may well have been Miss Whistler. I suspect she was a newcomer trained in fashionable Montessori principles, for she encouraged spontaneity and freedom from restraint. Once, however, her innovative zeal ran awry: to supervise 30-plus five-year-olds 'modelling' Plasticine was inviting trouble. Shaping stringy men and plump women became boring: better far to roll it into tiny balls and drop them down shirts and blouses; I did well at this game. That evening at bath time, Mother found the wretched substance clinging to a clean vest. Other mums too were exasperated. There were complaints. Sadly, Plasticine modelling was a single day's delight.

The second year brought a more traditional approach from Miss Green, a natural teacher who dressed to match her name. We recited the litany of multiplication tables and our reading skills rapidly improved. Yet, once, even Miss Green broke loose from classroom restraint and that was on 24 May 1933, Empire Day.

This anniversary of Queen Victoria's birth was celebrated throughout the sixth of the world she had ruled. In England some schools enjoyed a half-holiday and in deprived areas up north parsimonious councils condescended to treat hungry mouths to a sticky bun. Miss Green's salute to fading imperialism came with the aid of a maypole garlanded with paper streamers around which we frolicked. A photograph shows a golden-haired

Queen of the May proudly surrounded by her court. I am in the front row with a child's violin under my chin, poised to make music. This, however, I did not do; alas, never have I played a stringed instrument. Miss Green, I suspect, cherished the image of the violin prodigy who had won the hearts of motherly music lovers. Why she cast me for that role I have no idea. Apart from a big head, I bore no resemblance to the young Yehudi Menuhin. Miss Green put a record on her portable gramophone and we again danced around the maypole before standing solemnly to attention and singing the first verse of the national anthem, which we knew by heart. Miss Green beamed, content with the cameo her imagination had conjured up. But what can she possibly have seen to link a May Queen, a No Menuhin and King George V's empire?

Soon afterwards my parents took me out of the council school and into the fee-paying private sector. In many ways I was sorry but perhaps I had outgrown the curriculum; I was keen to start learning French. Mother selected Park School where a friend's son was a pupil a few years back and could now even think in French, his mother proudly said. The school comprised two attached late-Victorian houses on Cranbrook Road, opposite the boating lake in the park; the 'only preparatory school in Ilford', a prospectus claimed. Although aspiring to reach the standards expected in a prep school it lacked the tradition, steady income and high principles that motivated the best of them. Boys were prepared for the Essex public schools but not for more famous foundations.

The school uniform was plain, with grey shorts, a black blazer and a cap with PS on it, entwined in decorative script to counter any impression of an afterthought. Once a week we trailed up The Drive in a crocodile to the PLA sports ground, where in summer we played at cricket and in winter kicked a ball about, wearing black and white striped shirts, like Ilford F.C. Small classes enabled us to make rapid progress at basic subjects including French. We heard the legends of English, Roman and Greek history. There was no science and definitely no sex education. Latin provided the greatest fun. Our textbook, *Latin with Laughter*, was illustrated with line drawings. *Julia vaccam amat* (Julia loves the cow), page 3 told us… *Vacca Juliam amat* came the next sentence, assuring us the cow loved Julia too; a marginal picture depicted Julia with her arm fondly round a cow, looking so smug that she must just have broken the high jump record over the moon.

We used to think the headmaster bore a passing resemblance to Will Hay, the subtly ironic straight man of British film comedy, but life was more earnest for our Mr Hughes. His muscular faith prompted him to wield a cane too readily and too hard. Yet he had good qualities too: he was a generous charitable donor to Ilford's new hospital and, though he taught little, as a Licentiate of the Royal Academy of Music he made certain any boy who could, sang in tune, but he did nothing to throw his voice and control his breathing. For this I have always been grateful.

He must also have possessed considerable powers of persuasion. Every year he hired the Cecil Hall community hall in St Clement's Road for The Concert, an occasion when we sang to doting parents and received prizes, if merited. In 1935 this event coincided with the opening of a ward at the new hospital by *the* film star of the year, someone we had seen recently in Hitchcock's *The 39 Steps,* and rumour said she would be at The Concert. We asked a teacher but he said nothing. And so with hair brushed, ties tightened, and kinks pulled out of long socks, off we trailed to the Cecil Hall.

Some forty minutes later we are 'Heigh Ho come to the Fair'-ing when there is a clatter on the uncarpeted stairs. Mr Hughes stops playing, with a definitive chord. A posse of strangers enter and suddenly, to our amazement, we find the rumour is true after all: Madeleine Carroll is there in person, among us on the stage. To her amazement, too, I suspect. For, as I worship my film goddess of the moment from a few feet away, I see her Irish eyes dart quickly about her as if she wonders where she is and why. Mr Hughes welcomes her with rare brevity, we clap madly, she smiles patiently and duly presents the prizes as speedily as courtesy permits. I am so elated at shaking her hand that I do not even glance at the book she hands me but only at her. Then, as swiftly as she came, she and her escort bustle down the stairs. The magic goes from the hall. We are back in the monochrome reality of Ilford on a winter's evening, still heigh ho-ing to that wretched fair. I look at the book's title: *Random Gleanings from Nature's Fields*. Perhaps I will read it one day.

Twelve months later it was time to put Park School and Mr Hughes behind me and move on to secondary education. I was not eligible for Ilford County High or for co-educational Wanstead High, a happy school where Derek Tatnall was to go. Among local independents Bancroft's at Woodford Green had most to commend it, not least because it was easy to reach: a no. 145 bus took only 20 minutes to cover four and a half miles from Gants Hill to a stop in Whitehall Lane outside the school. I was told some years later that at first the fees – a basic £81 per annum for a day boy – made Dad hesitate. He calculated, however, that he could meet the sum if he supplemented his salary by teaching shorthand two evenings a week at an LCC 'night school' in Stepney rather than the one evening to which he was already committed. Grandfather Perriam offered to give me pocket money, a princely half-a-crown a week (two shillings and sixpence, 12.5p), of which one shilling covered bus fare.

It was too late for the main entrance examination but there would be another before Christmas, providing a small intake in January 1937. The thought of becoming a Bancroftian thrilled me, not least because I would wear the long black-striped trousers of manhood in winter and grey flannels to go with a blue blazer in summer, as well as always playing cricket in whites. I never wore shorts again until issued with tropical gear in the navy.

I knew little about the school and nothing of the benefactor whose name it preserves. Like many similar foundations, Bancroft's owes its inception to a London worthy who wished to approach death with a trouble-free conscience. In 1720 Francis Bancroft, a canny revenue official in the Lord Mayor's household, had the good sense to retire just before the South Sea Bubble burst. Eight years later he died, leaving most of his £28,000 fortune in trust to the Drapers' Company to found a school and almshouses in what became the East End.

'Bancroft's Hospital', as it was originally called, flourished at Mile End for a century and a half. Old prints show an attractive Georgian building facing a long lawn with a group of almshouses on either side but by 1880 Victorian industry's sooty fallout was attacking the fabric of the school and almshouses, and 17 weeks in which a grey, yellow, choking fog enveloped the East End spurred the Drapers' Company to decisive action. They looked towards Essex, the county from where Francis Bancroft had derived most of his income, and a new Bancroft's School opened in 1889 at the northern fringe of Woodford Green.

I had seen the school many times before Mother took me there for the entrance exam on 2 December 1936. Two years previously Auntie Bessie had moved from Forest Gate to Woodland Way, backing on to Knighton Wood, south of the main school entrance. The architect, Sir Arthur Blomfield, took full advantage of the site, high on a ridge, that carries the historic road to Ware and Cambridge through Epping Forest; trees and bushes come down to the school boundary. As he drafted plans at home in metropolitan Surrey, Blomfield may have found inspiration in Hampton Court, for Bancroft's is strongly reminiscent of Wolsey's magnificent palace; a red-brick gatehouse with a three-storey tower 80 ft high, battlements, mullion windows and corner turrets.

About two dozen mothers and their offspring clustered under the tower that December afternoon. We boys were taken into a hall, cold and barn-like; I was too young to appreciate the hammer-beam roof. All that registered with me were rows of desks with sunken ink-wells and facing us on a dais a gowned figure, the headmaster; he looked taller than any previous teacher I had met.

Thomas Grantham Wells, a scholar with an Oxford Double First in Greats (Classics), was appointed head in 1931, aged 29. He immediately began to raise Bancroft's educational standard to an unprecedented height. He was a true classicist, who gave his spare moments to the beekeeping commended by Aristotle and celebrated by Vergil in the *Georgics*. Some elderly masters, particularly war veterans, did not give 'young Wells' the support he deserved but he was a shrewd talent spotter and he brought in gifted newcomers. Here, the school governors felt, was a great headmaster in the making.

Disastrously, four years after his appointment, Mr Wells made an error of judgment that unleashed tragedy. Examination of the annual accounts for 1934 led him to suspect pilfering was rife in the kitchens. He called in the local police, and the school matron, her brother-in-law and the cook were arrested. On 27 February 1935 the matron came before the Stratford magistrates charged with stealing a pie, a haddock and dripping. The value of the theft can hardly have been more than £1 but her appearance in court left the matron with a deep sense of shame. Next day she was found dead on Wimbledon Common, having poisoned herself.

The London evening papers gave the affair wide publicity and rounded on Mr Wells for pressing charges over such a trivial matter. He was appalled by the chain of events, retreating whenever possible from the public eye. A few months later he married but his wife was shy and frail in health. Two sons were safely born, a third died in infancy. In 1943 Mrs Wells gave birth to a daughter but contracted pneumonia during convalescence and never recovered. Her husband found a nurse and friends who took care of the children while he sought to carry on. The task was beyond him. On 11 September 1943, a week before the start of term, he spent an hour coaching a pupil who was seeking (successfully) an open classics scholarship at Oxford. Then he walked across to the chemistry laboratory and swallowed prussic acid, meticulously washing the glass before collapsing on the floor. He was seven weeks short of his 42nd birthday. His death was a tragic loss, not only to his family, but to a school that must always remain grateful for his academic legacy.

I knew nothing of Mr Wells' background when I took the examination, though I felt awed by his glacial solemnity. The exam was straightforward: some simple sums and a question to test our literacy; we were to write about any figure in English history who interested us. While we scribbled away, Mr Wells summoned us up to the dais one by one. 'Who are you writing about?' he asked me. 'Julius Caesar, sir,' I replied, adding that I was much more interested in Napoleon but *he* wasn't part of English history. 'Do you think Caesar was?' he queried. 'Yes, sir,' I explained; 'he landed in Kent, and Napoleon didn't.' The stern expression mellowed, with a slight smile; he gave a nod of approval which I interpreted as a sign to go back to the desk.

When we rejoined our mothers, some seemed strangely solicitous. Over tea and scones at Auntie Bessie's, mine explained to me that after our departure, they were standing in the quadrangle when a grim-faced senior boy emerged from a room on the far side with a cane in his hand and walked purposefully past them to a door beside the one through which we had entered the hall. She was amused by what seemed to her a young man's gesture of self-importance. Long afterwards, during discussion of a planned school history, I recalled the episode and found that the cane carrier was Frank Winmill, who was present that evening. It was, Frank told me, a joke to raise a frisson of alarm among loving mums. This it certainly did; but with three years of Park School behind me Frank's action didn't strike me as odd. After all, the school colours *were* black and blue.

On 16 January 1937 I was back again, one of four boys successful in the examination. George Haines, school porter for the past 50 years, took the four of us to Form 1's French class, taken by Mr Jenkins. 'So you are the new boys?' he said. 'Humph! Ugly bunch, aren't you? Ah, well,' he sighed resignedly; 'sit down the front.' In later terms I profited from Ifor Jenkins' wide range of interests:

a love of France past and present, French songs and French wines, as well as playing the double bass and supporting Llanelli Rugby Club; a delightful man, his lessons were salted with dry humour. But that first greeting hardly put us at ease.

Settling in took at least two terms. Bancroft's was a small school, with less than 300 day boys, 100 boarders and a teaching staff of 20. But, like any independent school, it had accumulated arcane traditions tightly preserved: the half envious contempt of boarders for day boy 'new bugs'; 'quad walks', when a minor offender had to go round and round the quadrangle for half an hour in enforced silence; school monitors who could administer beatings for such grave offences as dropping litter in the locker room or, worse still, taking a shortcut across the cricket square, the carefully tended First XI pitch on the main field. There was also a strange argot to learn. Masters had nicknames, generally opprobrious and prompted by their surname: thus Messrs Herring, Stainsby and Belchamber became Fishy, Oily and Burp. Changing rooms were 'swappers', an asphalt playground 'the assy'. Newly built boarders' lavatories were dubbed ironically 'the palace' while we day boys made do with 'bogs', like any other school. At first I could not understand references to 'Vis Day'; it stood, I soon discovered, for July's annual 'Visitation Day' – the prize-giving occasion known as 'Speech Day' in most schools. The name was retained as a relic from the Bancroft's Hospital era.

Moving around to different venues proved a particular problem, as it must to newcomers at any secondary school.

To walk to the farthest playing field, at West Grove, south-east of Woodford Station, took almost half an hour and, except in cross-country running weeks, was made every Tuesday and Thursday. School rugby XVs and cricket XIs turned out on Saturday afternoons too, playing on the field beyond the quadrangle, looking towards the Lea valley.

The internal geography of the school itself had to be mastered speedily or you were in trouble. Woe betide a boy who dallied on his way to the chaplain's class! The Revd Arthur Stainsby – cassock-clad whether teaching English, Geography or Divinity – gave a whack with a hammer handle across the backside of late comers. As chaplain, however, he was a good pastor, ready to accommodate individualistic spiritual practices within the evangelical ethos of public school religion. Thus in 1942 his confirmation class concentrated, not on a devotional book, but on the teachings of Archbishop William Temple's *Christianity and Social Order*. 'Sensible of him; couldn't have done better,' a very senior retired bishop commented 62 years later.

All who enjoyed schooldays remember with gratitude teachers whose character and influence shaped their lives. For me, three masters stand out in my memory: Ifor Jenkins, of course; E.T.S. Wheeler, the head of English; and D.C.R. Francombe, who taught Latin and much else besides, including singing. 'Boss' Wheeler was a Flanders veteran who had first been educated at the church school in Gloucester Green, Oxford, and retained the burr of his native county throughout his life. He loved not only Shakespeare and Chaucer but essayists from Bacon down to 'Alpha of the Plough' (A.G. Gardiner), and he encouraged me to write and read widely. So too did Donald Francombe, the most gifted of all our teachers, a stimulating and gently provocative conversationalist with a natural wit, never malicious. The actor Denis Quilley, some months my junior, rightly paid tribute to him in *Happiness Indeed, An Actor's Life*. As producer of the school plays in which Denis began his career, Don Francombe triumphed over wartime restrictions, particularly with a fast-moving *Androcles and the Lion.*

The longest lasting friendships I made were with boys who entered Bancroft's in 1939, with the upheaval of war: Desmond Perry came from Cooper's School and Ted Ellis from Newbury Park. Another newcomer in 1939 was Richard (Keir Pethick) Pankhurst, son of Sylvia Pankhurst, the socialist second daughter of Mrs Emmeline Pankhurst, leader of the militant suffragettes. His father was Silvio Corio, an anarchist who sought refuge in England ahead of the establishment of Fascism in his native Italy.

I became friendly with Richard soon after he arrived at Bancroft's, though we did not so much do things together as simply talk, mostly about politics and recent history. I was fascinated by mementoes he showed me from his mother's visit to Moscow soon after the Bolshevik revolution, when she met Lenin. On her return to England she helped found a British communist party. Evidently her independent spirit was too much for her comrades who within a few weeks expelled her from the party; 'I was more communist than they were,' she told me. I remember her as imperiously gracious, her face leathered by the strain of 35 years of vigorous campaigning for causes in which she passionately believed. During the time Richard was at Bancroft's she was supporting the cause of the exiled Emperor Haile Selassie of Ethiopia. On his return to a country liberated from Italian rule she raised funds for a hospital and, after the death of Richard's father in 1954, she and her son settled in Addis Ababa. There Sylvia was widely respected and on her death in 1960 she was given a state funeral. I met Richard and his wife in London a few months later but to my regret have lost contact with him since then.

In one respect I was luckier than these wartime arrivals at Bancroft's for I had come there in time for the school's 1937 bicentenary celebrations. The ever-generous Draper's Company donated £50,000 for new buildings. We gained art rooms, a woodwork shop and additional science laboratories. At the same time the hall where I sat the entrance exam was drastically changed, with a false floor giving it two storeys. It housed a spacious library, with a good history section and an ever-expanding collection of books on cricket that went back beyond *The Age of Grace*. On Visitation Day 1937 the Earl of Athlone laid the foundation stone of a new Great Hall which was built with astonishing speed. It was as good as a medium-sized theatre with a permanent stage, a gallery, a sloping floor and chairs for an audience of over 900 people. When in 1945 Mr Churchill received the Freedom of Wanstead and Woodford the ceremony was held in Bancroft's Great

Hall because there was no assembly place so spacious elsewhere in his constituency.

Unfortunately my mother's first visit to the Great Hall coincided with the Munich crisis. As war clouds gathered over Czechoslovakia in September 1938, parents were invited to the hall to hear details of the plans for evacuation; Mother went on her own because Dad was teaching that evening in Stepney. She heard that Bancroft's would be evacuated to a Drapers' Company girls' school in North Wales. Parents were told what each boy would need to take with him. She returned with a sheaf of notes. She need not have bothered. Two days later the crisis deflated. It was, however, too late to change my twelfth birthday: a torch, woollen gloves, a hand towel and a small blanket; books followed once the daily routine returned to normal.

Most independent schools continued to prepare for a war their governors thought inevitable. In some, work began on air raid shelters; others rehearsed action to take in case of an 'alert'. At Christ's Hospital there was a practice blackout. In metropolitan London arrangements for evacuation were completed jointly by governors and headmasters: Westminster School would double up with Lancing College; Dulwich with Tonbridge; St Paul's with Marlborough. At Highgate the headmaster, Geoffrey Bell, sensed the approach of war as early as May 1938 and during the Munich crisis an advance party, 100-strong, reconnoitered Westward Ho!, where the school did indeed go 12 months later.

By contrast, Bancroft's did nothing, outwardly. The

word 'evacuation' was never mentioned. We learnt much later that this apparent inaction was caused by an on-going dispute with the Board of Education. Was Bancroft's in inner London, in which case the 1938 proposed move to Wales would be implemented? Or was it in rural Essex, where evacuation was optional? Essex finally won but the problem was not resolved until after the end of term. Only then did work begin on providing air raid shelters.

School life continued as normal through the summer. On Visitation Day in July, I won a prize for English Subjects and we enjoyed lunch in a marquee on the school field. I was in high spirits, elated in a 'Hooray for the hols!' mood. Eight weeks without schooling lay ahead.

I miscalculated. At the end of the sixth week came war; the start of term was delayed for a month. Not until 18 October were the shelters considered safe for the school to re-assemble. Even though I had a gas mask in a box over my shoulder as well as carrying my school bag, it felt good to head back after so long a break. That morning I clambered up the bus stairs more willingly than ever.

FOUR

Children's Hours

The process of learning has never been limited to what was taught within a school, and by the early 1930s the knowledge and specialised skills long passed on to boys and girls from parents, family or friends could be supplemented at home by radio. The Calvinistic mission-inspired mind of Sir John Reith, director-general of the BBC from 1926 to 1938, brought order and purpose to any wireless venture. Thus in 1927 was born *Children's Hour*, a programme that welcomed boys and girls into a family of surrogate uncles and aunts with high moral standards. Against all the odds, it survived, cosy and clean, into the swinging 1960s, with only a few discreet modifications. At its peak in the last pre-war years *Children's Hour* could attract 4 million listeners.

Like many youngsters, my earliest memories are of *Toytown*, a favourite with many adults too. But *Children's Hour* also offered more mentally stimulating entertainment: plays, readings from children's books and, above all, weekly 15-minute talks by specialists. On Mondays David Seth-Smith, the 'Zoo Man', would tell us about animals and birds in their habitats as well as in zoological gardens. Then on Wednesdays we had 'the Stargazer', Lieutenant-Commander Gould, who talked not only about the galaxies but weather phenomena, too. One afternoon in 1935 he suggested that just possibly a man might land on the moon before the end of the century. 'There, Alan, think of that,' Mother said. I duly thought but not for long. I have never fancied science fiction. Thirty-four years later Neil Armstrong, then a toddler in Ohio, was to confound my doubts.

The outstanding specialist was Commander Stephen King-Hall. On Fridays between 1930 and 1937 he made world politics comprehensible to youngsters. From him I gained some understanding of the League of Nations, was prompted to find Abyssinia in my atlas and seek to follow the war waged there by Mussolini's fascist legions, discovered how British and American concepts of democratic government differed, and first heard of Franklin D. Roosevelt and the New Deal.

King-Hall's microphone style was unique and by modern standards patronising, yet the breezy, no-nonsense quarter deck manner with which he tackled complex international issues was reassuring. Ironically, though spared the absurdity of 'uncle'-ing, he was by nature the most avuncular of *Children's Hour* personalities; each Friday he signed off with the same message to his youngest listeners: 'Be good but not so *very* good that someone at once says to you, 'Ah, and now what mischief have *you* been up to?'

One of my ambitions was to visit Broadcasting House

and watch a programme put out. A chance came shortly before the war, thanks to a general knowledge competition for under-14s. Answers were sent in over several weeks by post. The prizes – a silver pencil and an artistic collage of story-book characters – would be presented in a *Children's Hour* broadcast during the school holidays. I won the boy's prize and was invited up to Portland Place in January 1939, accompanied by a parent. Even in the fading light of a wet winter afternoon Broadcasting House looked imposing, the pristine whiteness of its stone still repelling heavy rain despite seven years of London fumes and smog. Mother and I entered beneath Eric Gill's punning sculpture of Prospero sending Ariel out into the world. Sir John Reith's term as director-general had ended in June but his influence remained omnipresent. There hushed bustle, almost reverential. Along the wall of the reception hall ran a Latin inscription which I tried to translate as we waited. I had got as far as a dedication to Almighty God of 'This temple of the arts and the muses', when a young 'aunt' greeted us and introduced the girl winner and her mother to me. We went down in a lift to the sub-basement, then along a thickly carpeted corridor to Studio 2BB, the silence broken only by a faint rumble of a train on the Bakerloo Line, not far below.

The studio surprised me by its size; I had expected a box-like affair. 2BB seemed spacious. It even had a gallery, where our mothers were given seats. At the start of the programme 'Uncle Mac' presented my girl companion and myself with the prizes; we thanked him, speaking into the microphone, and were then led up carpeted stairs to sit with our mothers and watch *Toytown* unfold. At a quarter to six we hurried down from the gallery to collect autographs in the studio before heading for the nearest Lyons teashop well content. The visit left me with a lasting admiration for the courage and tenacity of Derek McCulloch, 'Uncle Mac'. From a broadcast feature on the Battle of the Somme I knew that in 1916 he had been gravely wounded and lost the sight of an eye, and in the spring of 1938 I read in the *Evening Standard* of an accident on a Greenline coach at Banstead which necessitated the amputation of his left leg. Yet, only some nine months after the operation, here he was in Studio 2BB greeting us, bleating Larry the Lamb in *Toytown* and directing the programme with the energy of a fit man. I did, however, notice that several times he screwed up his face, unable to conceal spasms of pain.

Some 40 years later I had a chance to finish reading the Latin inscription in the reception hall. 'May all that denies peace and purity be banished from this place' in favour of 'what is beautiful, honest and of good report', ran the last sentence. These were noble aspirations for the BBC to uphold, a prayer that preserved Reith's sense of mission through the World War and into the Cold War that followed it. But standards of morality change rapidly: what is sacrosanct to one generation becomes humbug to the next. Small wonder 'the Beeb's' critics came to refer to Reith's creation as 'Auntie'.

Producers began cautiously challenging Reith's earnest restraint while he was still in office. *Band Waggon*, the hit comedy show of 1938-39, was the most enjoyable of pre-war entertainment programmes and yet it was set – almost sacrilegiously – in a fictitious flat on the roof of Broadcasting House accommodating 'Big Hearted Arthur' Askey and 'Stinker' Richard Murdoch. Their domestic needs were met by Norah Bagwash, radio comedy's earliest charwoman. In one programme Norah accidentally discovered a magic stain-remover which the flat's residents thought could be promoted by the slogan 'Askeytoff will get it off'. An enterprising shop put a substance labelled Askeytoff on its shelves before the end of the week. A threat of legal action ensured it was hastily removed: Auntie Beeb was not amused.

Other shows we heard avoided any such faux pas. On Saturdays Eric Coates's *Knightsbridge March* was faded out, so that we could 'meet some of the interesting people *In Town Tonight*'. Two evenings later we tuned in to a magazine programme, *Monday Night at Seven,* an odd medley that made good listening. It included a rag and bone man who soliloquised 'day after day, as I'm on my way', and 'Inspector Hornleigh Investigates', an ingenious detective puzzle for listeners to solve each week. The clue to the identity of the culprit was always a verbal factual slip. In seeking to identify 'this week's deliberate mistake' we became wireless Dr Watsons.

Paradoxically, lazy listening stimulated a growing interest in outdoor sport. The *Radio Times* helped readers ahead of major Rugby Union matches by printing a rectangular diagram divided into eight squares. During the game a sepulchral voice in the background would enable listeners to keep up with play by interjecting 'Square 5' or 'Square 2', etc. as the commentator was reporting a scrum, a line-out, or three-quarters passing the ball across as they ran forwards. This was a highly effective way of making a match audibly visual. I do not think there was a similar method covering football matches. Perhaps the cut and thrust of soccer is easier to envisage.

Less time was devoted to cricket than later in the century; commentaries fitted into scheduled slots and lacked the clubbable effervescence of *Test Match Special*. I do, however, recall hurrying home from school on a Monday in June 1934 in time to hear that Hedley Verity had taken seven wickets in an hour to give England its only Ashes Test victory at Lord's during the twentieth century. Although Verity was a Yorkshireman and I felt a natural loyalty to my native county, he became a cricket hero of mine and I continued to follow Yorkshire's fortunes closely until the very eve of war. Of course, when Essex brought championship cricket to Ilford in Silver Jubilee year I was there to support them, clapping madly at the cavalier hooking of Jack O'Connor and the relaxed speedy accuracy of Stan Nichols' bowling.

Like so many of our generation, Derek Tatnall and I had collections of lead soldiers. They were intended for re-enacting battles or colourful parades. But our armies fought no modern wars. They had an auxiliary function. The ones with bent arms carrying rifles were seconded as batsmen in a table cricket game Derek and I invented, with matchsticks as bats and particularly small marbles 'bowled' by us at matchbox wickets. The matchsticks were inserted in the bend of the arm; one of us held the soldier between our fingers and played scoring strokes; the other held a non-bent-arm soldier as a bowler/fieldsman and if he was moved quickly enough along the table to take the ball on his chest, the batsman was out 'caught'. As often as not the batsman kicked the ball away from the wicket and play was interrupted by noisy 'leg before wicket' disputes. This fantasy cricket was a travesty of the finest of sports but it had the advantage of being playable in bad weather or during the winter.

There were many personal 'children's hours' like this: times spent amusing ourselves at home. Both of us had a model theatre. Dad made mine, with plywood, a fretsaw and plenty of glue; Derek's was a fine affair, in the 'penny plain, tuppence coloured' tradition associated with Benjamin Pollock of Hoxton. The great man did not die until we were 11 and so some of the scenery and cut-out figures may have been Pollock originals. Derek, who in later years became an architect, practised his skill on additional scenery while I wrote some scripts, though we often improvised, just for our own amusement.

Birthday or Christmas parties in the mid-30s tended to be jelly, trifle and creamy cake affairs, with less sophisticated entertainment than youngsters expect in the cyber digital era. Every household seemed to possess a piano, generally an upright, though Auntie Bessie had a compact grand. 'Musical chairs' was therefore a party stand-by. Occasionally a boy or girl would play a piano solo, and I was guilty of inflicting songs on our guests, with Mother playing the accompaniment. But there was fun in store for them, too. Mrs Tatnall's brother would provide a screen and projector for hired Charlie Chaplin or Buster Keaton films. I was extremely lucky, for Dad's brother Warren was a first-rate conjuror, a skilled member of the Magic Circle whose tricks enthralled us year after year. He would discover china eggs behind our ears, make badges and brooches disappear from a box and restore them at the tap of a wand, and garland a stage, large or small, with an endless chain of handkerchiefs pulled from his hat. He and Aunt Beattie lived in Ilford and we saw them and their children, my cousins Jean, Tony and Madeline, frequently. Jean was a year older than me and had a daredevil quality in her character that made me think her wonderful.

For a long time one prized suburban accessory was missing in our household. The Greys at no. 44 Clarence Avenue had a dog; so did the Tatnalls at no. 40 and the Smiths at no. 34; the Palmers at no. 38 did not. But at last, to my delight, in the spring of 1936, I was given a puppy, a present from my Palmer grandparents who lived on the Suffolk-Essex border. He arrived in a basket dropped off by my father's brother, Albert, as he drove his family home to Devon. The newcomer stepped unsteadily towards the front door, paused, and put his head ruminatively on one side as he saw a spider climbing the wall. That decided his name; 'Bruce'

he must be, for Scotland's King Robert the Bruce is the
only legendary hero inspired by the persistence of a spider.
But from what canine clan did the puppy come? Uncle
Warren knew; 'He's a Suffolk tripe hound,' he solemnly
assured me. Why, I wondered, did people laugh when they
asked me his breed and got that as an answer?

Bruce became my closest companion, getting me away
from the wireless and into the park, where he rambled
in thickets I would never have thought of penetrating.
He was a small, sleek brown terrier – at least that was his
colour so long as his liking for green slimy ditches could
be held in check. Probably my dog-yearning sprang from
the misadventures of William Brown and his Outlaws in
Richmal Crompton's books. Bruce was to me a Valentine's
Park incarnation of Jumble, William's devoted mongrel.
The 'gang culture' in which the Outlaws flourished was
as natural and harmless as the penknife that William,
like me, carried stuffed away in a pocket. My knife had
a hooked scalpel for getting stones out of horses' hooves
attached to it, an emergency that never arose. What a lucky
generation we were! No paedophile shadow encroached
on our movements: think of the freedom that Arthur
Ransome's Swallows and Amazons enjoyed, unmolested
in the Lake District.

Books for children about children were never a British
monopoly. Apart from Tom Sawyer I did not think much
of the American tales, but one book from Continental

Europe I particularly liked. Erich Kästner's *Emil and the Detectives* had been published in Berlin in 1929 and was translated soon afterwards. It describes how, in pre-Nazi Germany, a gang of children tracked down a thief who had picked young Emil's pocket while he dozed in a Berlin train. By their ingenuity the children were thus able to unmask and catch a wanted bank robber. I warmed to the characters, just as I had to William's Outlaws: Emil Tischbein, the country boy making a first visit to the big city; his cousin Pony Hütchen, proud of her new bicycle; and mischievous Gustav, the young Berliner with a motor horn. The novelty of the setting, a foreign capital so unusual that it could name a major railway station 'Zoological Gardens', intrigued me. I did not know that by the time I discovered *Emil*, the book was already banned in Germany and publicly burnt by fanatical Nazis: Kästner was a liberal-minded writer who despised political pretence and saw no reason to compromise his beliefs. When Hitler came to power, Kästner settled in Switzerland. Kästner outlived the Führer by almost 30 years; the young detectives he created deserve to live on forever.

By 1936 I was spending hour after hour with eyes glued to a book. Ilford's enlightened borough council appreciated the value of reading for young and old. There was a well-stocked central library in Oakfield Street, south of the High Road, and in 1938 a branch library opened in Cranbrook Road North, within easy walking distance of home. For the next seven years I profited greatly from up-to-date non-fiction shelved at this Gants Hill branch.

We had plenty of books at home. The most attractively produced were two sets of novels made available very cheaply to subscribers who read the *Daily Express*. The complete works of Dickens were bound in eye-catching blue. Other prose authors including Thackeray, Jane Austen and Walter Scott were in pillar-box red. I was also beginning to build up a library of my own, partly by discovering the excitement of browsing in Foyle's when we were in town, but also thanks to Allen Lane's paperback revolution of 1935 which, as André Maurois quipped, made Britain 'a penguin island'. My earliest Penguin is H.C. Armstrong's *Grey Wolf,* a biography of Mustafa Kemal Ataturk, with the date of purchase scribbled on the flyleaf as July 1937, 16 months before Kemal's death.

For leisure hours we often went to the 'flicks'; the 1930s were peak years for the film industry. Luckily we could visit the Super, an elegantly spacious Gaumont cinema opposite Ilford station, or from 1934 the Savoy, at the apex of Eastern Avenue and Perth Road in Gants Hill. I was thrilled by early Hitchcocks and picked up some American slang from the Hollywood invasion but made certain I never missed a good English Will Hay comedy. Many films I liked were frothy and lightly operatic: the tenor Richard Tauber in *Land without Music* and the soprano Deanne Durbin in *Mad about Music*, for example. For me, however, the outstanding British triumph of the decade was Anthony Asquith's 1938 version of Bernard Shaw's *Pygmalion,* with Leslie Howard as Professor Higgins and Wendy Hiller as Eliza Doolittle. Shaw added additional dialogue and won an Oscar but is said to have thought

Leslie Howard made Higgins more attractive than the egocentric academic created for the stage but audiences loved Howard's Higgins, and Anthony Asquith's film too.

Theatre-going I associate mainly with the West End at Christmas. I remember pantomines at Drury Lane, *Peter Pan* at the London Palladium, and the fascination of the revolving stage at the Coliseum. We had first seen it used in the autumn of 1936 for *The Desert Song* but it was more effective when *Cinderella* was presented that Christmas. In 1937 the application of refrigeration to half the stage enabled the Coliseum to present London's first 'ice spectacle', *St Moritz*, which I thoroughly enjoyed. My Christmas treat a year later came outside traditional theatreland. We went to the Victoria Palace to see Lupino Lane as Bill Snibson 'doing the Lambeth walk' in *Me and My Girl*. The play continued its run there until the coming of war.

Yet the finest 'theatre' London offered needed no stage. It was played out along The Mall and Whitehall, on Horse Guards Parade or at Westminster Abbey and St Paul's. London in my boyhood remained the capital city of a great empire. We could watch the rich pageantry of state for no cost beyond the fare to town. During the 1930s there was plenty in the royal peepshow for us to see and hear.

FIVE

The King Riding By

At the start of the twentieth century there were 43 empires, kingdoms, duchies or sovereign principalities in Europe and only two large republics, France and Switzerland. A third of a century later the empires had gone; there were still 13 hereditary rulers, one self-proclaimed king in Albania, and in Hungary a vacant throne under a nominally elected regent who was an admiral without a fleet. In the remaining 15 states, republicanism prevailed.

In London, however, the throne seemed as secure as ever. When King George V and Queen Mary travelled around England, Scotland and Wales they were received with a natural deference that bordered on affection; only in the Irish Free State was there a strong nationalist republicanism. Their two eldest sons were also widely popular. As a roving ambassador Edward, Prince of Wales, could, when he wished, radiate charm. Prince Albert, Duke of York, enjoyed respect, both as a family man and for seeking each summer to break barriers between boys from working-class families and those from independent public schools at his camp, generally held at Southwold.

By the early 1930s even scoffers in fashionable society condescended to treat the monarchy with resigned tolerance.

At heart King George V was a Norfolk squire, devoted to his wife and the wellbeing of their children, even if he did not always understand them. Socially he was conservative, culturally a philistine, as Queen Mary commented more than once. He was happiest at the helm of his yacht *Britannia* in Cowes Week or stalking deer at Balmoral, though he was glad to go into residence at Sandringham, where he would shoot partridges, snipe and pheasant while taking a paternal interest in the welfare of workers on his estate. Ever since he was commissioned as a naval cadet at the age of 12, King George's life had been shaped by the obligations of a recognised code of service. In 14 years at sea he became accustomed 'to mixing with my fellow creatures', as he once explained to the first Labour prime minister. Three days after his death in January 1936 the socialist *New Statesman* mourned the passing of a 'country gentleman', a ruler whose 'industry and devotion to duty were beyond praise'.

His naval background helped the king establish a rare empathy between sovereign and subjects. With them he suffered all the vicissitudes of the Great War. Twice he crossed to France and Flanders, on the second occasion being forced to return to England on a hospital ship after his chestnut mare slipped in the mud and rolled on top of him. On the Home Front he conscientiously toured munition factories, where he would speak encouragingly to the workers, and visited charitable enterprises and the wounded in hospital. Queen Mary generally accompanied him on these sad engagements.

This modern variant on the royal progresses made by sovereigns in earlier centuries continued in the immediate aftermath of war. No previous monarch was known by sight to so many of his or her subjects. Yet if King George was *seen* by thousands of people in the second half of his reign he was *heard* by millions. His voice first crackled through early wireless sets at the opening of the British Empire Exhibition at Wembley in April 1924 and over the following years he grudgingly accepted the presence of a microphone at official engagements. He disliked both public speaking and technological innovation and repeatedly resisted attempts to induce him to broadcast directly to his subjects. However, with the opening in 1932 of the BBC's Empire Service from a powerful new transmitter at Daventry, he agreed to send a message from Sandringham to his peoples across the world on Christmas Day.

The broadcast was a great success. The text, drafted by Rudyard Kipling, came to no more than 250 words, simple but vividly evocative: 'I speak now from my home and from my heart to you all, to men and women so cut off by the snows, the desert or the sea that only voices out of the air can reach them.' The King read his message slowly but very distinctly; he spoke in a natural baritone, ideal for the wireless. Appreciative letters arrived, not only from homes in the British Isles, but from excited listeners in the dominions, colonies and the Indian sub-continent. King George recognised that he had harnessed a new institution which would tighten the bonds of imperial monarchy. With some reluctance he accepted the obligation to speak to his subjects at Christmas year after year.

I saw the King for the first time on his 68th birthday, 3 June 1933, ten days after we had celebrated Empire Day at Valentine's School. He was riding down The Mall on a glorious sunny Saturday for Trooping the Colour on Horse Guards Parade. We had arrived early and secured a good vantage point about halfway between Buckingham Palace and Admiralty Arch; never before had I seen the pageantry of a state occasion. Unfortunately the gaiety of onlookers in holiday mood, the sound of bands and the rhythmic marching feet excited me so much that Dad had to hustle me behind a convenient tree, which I duly watered. For a moment it seemed I would miss the climax of the procession. But I *did* see the King go riding by – bearded and upright, the feathered plumage of his hat rustled by the breeze, a gleam of sunlight flashing back from medals across his scarlet tunic. Then people in the crowd began to shuffle around, trying to give names to the uniformed figures riding behind him. 'There's the Prince of Wales,' Dad said; but all I could see was a vast busby that looked as if it would soon engulf the wearer's face.

I fared better two years later. The spring of 1935 held the promise of being the finest in a cycle of sun-baked summers and the Silver Jubilee of King George's accession fell in the first week of May, at a time we could enjoy hour after hour of sunshine, with shade temperatures in the mid-70s Fahrenheit (25°C). There were several days when we had no school. Families flocked up to the West End to cheer the processions that brought the King and Queen to St Paul's on Monday and later in the week to Westminster Hall. By now the BBC had perfected outside broadcasts and we could hear the clank of carriages and the clatter of horses clearly as we sat around the wireless.

Mother did not feel well enough to cope with jostling crowds in such heat on the processional days but she remembered from her girlhood the celebration of Queen Victoria's Diamond Jubilee and 38 years later thought I should share the current jollity. So up we went to London on Tuesday afternoon, admiring the flags as the bus took us along the Strand and then wandering among floral displays at Westminster. Dad joined us and we stayed until nightfall. We walked across St James's Park, with the old iron suspension bridge over the lake lit by Chinese lanterns. On the pavement opposite the Queen Victoria memorial a crowd cheered intermittently. We hurried out of the park to join them, in time to see a small group assembling on the newly floodlit balcony of Buckingham Palace. 'Look, Alan, there's the King and Queen,' Mother said. I was surprised by what I saw. Astride a horse in The Mall two years back, the King had seemed a big man. Now my eyes focussed on a distant, diminutive figure. But the majesty was there, just the same. As I watched, he raised his arm in a gesture not as formal as a salute nor as casual as a wave; it mingled dignity and affability.

By now I knew the King's voice well. Inevitably I associated it with puddings, crackers and paper hats, for we had listened to each Sandringham broadcast seated at my grandfather's dining table, cluttered with remnants of the Christmas meal. But I was very conscious the Jubilee was a special occasion. At eight o'clock in the evening after the Thanksgiving Service at St Paul's, the King broadcast again. This time it was a tired voice, though he was still a month short of his 70th birthday. He began with a message of gratitude to 'my very, very, dear people'. Then suddenly I heard him say, 'I am speaking to the children above all. Remember, children, the King is speaking to *you*.' It seemed as though he was indeed talking to me directly, slowly and distinctly, a firm but kindly uncle commanding my attention and I gave it. 'I ask you to remember,' he said, 'that in days to come you will be the citizens of a great Empire… When the time comes be ready and proud to give to your country the service of your work, your mind and your heart.'

Six months later the King made his fifth Sandringham Christmas broadcast. He sounded very frail; three weeks earlier his favourite sister, Princess Victoria, had died and he grieved for her. Back in July he had reviewed the fleet at Spithead and he sailed *Britannia* at Cowes but there had been no pictures of him at public events since early August and he felt unable to lay his wreath at the Cenotaph on Armistice Day.

The weather, so fine throughout the summer, turned wet and cold early in December. From the school window we could see a thin layer of ice on the lake in Valentine's Park, rare before the end of the year. Snow did not fall in London until the start of term in mid-January and then it came as no more than light flakes. A neighbour took me to see Ilford play St Albans City at Lynn Road, Newbury Park, but there was such a biting wind blowing from the east that the afternoon treat sent me off to bed with bronchitis for several days.

If the weather was raw in metropolitan Essex, how much worse it must have seemed at Sandringham, for there is no natural windbreak to protect north Norfolk from Siberia's icy blasts. The papers first showed alarm over the King's health on Friday, 17 January, after Queen Mary summoned the Prince of Wales up to Norfolk from Windsor and reporters discovered that the royal physician, Lord Dawson, had also arrived. By Sunday evening we were getting official bulletins regularly over the wireless and they continued throughout Monday, 20 January. After I had gone to bed that night my parents heard Stuart Hibberd, the BBC's chief announcer, read the famous penultimate bulletin, 'The King's life is moving peacefully towards its close.' It was then a quarter of an hour before midnight. George V died ten minutes later.

Daily and evening newspapers appeared with black borders and so did the placards advertising them. For a week Dad went to work wearing a black tie; it was my first encounter with the observance of mourning and I was deeply impressed. Cinemas remained open and on Saturday afternoon we went to a matinee at our local Savoy. I cannot recall what film we saw but I remember coming out into steady drizzle and Dad buying an evening paper with pictures of the long queue waiting to enter Westminster Hall and file past the catafalque on which the coffin rested. In four days almost a million people walked in that slow silent procession.

There was no school on Tuesday, 28 January, the day of the funeral. Although banks remained open many offices in London closed as a mark of respect, including Martineau and Reid. My parents and I remained indoors, glued to the wireless set, but despite light rain and mistiness, thousands lined the streets from Westminster to Paddington as seamen hauled the gun carriage bearing the King's coffin to the special train that carried it to Windsor. The interment in St George's Chapel was not carried by the wireless. But we heard the monotonous iteration of the minute guns while the cortège was still in London and, like many other people, we observed two minutes' silence at the time the coffin was due to be lowered into the vault.

Next day's papers carried pictures of the funeral procession. Five foreign sovereigns were there, together with President Lebrun of France, Prince Regent Paul of Yugoslavia and several other heads of state. Many years later I was interested to find in the Public Record Office a handwritten note from the new king that had caused consternation at the Foreign Office. He suggested that, as a gesture of reconciliation, the Hohenzollern dynasty of Prussia and imperial Germany should be represented by his second cousin, the ex-Kaiser's eldest son Crown Prince William, titular commander of German troops in the battle for Verdun. The presence of 'little Willie' would have been an embarrassment, for the army of our closest ally was represented by Marshal Pétain, then still honoured in France as 'victor of Verdun'. A diplomatic compromise ensured that a less controversial Hohenzollern was present: Prince Frederick, the fallen Kaiser's young grandson, lived in England.

There were two other foreign marshals in the procession, Mannerheim from Finland and surprisingly from the Soviet Union, Tukhachevsky, who was to perish a few months later in the first of Stalin's purges. Only the *Daily Mail* bothered to comment on a soldier who walked behind the marshals in the procession; he was the Spanish Chief of Staff, a 44-year-old general named Francisco Franco. He, too, would soon be in the news.

Despite the presence of these foreign dignitaries, King George V's funeral was above all a momentous *British* event. Those rain clouds over the procession hid the setting sun of Empire. We still used the word 'imperial' with pride and for 22 more years 'Empire Day' continued to appear on official calendars but it was no longer celebrated as a festival by schoolchildren in all the 32 lands and territories enamelled patriotically pink on globes in the toy shops. The Commonwealth of Nations may flourish as an afterglow but Victorian Imperialism – a creed with forgotten virtues as well as grievous faults – slipped away with the death of the Queen-Empress's grandson.

It was therefore natural for press cameras to focus on the heavily veiled Queen Mary and her eldest son. Now he was proclaimed 'Edward VIII, by the Grace of God, of Great Britain, Ireland and the British Dominions beyond the seas, King, Defender of the Faith, Emperor of India', a splendid title. But my immediate reaction to the change in kingship lacked profundity; it was a schoolboy's response. I simply found it hard to imagine this fair-haired perpetually young prince, whose picture was so often in our papers, ruling as sovereign in London. A king of England without a beard? It didn't seem right somehow.

SIX

Crown Imperial

On the evening of 30 November 1936 the widowed
Queen Mary, who had gone into residence at Marlborough
House in October, looked from her window across St
James' Park and was 'horrified' by what she recorded in
her diary as 'a very sad sight'. Hundreds of Londoners
saw it too, many of them hurrying to a theatre before the
curtains went up at 8.30. My aunts, emerging from the
Tube at the top of Lower Regent Street, found the Duke
of York's column silhouetted against a red sky; a bad fire
across the river, they thought, in Lambeth or Southwark.
But it was much farther away than that. The nine o'clock
bulletin from the BBC broke the news: at Sydenham the
Crystal Palace was burning and the blaze could be seen
across the capital and out into the suburbs. We heard later
that a pilot flying the regular service from Le Bourget to
Croydon spotted it mid-Channel and homed in on it like
a carrier pigeon.

Gants Hill is some 13 miles from Sydenham as
a pigeon flies. I had gone to bed early; the Bancroft's
entrance exam was two days away. Unexpectedly Mother

came in and gave me the news from the wireless. I dashed to the window and pulled the curtains back. Sure enough, the sky above the trees of Valentine's Park reflected a great blaze. As my eyes grew accustomed to the spectacle, I saw quite distinctly a central flame, like a low flickering candle but strong enough to project an arc of light that played along a line of fast-moving clouds. I suppose I must have looked out at the night sky for half an hour or more. Every now and again the flame grew brighter, as another tongue of fire shot up and the base of the arc broadened. Once there seemed to be a cascade of sparks; presumably stanchions that had supported Joseph Paxton's glass and iron triumph for 82 years were crashing to the ground and brought with them wooden rails to feed the flames. At last, out of sheer tiredness, I slipped into bed – only to wake in the small hours and hurry to the window. The flames and russet glow had gone. Something paled the clouds to the south; grey smoke from a smouldering ruin, no doubt. Otherwise it was a dark night, mistily crisp, as befitted the first day of December.

The great years of the Crystal Palace were long gone. At that moment there was more interest in north London's Alexandra Palace, where the BBC's regular television service had been launched four weeks previously. Back in the 1860s and 1870s the Crystal Palace had provided 'a means of instruction and wholesome recreation' to more than 40 million visitors. Even before the accession of George V, new habits and interests limited its appeal but his coronation was marked by a Festival of Empire and plans were now well advanced to celebrate Edward VIII's crowning with a party for thousands of children. After the Great War the palace still housed 'wholesome' Victoriana in its galleries and hosted flower shows, dog shows, cat shows, bird shows and a national cycle show. The organ and choral recitals were famous, with an annual three-day Handel festival a sell-out. Briefly in 1919-20 the palace found space for an embryonic Imperial War Museum, and in 1933 John Logie Baird made the south tower the home of his television development company – only to lose most of his equipment in the fire, poor man. The greatest crowd-pullers were the annual brass band contest and, ironically, Brock's firework displays on summer Thursdays at his 'temple of pyrotechnics'.

Londoners north and south of the river looked on the palace with affection: 'I don't envy the next generation of boys that will grow up without a Palace,' Robert Cockayne wrote in *The Star* on the evening after the fire. Now all that remained of Sydenham's familiar landmark were Brunel's two flanking water towers, 280 feet high and almost half a mile apart. They stood like gaunt guards over groups of plastered prehistoric animals poised above the parkland.

The blaze remained London's talking point: Queen Mary insisted on being driven out to Sydenham the following morning; the enterprising Cameo News cinema in Charing Cross Road advertised a special 'film of the fire' while the skeleton of the palace still smouldered.

Mercifully no lives were lost and speculation began to concentrate on the cause of the blaze: a cigarette end thrown down near a paint shop, it was said. But was the fire 'a portent'? Did a conflagration engulfing Europe lie ahead? Ancient soothsayers might have made much of the coincidence that 30 November was Winston Churchill's 62nd birthday. 'This is the end of an age,' he is said to have observed as he was being driven from his home in Kent to Westminster.

It was left to the *Nottingham Evening Post* to suggest later in the week that the fire portended disaster, not for Europe, but for the British monarchy. For, while London dailies on 2 December still grieved for the palace, Fleet Street was scooped by the provincial press. In Yorkshire, Manchester and Birmingham the papers took up remarks about the coming coronation made on the previous day by Bishop Alfred Blunt of Bradford to his diocesan conference; Dr Blunt hoped King Edward was aware of the sacramental character of the ceremony and accepted the need for self-dedication 'to do his duty properly'. The *Yorkshire Post* referred to 'rumours… in the more sensational American newspapers' but like the bishop, mentioned no names. London editors, who for months had loyally ignored Edward's private life, felt they could do so no longer. What, they reflected, should tomorrow's editions say about Mrs Wallis Simpson?

As yet we knew nothing of her, nor did our friends. Many of us had closely followed the King's movements over the last ten months. We were relieved no harm came to him when a loaded revolver was thrown towards him as he rode up Constitution Hill in July. A month later we read of his journey to Šibenik for a cruise in a chartered yacht down the Dalmatian coast and on to meet Turkey's President Kemal Ataturk in Istanbul. Most recently had come a widely reported journey through the depressed areas of South Wales, where there was obvious sincerity in the sympathy he showed towards long unemployed steelworkers and miners. But to Americans, and to many on the Continent, he was a much photographed celebrity, with different qualities from those we admired. In Dubrovnik, Yugoslavs and tourists applauded 'the young king' and the raven-haired companion he treated with such solicitude. Cameras clicked or flashed – and another clutch of pictures went off to the dailies of New York and Chicago. At Westminster anyone with close connections outside Britain had known of Edward VIII's infatuation for at least 18 months – the printed diaries of Harold Nicolson and Chips Channon are testimony to that. But for suburbia's man-in-the-street and his family the private life of their king was a closed book. All the greater came the shock when they unfolded their papers on 3 December to find King and Country locked in constitutional crisis over a love affair.

We had two papers delivered to us each day: Dad's *Express* and Uncle Bill's *News Chronicle*. Neither saw any objection to the King taking a twice-divorced American as his consort. The *Chronicle* aired the possibility of a morganatic marriage. This meant Mrs Simpson would be a wife but not become queen, Mother explained; any children could not inherit the throne; 'Something grand dukes did in Russia,' she said. (She might have cited, too, the victims of the Sarajevo assassination in 1914, Archduke Franz Ferdinand and his consort.) Other papers insisted such unions were outside English law and Parliament would never accept hurried remedial legislation. Though we did not know it, the Cabinet had already given the idea of a morganatic marriage short shrift.

The *Express, Chronicle* and *Mail* continued to back Edward throughout the week. So too did Sunday's *Observer*. We generally glanced at the *Telegraph* when we were at my grandfather's. In retrospect, I realise that the paper was a mouthpiece for Stanley Baldwin, the prime minister, but it accurately reported the hostility of Australians, South Africans and most Canadians to a possible 'Queen Wallis'.

Three comments overheard then stick in my memory: 'And *twice* divorced!'; 'What do you expect from Americans?'; 'It's all Hitler's doing.' The two divorces seemed the most widespread objection. Although by now divorce was a common feature of London society, it was still rare in suburbia and twice divorced was more than twice as rare. Only a few acquaintances of ours were anti-American. The 'blame Hitler' camp suspected the machinations of the German ambassador, an arrogant Nazi named Ribbentrop, who had arrived in London in October and was already getting a bad press. Whatever the reasoning, by 8 December, people had become less sympathetic towards the King. I heard Dad say, 'He'll be going soon'; he shook his head and pursed his lips resignedly.

The formal Instrument of Abdication was signed on 10 December; it became effective the next day. That morning it was decided Edward VIII would broadcast a farewell message in the evening. As it was a Friday I was allowed to stay up and hear the broadcast, at about ten o'clock, I think. A very solemn voice – the BBC's director-general, Sir John Reith – announced: 'This is Windsor Castle, His Royal Highness Prince Edward.' 'Not the King?' I queried, but was immediately shushed. The public renouncement of the throne followed, including the frequently quoted affirmation, 'I have found it impossible to carry the heavy burden of responsibility and to discharge my duties as King as *I* would wish to do without the help and support of the woman I love.' Mother sighed when the broadcast was over, 'What a waste!' I went up to bed puzzled by it all but was soon asleep. Some late editions of Saturday's papers gave the news that Edward had crossed to Boulogne in a destroyer and would settle abroad; his successor was to be styled King George VI, not King Albert, and had given his brother the title 'Duke of Windsor'.

The general furore died down with surprising rapidity: Christmas was soon upon us. Early in the new year we learnt we were not to be deprived of a May coronation after all. Preparations were too well advanced for postponement: a 'huge working model of the coronation procession' was the great attraction of a Christmas gifts exhibition at Dorland Hall, Piccadilly, sponsored by the Lord Mayor in aid of charities, including the British Legion; William Walton had been commissioned to compose a patriotic march for the service; and the potters of Hanley were already turning out coronation mugs. In front of me as I write is one we purchased: King Edward is in profile, as on a coin, encircled with the Order of the Garter's *Honi Soit Qui Mal Y Pense*, surmounted by a crown. Around the rim runs the inscription, 'Coronation of King Edward VIII, May 1937'.

Early in the new year, Wednesday, 12 May was confirmed as the date of Coronation Day. Provisional arrangements put aside at the abdication were revised and augmented. The potters of Hanley were quick off the mark. Beside the mug purchased before Christmas I keep a similar one that we bought at Easter. This time it carries a double profile and the words 'King George VI & Queen Elizabeth, May 1937'. The Garter motto is omitted, presumably because the Queen was not a Lady of the Order when it was cast.

On the Saturday preceding the coronation Dad, Mother and I went up to town, as we had during the same week of the year in 1935. This time, however, there were no buses: a month-long strike kept them off the roads. We walked the route the procession would take from Buckingham Palace to Westminster Abbey. Flags along The Mall were only to be expected but I was amazed to see the West End as a whole beflagged beyond recognition: half a dozen white ensigns fluttered above the Admiralty wing in Cockspur Street; a huge crown was over the carriageway of Admiralty Arch through which the golden state coach would pass; floral festoons dipped like paper chains under the pediments of shipping offices; and silver and gold drapery transformed lamp standards in Whitehall and Trafalgar Square into decorative masts. The fronts of public buildings were draped in scarlet, with golden GR VI ciphers and crowns on them. At Westminster Abbey an ingeniously designed annex blended unobtrusively with Hawksmoor's west front. Red and white striped canvas-covered stands for privileged spectators encroached as close as Broad Sanctuary and the gateway to Dean's Yard. So extensive were the changes that the Royal Maundy service, which had been held in the Abbey on the Thursday before Easter for as long as my parents could remember, was moved to St Paul's Cathedral.

The great day began with spring sunshine, though the sky soon clouded over. The procession followed a circuitous route back to Buckingham Palace and a heavy shower poured down as the state coach came up to Hyde Park Corner. But, as we could hear on the wireless, the thousands lining the streets took little notice of the rain and cheered with vigour as the procession passed by.

About another thousand people were lucky enough to catch the pageantry outside the Abbey on small television screens in their sitting rooms, for the Alexandra Palace transmitter could send a reasonable picture within a radius of 35 miles and flickering images farther out. Those of us without television had to wait until the following week to see the procession and the ceremony in the Abbey: a film, duly vetted by the Earl Marshal as master of ceremonies and the Archbishop of Canterbury, was released worldwide. On the day itself we relied on the BBC's team of commentators and they did well.

During the Silver Jubilee broadcasts, the jingle of

horses and carriages on their way down The Mall had fascinated me, while the service from St Paul's left no lasting impression. Before the coronation, however, an official programme went on sale and this time I could follow every detail of the ceremony within the Abbey. I remember two musical delights: the impact of the opening anthem sung by the choir, Parry's 'I was glad when they said unto me…', and, at the end of the service, the grandeur of 'Crown Imperial'. For me, William Walton's march, vibrant with confidence, conjures up a memory of George VI's coronation whenever I have the pleasure of hearing it.

Fortunately the weather soon improved. Festivities, in one form or another, continued over the weekend across the kingdom. It was a great time for crowns and coronets, a long-running festival of monarchy. Cigarette manufacturers had anticipated the mood: John Player's collection of cigarette cards, previously giving us stars of film or sport turned instead to England's kings and queens. No taken-from-life portraits exist earlier than the Wilton triptych of Richard II, and the cards must owe much to imagination, but it was fun collecting them. My father normally smoked his way through several packets a week and I thought it would be easy to fill an album. I had reckoned without Bluff King Hal: Dad opened four packets on successive evenings and each time Henry VIII turned up. It took hard bargaining at school to catch an elusive Richard III and complete the collection.

Film studios on both sides of the Atlantic contributed to the celebrations. Herbert Wilcox directed Anna Neagle and Anton Walbrook in *Victoria the Great*, the first time a British sovereign whom many could remember was portrayed in a cinema. Hollywood's royal offering was more to my liking. For 1937 was the year that Ruritania came to the screen. An Elphberg coronation in a cardboard Strelsau might lack the authentic traditions of Westminster, but *The Prisoner of Zenda* made first-rate schoolboy viewing: sharp swordplay with much swashing of buckles; court intrigue; castles and hunting lodges; a princess in distress saved by a stiff upper-lipped Englishman who impersonated a kidnapped king. And what a cast David Selznick assembled! Ronald Colman, Raymond Massey, C. Aubrey Smith, David Niven, Douglas Fairbanks and, to my delight, Madeleine Carroll as Princess Flavia. The film sent me hurrying to Anthony Hope's original book. It soon gripped me.

One coronation celebration I was sorry to miss. The naval review took place on Thursday, 20 May, while we were at school and I could follow the spectacle only in newspapers and on subsequent newsreels. Four lines of warships gathered off Spithead, awaiting the ageing royal yacht *Victoria and Albert* with the Jutland veteran, King George VI, aboard, together with the Queen and Princess Elizabeth. Foreign governments sent warships on courtesy calls. Among them were the fast German 'pocket battleship' *Admiral Graf Spee*, France's *Dunkerque* (specifically built to counter this threat from Germany), the USS *New York* and the Soviet Navy's venerable dreadnought *Marat*, once the Tsar's *Petropavlovsk*. In the afternoon listeners at home heard a commentary on the ceremonial passage of the royal yacht up and down the avenues of warships from HMS *Nelson* by Thomas Woodrooffe, a 38-year-old retired lieutenant-commander who had covered some events in the Berlin Olympics the previous summer and, more recently, an innovative actuality programme describing an evening's policing of London. The best to which I could look forward was his commentary on 'the illumination of the fleet' as soon as night fell.

Mother, Dad and I gathered round the little Ekco. The announcer told us that they would be broadcasting from Spithead and that we would shortly hear a description of the scene. From the start it was clear that we were in for original entertainment. Woodrooffe explained that the whole fleet was lit up but then, much to our surprise, went on to say that it was alight with fairy lamps! This he kept repeating again and again – he even went on to say that the royal review was 'forgotten" and we were in fact, in fairyland. And just in case we had not got his message, he added (in rather slurred speech with long pauses) that the colossal fleet was all lit up by little lamps.

So the commentary ran on cheerfully towards the time when all the ships would be darkened ahead of the firework display. This stage in events had clearly been forgotten by our commentator as Woodrooffe broke off in mid-sentence, to continue excitedly that the fleet was all gone, that it had disappeared! And finally with a dramatic flourish, he declared that there was nothing between us and Heaven. There was nothing at all.

At this point, just four minutes after the commentary

had begun, the wireless went silent. A few seconds later the announcer apologised for having 'unfortunately lost the line to Spithead'. Dance music was faded in as a substitute. The people of Portsmouth, Southsea and Cowes enjoyed the spectacle of fireworks and the illuminations. They had a good evening. So, too, in a way did listeners across the country; we schoolboys were still laughing at the commentary-that-never-was the next morning. Despite the excellent broadcasts on Coronation Day it was satisfying to find the BBC subject to human frailty. Tommy Woodrooffe became a favourite of us all. At Christmas 'the fleet lit up' London's theatreland, for the shrewd impresario C.B. Cochran chose the catchphrase of the day for the review he presented at the Hippodrome.

How, I wonder, would King George V have responded if these events had taken place at the Jubilee review two years previously? As it was, Woodrooffe explained to the director-general that the majesty of the occasion had left him overcome with emotion; Reith, normally a stickler for convention, treated him benignly. Ten months later he was chosen to present television's first live cup final from Wembley, where Preston North End, the previous year's finalists, were facing Huddersfield Town. With 20 minutes of the match to go, there was still no score, although Huddersfield repeatedly looked threatening. Confidently Woodrooffe committed himself, 'If Preston wins now, I'll eat my hat.' He should have known better. In the last minute of extra time Mutch, the Preston centre, obliged with a penalty. On the following Monday viewers of the TV magazine programme, *Picture Page*, watched

Tommy Woodrooffe keep his word, though, as they may have guessed, the straw boater was made of marzipan.

When war came, Lt-Commander Woodrooffe returned to active service and in 1943 I heard him again on the wireless, reporting from an aircraft carrier in the Mediterranean. He spoke soberly and with authority, for he was no extrovert buffoon. In 1958 he published a historical study on Britain as an 'oceanic' sea power. He also wrote his memoirs, for which his publishers could think of only one possible title. Yet the book got no farther than a typescript and those familiar words never illuminated bookshop windows. In a desire to be remembered as a serious naval historian, Woodrooffe seems to have had second thoughts over publication. But to those of us who recall these distant days his review commentary remains *the* joke of Coronation Year and memory of that evening when Broadcasting House 'lost' the line to Spithead always brings a nostalgic smile to my face.

SEVEN

Foreign Shores

In Victorian and Edwardian Britain few people travelled abroad for pleasure or relaxation. Journeys to the Continent were taken for granted by the aristocracy and welcomed by the newly affluent as a token of social recognition. For most families a holiday, if able to be taken at all, would be spent either with relatives or at a boarding house at a coastal resort. But the Great War broadened the horizon for thousands of men and women who served overseas. They looked to the Continent and turned to travel agents like Thomas Cook and Polytechnic for advice, bargain breaks and insurance.

Like many other couples in southern England my parents had taken day trips to France before 1914 but they never thought of going deeply into Europe or staying abroad for any length of time. Mother was particularly alarmed at the prospect of a night crossing. One evening in 1907 she had waved to passengers on the boat train for the Hook of Holland as it went through Forest Gate only to be shocked next day by news that over a hundred of them had drowned in a disaster that left the SS *Berlin* sinking in the dark as she approached the Dutch quay.

In 1932, however, we took a short holiday at Felixstowe. Each day I watched steamers come down the River Stour from Harwich. Upriver I saw the impressive line of LNER ships berthed at Parkston Quay. 'Dad, I do wish *we* could go on one,' I said. So at heart did he, and gradually over the winter months he convinced Mother that, after 25 years, improvements in safety made another *Berlin* disaster unlikely. My parents had a friend who worked at Cook's head office in London and she gave good advice on where to stay. So to my delight on 18 August 1933 the three of us set out from Liverpool Street for Harwich and a fortnight on the Belgian coast.

At Parkston Quay we boarded the SS *Archangel*. Dad had sailed in her once already: in 1918 she brought him back from Le Havre, fighting the onset of Spanish influenza at the end of his service in Salonika. For me a bunk in a cabin of what seemed a vast ship was intensely exciting. They let me stay up and go on deck to see Felixstowe's familiar lights slip away and watch us pass the *Cork* lightship. This was bliss. *When I grow up, I'll be captain of a steamer*, I decided.

Next morning there was Zeebrugge Mole to see out of a porthole. And then ashore in a foreign country, aboard a tram more like a train than London's clanging double deckers and running the length of Belgium's coast. We stayed at the Hotel de l'Univers in Heist, the first of three visits there over the next four summers. My father persisted with these holidays because he calculated that Heist was cheaper than any British resort likely to appeal to us. Even though Britain was off the gold standard, the exchange rate still benefitted sterling, and in 1935 devaluation of the Belgian franc by 28 per cent made the pound stretch further still.

Not that I knew about such matters. For me and for Mother it was enough that Belgium's sands were clean and there were plenty of English boys and girls around to join in beach games. Curious novelties caught my eye: oblong lumps of sugar wrapped in paper instead of our familiar cubes; dogs harnessed to small carts that delivered milk daily in big churns; no Punch and Judy shows, but men on stilts at a carnival instead; and at Sluys, just across the Dutch border, women with strange coverings on their heads – sometimes they were in wooden clogs as well. Teatime delicacies abounded: sickly cakes and glutinous chocolate creations at Duinbergen; speciality ice-cream at Knokke; delicious currant bread at Sluys.

I turned up my nose at the smell from the Bruges canals and wafts of rotting turnip and fertiliser rising from low lying fields. Yet I recall only one morning of dismay. The dunes, such fun when first I tried to scale them and tumbled down in soft sand, turned against me a few days later. A high east wind seemed ideal for kite flying. Alas, the gusts proved too strong. I could not keep hold of the cord. Miserably I watched a brand new kite fly out to sea. 'Never mind. Perhaps we'll find it back in England,'

Mother said helpfully. Her words brought no comfort. I knew full well that England was too big for a wayward kite hunt to succeed.

No child whose father and uncles served in the Great War could fail to know something about the tragic conflict. I had heard of the fighting in Flanders mud and the proto-commando style raid on Zeebrugge on St George's Day 1918. When the *Archangel* berthed I was excited to see scars of battle on the Mole and later to clamber around the Kaiser Wilhelm battery at Knokke. One afternoon we took a tourist excursion to Ypres. A British tank was preserved in the centre of the town and there were trenches to scramble along at Hill 60, where Dad bought a spent bullet for me from the museum shop. Work was continuing on restoration of the Cloth Hall, much of it still a jagged line, looking to me like broken teeth, the first war damage I had seen. The serried uniform gravestones in Tyne Cot cemetery sobered my excitement and left me silent; everyone seemed to speak in whispers as if we were in church. But my clearest memory is of Mother searching for the name of a childhood neighbour on the panels of the Menin Gate and of a woman draped in black who followed us down the steps weeping. When Armistice Day came round in November and Mother pinned a poppy on my blazer, I had some awareness of the sacrifice it symbolised. Not until 2001 did I visit Ypres again but so deep was the impression left after 68 years that I guided my friend Christopher Johnson, in whose car I was travelling from Blankenberg, to the back entrance of Tyne Cot and down the Menin Road to the Cloth Hall as if I had been there the day before.

The fortnight at Heist was so successful that Dad decided in 1934 we would experiment with a bargain holiday in France. He chose Wimereux, a mere 110 miles from Ilford. The wedding of a close friend meant that we could not cross to Boulogne until the afternoon of 1 September, and off-season Wimereux was not so jolly as Heist the previous summer. There were interesting trips to make along France's 'opal coast'; Ambleteuse, where Mother told me King James II had landed, though I was rather hazy when and why; Cap Gris Nez close-up – not a patch on Beachy Head I felt patriotically. We explored Calais and Boulogne, with its domed cathedral. One morning a smoke-stacked train took us to Le Touquet, where men in plus-fours strode purposefully out from smart hotels with golf-bags in hand and Mother glanced admiringly at slim young women with big hats which by my reckoning were silly for the seaside. The beach at Paris-Plage looked good; odd not to see buckets and spades on it, of course, but the sand yachts were a novelty well worth watching.

Shadows of past wars linger in Picardy as they do in Flanders, and one afternoon we saw the huge military cemetery at Étaples, where thousands of dead from the Battle of the Somme are buried, British and German alike. On another day we trudged two miles uphill from Wimereux to the heights where from 1803 to 1805, Napoleon kept 160,000 men of the Army of England under canvas, waiting for a few hours' mastery of Channel waters in which to send his invasion sloops across the Straits. This was my first exposure to the Napoleonic legend and I looked out to the grey smudge of Dover's cliffs some 20 miles away, thrilled by a sense of past drama. We had not the faintest inkling that an even greater drama would be played out over those waters in six years' time.

By 1930 a network of government-subsidid airlines threatened the near monopoly of cross-Channel passenger traffic the railway companies had enjoyed for 70 years. In May 1929 this mounting competition induced the Southern Railway and the French Chemins de Fer du Nord to introduce the Golden Arrow, an all-Pullman first-class express service to Paris. The new single-funnel luxury steamer *Canterbury* provided a faster crossing from Dover to Calais than any previous ship. It was, however, a bad time for such a venture. The world slump forced railway companies to abandon their original concept, although they were determined the Golden Arrow would retain its prestigious character. The *Canterbury*'s interior was modified, with space set aside to accommodate second-class travellers. Trains would have second-class carriages, next to the engine at the far end of the platforms. These changes were to our advantage: early in 1936 our friend at Cook's let Dad know of an Easter bargain break in Paris with four nights at a small hotel. Outward and return journeys would be on the Golden Arrow. Dad booked the holiday by return of post.

We left Victoria at 11.00 a.m. on Maundy Thursday, crossing to Calais aboard the *Canterbury*. By 2 p.m. we were rumbling down familiar tracks through Boulogne and Étaples. We paused at Amiens and, beyond the station, I saw for the first time the majesty of a French Gothic cathedral. The landscape of rural France, with woods and broad fields and clusters of compact villages dwarfed by their churches, looked more attractive from the Golden Arrow than it does now from Eurostar, speeding down the straight line from Lille.

As the train neared Paris I watched out for the Eiffel Tower and caught a glimpse of it spectrally on our left. To the right I was amazed to see high above us the starched white cupolas of a church that looked mysteriously Indian. 'That must be the Sacré-Coeur,' Mother said, glancing at the Cook's dark blue guidebook on her lap. We took a taxi to the hotel; the driver's skill in getting us through crowded streets alarmed Mother. ('Sit back, Alan, and *do* hold on to that strap.') The light was almost gone when he reached the Luxembourg Quarter and turned into the Rue de Fleurus, where we were booked into no. 8, the Hotel de Fleurus. Our room on the first floor had long windows opening on to a wrought-ironwork balcony. I was out on it before Mother could stop me. Facing us was the Café de Fleurus, out of fashion now, so someone told Dad, though still traditional in character and lively. But what caught my eye was the view down the road. There, barely 50 yards away, stood the gates of the Luxembourg Gardens. Beyond them, well above the chestnut trees, came the semi-gilded dome of the Pantheon. Even now, more than 80 years later, impressions of that first hour in Paris stand out vividly in my mind: rabbit-warren roads opening on to grand boulevards; the spaciousness of the

Place de la Concorde; and the pavement culture of the Left Bank – all these contrasts left me entranced. *Surely Paris must be the most wonderful capital in the world*, I thought. None of the 39 capitals I have since seen has shaken that belief.

The next three days were hectic. I spent hours in the Luxembourg Gardens, with ponies to ride and sailing yachts to hire and push out on the central pond. Around us, in front of the Luxembourg Palace, I watched show-offs with tennis rackets hitting the ball really hard. Men in blue berets endlessly gesticulated as they threw what looked to me like oversize metal marbles at an off-white dusty jack; for them boules was a serious pastime. So too for its players was a mysterious game, in which they noisily trumped each other's card with a great flourish. Behind them quieter men at tables beneath the trees pondered chess moves. I do not remember noticing women in any of these activities. No doubt at Easter *Parisiennes* fulfilled other obligations: spiritual, domestic or simply social.

My parents *did* get me away from the Luxembourg Gardens from time to time. We went down the Boulevard St Michel, saw Roman remains at the Cluny museum, visited Notre Dame in an interval between Easter devotions and dutifully joined the throng at the Louvre. Dad and I took the lifts up the Eiffel Tower, leaving Mother firmly *terre á terre* but she joined us when we went to the Arc de Triomphe. She maintained, rightly, that you gained a better impression of Paris from a viewing platform 160 feet above the eight avenues of L'Etoile than from 900 feet up Eiffel's masterpiece. I was disappointed not to ride on one of the single deck buses with their open rear standing room but I liked the Metro, with clanging platform barriers and a smell that was far from attractive but different from the stuffiness of the London Tube.

Dad had booked two Cook's excursions. One, inevitably, was to Versailles. The sheer size of the palace overwhelmed me; I appreciated the Hall of Mirrors more two years later when there were fewer people but at least Easter ensured the fountains were playing as we wandered down to the Petit Trianon. The second excursion, around inner Paris, I found more exciting. Our guide was an enthusiast for France's past, from Napoleon onwards. He walked with a limp, resting at times on a stick. It was obvious he was a war veteran and I think he was Jewish. His hero was Georges Clemenceau, the radical republican who as prime minister in 1918 was the 'Father of Victory' and champion of France at the Peace Conference a year later.

When our coach drove along the Champs-Élysées the guide lifted his beret in salute to the statue at the corner of the Place Clemenceau, which was then barely four years old. The coach climbed up the side roads to Montmartre and we saw the contrast between the open-air jollity of the Place du Tertre and the sacramental reverence inside the Sacré-Coeur. But our guide also took care to show us the Mairie, where in 1871 the 30-year-old Mayor Clemenceau sought to check excesses during the bloody days of the Paris Commune and was lucky to escape with his life.

Across the Seine, at the Invalides, I was awed by

Napoleon's porphyry sarcophagus. The bronze tomb of Marshal Foch that I admire today was not then completed, but it filled a side chapel when we came to Paris two years later. The guide drew our attention to steel shutters in front of many shops and restaurants. They had been needed as recently as February 1934 when riots brought down the government. They were lowered again soon after we returned home, in the run-up to elections won by the Popular Front coalition that gave the Third Republic a socialist government and the nation's first Jewish prime minister, Leon Blum. I feel sure our guide would have welcomed the electoral victory of the Left but I dread to think of his fate if he was still in Paris four or five years later. He was frequently in my thoughts during those days; I wish I knew his name. I owe a debt to him for stimulating an interest in the Third Republic and its politics that I have never lost.

The Paris break ended on Easter Monday, a day when the weather turned suddenly cold; snow showers swept in from the east. There was a toyshop in the Rue Guynemer, around the corner from the hotel, and I came home with splendid recruits for my leaden army: Gardes Républicaines, Spas, and 'Turcos' from French North Africa. Before the train left the Gare du Nord I badgered Dad with one more request: I wanted a photo taken alongside the powerful locomotive that was ready to pull us to Calais. Although our carriage was at the front of the train we had to hurry along the last stretch of platform. I posed contentedly beside the engine. Suddenly a well-dressed stranger dashed up, threw an arm around my shoulder and stood waiting for the camera to click. There was no time to argue; not a word was said. So the snapshot was taken, with me sullenly resigned to giving the engine a different foreground from the one I had wanted. Then we clambered aboard the first carriage door and joined Mother as the train gathered speed.

I was puzzled, and with greater background knowledge have remained so since. Was the intruder a criminal on the run who thought attachment to an English family would fool the police? Was he a political activist, one of many communists informally convened in Paris during that spring and summer? Was he an actor whom we ought to have recognised? Sacha Guitry came to London that week; could it possibly have been anyone so distinguished? Or perhaps Monsieur Inconnu simply got a kick from embracing a nine-year-old boy wearing a school cap. But would a man like that risk confrontation with an irate father?

Of course the incident did nothing to lessen my enjoyment of the four-day break. 'Can we come to Paris again next Easter?' I begged Mother. 'Oh no,' she replied firmly. 'This holiday has already cost us £20! You can't expect *that* again.' I realised this was a considerable sum, well over £600 by 2015 values, and resignedly said nothing more of the possibility. Yet, all the same, Dad somehow managed to afford a fortnight back at Heist in August, with visits to Brussels, Ghent, Antwerp and the isle of Walcheren in Holland. In 1937 we took a Cook's bargain break to Lucerne, followed by Heist for the last time.

These pre-war holidays abroad sharpened my powers

of observation and heightened a sense of the past. I was too young to go hiking or biking, like many sixth-formers and students. Of course my picture of Europe was limited. Apart from the foray into Switzerland I remained a cross-Channel boy, familiar with the English coast from Orford Ness to the Lizard, and rivers on the Continent from the Scheldt to the Seine.

I felt, however, that I knew by proxy places we never visited. The first region to interest me was the Balkans. During two years at GHQ in Salonika Dad witnessed an attempt to assassinate the Greek radical nationalist Venizelos and he often saw the Serbian Prince Regent, who as King Alexander was assassinated on a state visit to Marseilles in October 1934. I felt very moved by a photo of the King's ten-year-old son Peter being whisked away from a Kensington prep school to become titular ruler in Belgrade under the regency of his uncle, Prince Paul. Five months later Venizelos was in the news for organising an abortive uprising against the Greek monarchy. These events and Dad's reminiscences alerted me to the deep tensions beneath the surface of Balkan politics.

Hungary I came to 'know' from a postcard of a floral display Auntie Bessie sent from Budapest, a city she first visited as a lady's maid attendant on a British 'grande dame' before the Great War. She admired the colours of the flowers shown on the card. I was intrigued because their pattern was irregular; they seemed to form a map. In 1938 I discovered that this was floral propaganda depicting lands lost in 1920 by the Treaty of Trianon, which deprived historic Hungary of two-thirds of its pre-war territory.

My proxy Austria was a land of music and sweets, thanks initially to a Mozart decorated box of delicious chocolates my aunts brought back from Salzburg in 1935. Operettas in film, recordings of Richard Tauber, and my liking for Strauss waltzes sustained this cosy illusion until March 1938 when it was shattered by the *Anschluss*, and newsreels showed Hitler welcomed in Vienna. Austria became a mere province of Nazi Germany.

Five months after the *Anschluss* we went again to France. We found a country more conscious than Britain of the threats to peace. Grandfather Perriam came with us he wished to celebrate his 80th birthday by seeing Paris for the first time. We crossed from Newhaven in the *Brighton*, smaller and faster than the up-Channel ships. Dad had booked a week at Dieppe, followed by a few days back at the Fleurus.

Dieppe was a puzzling town. It packed holiday amenities and commercial needs into the mouth of a narrow river flanked by high cliffs. Our hotel gave us a room listed as facing the sea. In reality we looked out across a green *plage* to a distant beach as shingly as Brighton. Half a mile away, above the south-west end of the promenade, stood a fifteenth-century castle, well sited to keep English invaders out. Beneath it was a modern casino, well sited to tempt English tourists in. Dad and Grandfather succumbed to the lure of roulette. Children were allowed no nearer than the foyer of the cinema, where – a sign of the times – the feature film was *Alerte en Méditerranée*. Outside, long, coloured pictures showed French warships at such high speed that they created bow waves. If there was a story line, it was not evident in any poster. Everything trumpeted the glory of the navy Admiral Darlan was building up for France.

Mornings were for the beach but early in the afternoon the *Brighton* or her sister-ship, *Worthing,* arrived from Newhaven. As soon as I spotted either steamer coming in I would dash out to the harbour entrance and keep pace with the ship as she turned cautiously to starboard before mooring beside the Gare Maritim. For half an hour I was content to watch cars lifted off the deck and on to the quay. I admired models rarely seen at the Gants Hill roundabout and was amused by the loving anxiety of their owners as they swayed in a rope cradle on the hook of a small crane.

We spent a day at Rouen and one afternoon a bone-shaker bus took us 30 miles south-west to St Valery-en-Caux, a miniature Dieppe, with a small harbour and castle tucked into a hollow of high white cliffs. But we mostly stayed around Dieppe itself. Whichever way we turned, walks began with a climb. We could go through the fish market and head westwards along cliffs behind the castle to Pourville or we could go round the harbour and climb steeply through the fishermen's *quartier* of Le Pollet and head for Puys and Berneval. There were cliffs everywhere; the whole coast from east of Berneval to west of St Valery was like Sussex's Seven Sisters. The coast was a natural rampart to thwart any invasion by sea.

Paris seemed unchanged, with the Luxembourg Gardens as attractive in late August as at Easter. We saw one gem we missed two years back – Louis IX's Sainte Chapelle. It remains a favourite of mine. In the Upper

Chapel, the sun does not shine through the soaring stained glass windows: it illuminates them. The warmth of their colour gives an illusion of height to the star-studded vaulted roof.

It was as well we visited the Sainte Chapelle in the morning, for by afternoon the weather was miserably wet. We found shelter in a new wing of the Grand Palais, where I watched a television programme. Such 'visual broadcasting' was even more a novelty in France than in England, a medium to be put on display. Earlier in the year I saw BBC television for the first time at the Science Museum, with Herbert Morrison explaining the LCC's proposals for London's green belt. The programme was more interesting in Paris although, like the naval film at Dieppe, it was ominously topical, concentrating on the Maginot Line, the recently completed defensive barrier along France's frontier with Germany, from the Ardennes down to the Swiss border. We saw pictures from a deep fort, with sleeping quarters far better than school dormitories; there were glimpses of men and supplies arriving on a narrow gauge underground railway.

Shortly before our holiday King George VI paid a state visit to France intended to reaffirm and strengthen the Entente Cordiale between our two nations. In Paris there was a grand reception at the Quai d'Orsay, at where the Queen's elegance charmed all who met her. Attractive tricolour designs were painted on the stones where the royal couple stepped ashore from their launch and had a blank centre: the canny French would never waste public funds painting stones sure to be covered by a red carpet.

Newspapers on both sides of the Channel hailed the visit a success. But was the *entente* all that *cordiale*, we wondered? In 1936 Parisians had troubled to help us if we asked the way to a Metro station or back to the hotel but now they seemed short-tempered and uncooperative. And as our last purchase we bought a lavishly illustrated souvenir of the state visit at a virtually give-away price.

We left for home on 3 September, taking a taxi to the Gare St Lazare. The driver evidently thought we came from south of the Pyrenees, for he spoke to Dad in Spanish, though he soon switched to fluent English. We heard how he had fled from his native Russia after fighting for the Whites against the Bolsheviks. Now, he said, Paris was sheltering new refugees, fleeing north from a civil war close to hand. A war with Germany would come soon, he predicted. With an alarming sweep of the hand as he turned into the station forecourt he exclaimed, 'Look at Czechoslovakia.'

Home in England we duly looked, and so did thousands of anxious families in the lands we had visited in the last five years. By the end of the month we were gripped by all the uncertainties of the Munich Crisis, tuning in regularly to every news bulletin. For the remainder of my boyhood the crooked cross swastika cast a baleful shadow across Europe.

EIGHT

The Crooked Cross

On 30 January 1933 Adolf Hitler, leader of the National Socialists, the largest single party in the Reichstag, was appointed Chancellor by President Paul von Hindenburg. At the time this ominous event caused little concern in Britain; the *Daily Herald* even mocked the newcomer as 'a stubby little Austrian with... a Charlie Chaplin moustache'. There had been some alarm in July 1932 when the press had reported that in Germany's parliamentary election 'Herr Hitler's nationalists' received 13.5 million votes and won 230 seats in the Reichstag, but interest waned during the ensuing months of coalition politicking. Six days before Hitler's appointment *The Times* had printed a letter from Neville Chamberlain, who was to become prime minister in May 1937 but was then Ramsay Macdonald's Chancellor of the Exchequer. While walking across St James's Park Chamberlain saw a grey wagtail 'running about... the dry bed of the lake', a sight so rare 'in the heart of London' that he thought *Times'* readers might be interested. Perhaps they were but most talk in that week was over a topic of more gravity than enterprising wagtails or Chaplinesque foreign politicians. Tempers were frayed over the Australian cricketers' response to England's resort to the dangerous practice of bodyline bowling in the current Ashes Test series. Not until 28 February, the day after a mysterious fire destroyed the Reichstag building, did Germany's problems again merit headlines in the London press.

I saw shots of the blazing Reichstag in a newsreel at the Super Cinema in Ilford but some 18 months went by before I felt personally angered by the evils of Nazi rule. On some Sundays I attended meetings of the Crusaders, an evangelical movement whose predominantly schoolboy members sang hearty hymns and reflected on biblical readings. One afternoon in 1934 we were addressed by a young man back from Germany. There he had heard a courageous pastor protest at the government's persecution of the Jews. He told us about concentration camps and how Jewish youngsters would be taken from their parents and left to an uncertain fate. Two brothers in a Jewish family from Seven Kings were particular friends of mine at Park School. I hated to think of boys as jolly as David and Nicky being set upon by Hitler's thugs.

From then onwards I scanned the pages of the *News Chronicle* for any reports from Germany I could understand and photographs of current events there. Berlin always caught my eye; it was the city I knew by proxy from *Emil and the Detectives*. There was a good choice of pictures, though mostly of building work. In May 1930 the International Olympics Committee had awarded the winter and summer Games for 1936 to Germany. It was a gesture many thought long overdue. Berlin would have hosted the VIIth Olympiad in 1916 had not the Games been cancelled because of the war. In 1930 the German government willingly accepted the 'higher aspirations' for a 'valiant humanity' that inspired Baron de Coubertin in 1894 when he revived the Olympics after a lapse of 15 centuries. The IOC was content and assumed the Games would remain non-political like their immediate predecessors in Paris and Los Angeles; no one foresaw the rapid rise of national socialism. As it was, Hitler had three years to determine the character of the XIth Olympiad, ample time in which to sweep aside Coubertin's ideals and prepare a propaganda triumph to dupe the world.

The Games opened on 1 August 1936 with a protracted ceremony broadcast from Berlin. A fulsome speech of welcome and gratitude to the Führer dragged on so long that the English commentator inserted light-hearted observations. The right-wing historian Arthur Bryant, writing in *The Illustrated London News* a week later, was shocked by such 'discourtesy' and by the failure of the British competitors to give the Hitler salute to their host but we schoolboys were untroubled by such matters. At first we were disappointed that the outstanding English athlete Sydney Wooderson could not compete because of injury and we were also disconcerted to see the German medal tally getting higher and higher. Soon, however, we were rooting for Jesse Owens, the black American with a broad smile who won four gold medals and was shunned by Hitler as a 'non-Aryan'.

Within days we could watch the opening ceremony

and many events in cinema newsreels. The pictures amazed me: there were banners everywhere, each displaying a swastika beside the five linked rings of the Olympic emblem. Even more surprising were shots of the new airship *Hindenburg* trailing a huge German flag above the city and the stadium on the opening day. Eyes inevitably focussed on the swastika at the centre of the white roundel. By now I was beginning to loathe the sight of that crooked cross.

All too soon I was to see it again. The last week of August we spent back in Heist. On one evening a fellow guest at the hotel told Dad the *Hindenburg* was heading down the coast on her way to America. As the French, Belgian and Dutch governments would not allow German Zeppelins to fly over their countries the *Hindenburg* had to turn northwards from Frankfurt and up to Bremen before altering course for the English Channel and the ocean.

The 'largest airship in the world' was several miles offshore when we first spotted it from Heist's esplanade, the swastikas on the tail-fins standing out clearly, even from that distance. In July the airship had made the Atlantic crossing in a record 46 hours and it was again travelling at speed, seeking to complete the flight in half the time of its ocean rivals, the 'blue riband' liners, France's *Normandie* and Britain's *Queen Mary*. 'It's as big as the *Titanic*,' our companion said in awe.

Until then I had not heard of the loss of the *Titanic*. Dad enlightened me as we made our way back to the hotel. It struck him as a strange comparison; 'Why not the *Queen Mary*?' he remarked. The parallel proved tragically prescient, however. On a thundery afternoon in May 1937 the *Hindenburg* was being secured to the landing mast at Lakehurst, New Jersey, when suddenly it was engulfed in flames. More than 30 passengers and crew perished in the inferno. Within a few minutes all that remained of Nazi Germany's pride of the skies was a tangled heap of glowing metal. An American radio reporter, sent to interview interesting arrivals, caught the whole drama in a recording broadcast around the world. We could hear the shrieks of horrified onlookers on our wireless.

In London we were shocked by the disaster, which came only six days before the coronation, a time of general rejoicing. Already there was a certain sympathy for the Germans among the upper classes, for during the Olympics year the smiling face of Hitler's Reich pleased many visitors. Friendships blossomed between official guests and their hosts: Lord Londonderry, Air Minister from 1932 to 1935, was on first name terms with Joachim von Ribbentrop, soon to become ambassador in London; and 'Chips' Channon, the gullible Tory MP for Southend, found Göring 'a most disarming man' with 'merry eyes twinkling'.

New sporting links were forged: contact was established between the Berlin Cricket League and MCC at Lord's, enabling the Gentlemen of Worcestershire, a highly respected club, to play three matches against a German national team in Berlin, where a small cricket league survived from before 1914. The Worcestershire team easily won all three matches. *The Cricketer* for 31

July 1937 assured readers that 'Herr Hitler has shown an interest in cricket'. This seems highly unlikely. The visitors only saw the Nazi leaders from a distance at a parade down Unter den Linden. Later evidence suggests that a non-playing interpreter was working for British Intelligence.

Travel agencies readily responded to this emergence of an apparently friendly Germany, with Polytechnic Travel's brochure displaying a swastika on the cover. Auntie Bessie was enticed by Cook's offers and revisited Frankfurt, a city she knew before 1914. 'The police are wonderful,' she told us on her return. '*So* strict about the traffic. We had no trouble crossing the roads.' She was cheered by the sight and sound of a river boat heading up the Rhine with lads and lasses in brown shirts or blouses singing 'something about the Fatherland'. Everything struck her as carefree and jolly.

We were unconvinced. For the previous two years uniformed members of Sir Oswald Mosley's British Union of Fascists had stirred up anti-Semitism across the East End. My father encountered these paramilitary blackshirt 'biff boys' several times when coming home from the evening classes he taught at Jubilee Street, Stepney. There was a pocket of active fascists within the largely Irish Catholic community around Duckett Street, half a mile east of Jubilee Street. Sometimes the fascists stood at street corners ranting abuse at any person of Jewish appearance, and more than once he heard the shattering of glass, as some object was thrown through a shop window. On one evening Mother and I watched from the top of a tram as a group of blackshirts ran along the pavement of Mile End Road intent on destruction.

Clashes between uniformed fascists and their left-wing opponents reached a climax on 4 October 1936, in the legendary 'Battle of Cable Street'. Mosley gave early notice of his intention to lead a BUF 'route march' through the East End, during which he would make four speeches. The Labour party's leader Clement Attlee, a former mayor of Stepney, was among protesters who urged the Home Secretary, Sir John Simon, to ban the march. Simon saw no grounds in law for doing so.

The blackshirts paraded in Royal Mint Street, 2,000 strong, and were inspected by their leader. Before the march began news arrived that their route was blocked by a derailed tram at Gardiner's Corner, while at Cable Street a lorry with a load of bricks had been overturned, providing the basic core of an improvised barricade. No less than 100,000 supporters of the Jewish People's Council against Fascism and all the parties of the Left had come together in Whitechapel, united in their resolve to defy the fascists.

The battle itself was brief. When mounted police tried to clear a path for Mosley, the defenders began to fall back. Charlie Goodman, a 16-year-old communist, climbed a lamppost and called out, 'Don't be yellow bellies. We are winning. Forward.' He was seized by the police and roughly handled, then and later, but the barricades stood firm. So determined was the resistance that the police commissioner phoned Simon and secured an order for Mosley to call off the march. The blackshirts headed back towards BUF headquarters in Chelsea, a pipe band at their head. Forty-five years later a fine mural was completed on the wall of the old Stepney Town Hall to perpetuate the memory of the afternoon London decisively rejected Mosley's British brand of fascism.

We remained in Clarence Avenue on Cable Street Sunday, hearing a brief factual account of events on the wireless and gathering fuller details from Monday's papers. Dad took his evening class as usual on Wednesday and encountered no trouble during the journey home. It was on the following Sunday that the fascists sought revenge: a group of biff boy hooligans ran amok in Mile End Road while a communist-led rally was celebrating the previous week's victory in Victoria Park. There were no instances of arson and no deaths, though one Jewish barber is said to have been hurled through a window. By nightfall much of Stepney looked as if a tornado had struck the streets, Dad was told when next he went to Jubilee Street.

Parliament responded with a Public Order Act which became law on 1 January 1937: the wearing of political uniforms was banned, so too was insulting language likely to cause a breach of the peace; the police were empowered to forbid political processions. Large indoor rallies continued until the eve of war but we witnessed no more violence in the streets. At the close of 1938 I enjoyed a happy evening with Dad and his students at a social in Jubilee Street. Many must have been Jewish but they came and went without molestation. All was festively quiet.

Not everyone who manned the Cable Street barricade was from London. By October 1936 Spain had been wracked by civil war for three months, with General Franco's nationalist fascist rebels seeking to overthrow the republican Popular Front coalition government of Manuel Azana. Mosley's march coincided with newspaper reports of a bloodbath in Toledo, where the nationalists had recently relieved their troops trapped in the Alcazar military academy and summarily executed many of the besiegers. A friend of ours from Devon motored up to Whitechapel overnight because he felt strongly about the 'killings in the bull-ring' and we heard of others who made long journeys to London in revulsion at the reports from Toledo.

I backed the Popular Front government, naively I see in retrospect, for both sides committed appalling atrocities. To some extent, I was influenced by the *News Chronicle*, the one London daily to support Azana consistently, but I was also thrilled to read of a British International Brigade. Here it seemed was a body of men, only a few years older than me, willing to fight for a cause in which they passionately believed. Such over-simplification did not allow for the dedication of veteran communists or the desperate search for work of the long unemployed but my romantic image was not entirely false. About one in five British volunteers shared the motives I attributed to them. Many came from universities or schools. Bancroft's had a sixth-former who slipped away one weekend on the long journey to the multi-national brigades' base at Albacete. He was too senior at school for a new boy to know personally but I heard, many years later, that he had come back safely to England. He was fortunate. So intense was the fighting that some 17,000 brigaders from 14 nations never lived to return to their homeland.

For many of us, the abiding memory of Spain's Civil War is the fate of Guernica. Historically the little market town on the edge of the Rioja wine region was the Runnymede of the Basque people, a race settled since earliest times at the foot of the western Pyrenees. Through successive regimes the Basques had safeguarded their own language, their culture and the communal liberties which were bestowed in the fourteenth century on a proto-parliament, assembled under an ancient oak tree in the centre of Guernica. The town had little strategic importance for Franco but in the spring of 1937 he sought to overrun Spain's four Basque provinces, capture the key port of Bilbao and secure the north-western frontier with France. It was Guernica's misfortune to be eight miles behind the front line at a crucial moment in the nationalist assault. On the evening of Monday, 26 April 1937, the town was carpet-bombed by Heinkel 111s and Junker 52s in the German Condor Legion, planes sent by Hitler to help Franco and to gain battle experience for the Luftwaffe. Guernica was destroyed and between 1,000 and 1,600 civilians killed.

German responsibility was confirmed by George Steer, *The Times'* correspondent in Spain, who reached Guernica soon after the attack ended and found bomb cases stamped with the Luftwaffe's eagle hallmark. His graphic account appeared in later editions of Tuesday's

Times and was syndicated across the world. 'Guernica was not a military objective,' Steer emphasised. 'The object of the bombardment was seemingly the demoralisation of the civil population.' By Wednesday, as we sat at peace in Ilford 900 miles away, we could read details of the three-hour attack in both dailies we took.

Accounts of the raid angered Pablo Picasso, who came from Malaga but was living in Paris. He at once began work on his black and white symbolic mural, *Guernica*. It was completed for the Chaillot international exhibition in Paris three months later and inevitably invited comparison with Goya's depiction of the savagery of war in Spain, back in Napoleonic times. Soon after the exhibition closed in September *Guernica* went on display at London's New Burlington Galleries to raise funds for war relief. It failed to draw in West End art lovers, probably because they sympathised with Franco rather than the Basques. In November, however, when it was shown in Oxford, the mural aroused more interest; the philosopher Gilbert Ryle and the young historian Hugh Trevor-Roper – neither of them avant-garde 'lefties' – were among those prepared to queue patiently to study it. The queues were as long when it returned to London in December, for this time it was displayed at the Whitechapel Art Gallery, half a mile from Cable Street.

My parents found all sorts of reasons for not taking me to the gallery as I wished, and I did not have an opportunity to study the full mural until 1984, but I had seen photographs of it before the Blitz struck London. A small reproduction is beside me as I write. Though nowadays I find greater depth in the symbolism than I could see as a youngster, I can understand why *Guernica*'s unfamiliar art form impressed me at the time. Some figures have a simplicity that make their meaning stand out clearly even to the uninitiated. Picasso's Cubism distorted all that was familiar to the people of a Basque market town in the way that an act of war mangles daily life even as it destroys it. The mural is not solely a protest at three hours of horror in 1937. No other work of art conveys so starkly the abomination of aerial bombardment as a scourge of humanity.

The Civil War continued relentlessly for two years after the destruction of Guernica. I tried to follow its twists and turns but became easily confused. We had not 'done' the geography of Spain at school and I had no idea of the constantly changing terrain, with rugged mountains dropping down steeply to fast-flowing rivers that criss-crossed red dusty plains. But isolated happenings remain stamped in memory: the visit of a Labour Party delegation led by Attlee to Madrid and the British battalion of the International Brigade; the destruction of an over-confident Italian armoured division sent by Mussolini to reinforce the nationalists near Guadalajara; dramatic pictures in the *Daily Express* of the sinking by three republican destroyers of the cruiser *Baleares*, flagship of the nationalist navy; and reports of the hard-fought infantry battle on the River Ebro in the summer of 1938 that reminded my Uncle Warren of the slaughter he had witnessed in Flanders.

I did not however know of the political in-fighting between Marxists, anarchists and traditional republicans in Madrid and Catalonia and I was surprised when Barcelona suddenly fell in the last week of January 1939, after heavy bombing by the Italians. It heralded the beginning of the end; Valencia and Madrid defied the nationalists for two more months before their defenders too were overpowered. On 1 April 1939 Franco declared Spain's Civil War at an end. It had claimed the lives of 300,000 fighting men and women and at least another 400,000 non-combatants – a terrible toll that was to mount higher under a regime that imposed harsh sentences of death or imprisonment on its opponents.

Long before the guns fell silent around Madrid our attention had shifted to other potential flashpoints. The partnership of Germany and Italy in Spain sealed the bonds of the 'Rome-Berlin Axis', a pact of friendship Mussolini proclaimed in November 1936. This understanding left independent Austria isolated, sandwiched between two aggressive dictatorships.

On 5 November 1937 Hitler summoned his service chiefs and the Foreign Minister, and Germany was ready to seek expansion in the East (*Lebensraum*). First he intended to take advantage of any opportunity that arose to achieve union with Austria (*Anschluss),* forbidden by the Treaty of Versailles. A second move would cause the break-up of Czechoslovakia. Use would be made of the *Volksdeutsche,* the 6 million Germans beyond the borders of the Third Reich.

Twelve days after this conference Hitler received Lord Halifax, a minister without departmental responsibilities in Chamberlain's Cabinet. They met at the Berghof, his mountain eyrie above Berchtesgaden near the Austrian border. During the talks Halifax conceded that changes in eastern Europe 'could probably not be avoided in the long run'; he mentioned Austria, Czechoslovakia and Danzig, adding that 'England was only interested in seeing that such changes were brought about by peaceful means'. Hitler dismissed his visitor as a nonentity: if Halifax was representative of Chamberlain's government, Britain was unlikely to be an obstacle to his immediate objectives.

Hitler's opportunity came three months later. Since August 1934 the Austrian government had been headed by Chancellor Kurt von Schuschnigg, an astute lawyer from the Tirol, politically right-wing but a 'good Austrian', firmly anti-Nazi. He was confident he could placate Hitler by assuring him that his policy was based on the principle that Austria was historically a German state. For two years this balancing act seemed to be working well, and when Schuschnigg was invited to the Berghof on 12 February he saw no reason to expect any change in relations with Berlin.

Schuschnigg found Hitler in a furious temper; he denounced, not only recent alleged insults by individuals, but the past record of Austria as an obstacle to the fulfilment of the German people's historic mission. Schuschnigg was presented with a series of demands which would have given pro-Nazi Austrians control of the government in Vienna. He was required to sign acceptance of the proposals and put them into effect within five days or the German army would cross the frontier. He signed, though explaining that the Austrian constitution also required the signature of the president, Wilhelm Miklas.

Schuschnigg played for time, hoping for foreign support. On Wednesday, 9 March, he announced that a plebiscite would be held the following Sunday. Voters would be asked to support a 'free, independent, social, Christian and united Austria'. A 'Yes' vote was almost certain. But would Hitler delay any longer and would other governments support Schuschnigg's defiance? It was a desperate gamble.

Fate was against him. Incomplete accounts of the Berghof meeting had circulated in London and the papers we read were at first sympathetic to the Austrians. Then suddenly on 28 February our attention switched away to Westminster: the Foreign Secretary, Anthony Eden, unexpectedly resigned after differences with Chamberlain, primarily over Italian policy in Spain. On 1 March Halifax became Foreign Secretary. It was he who, on 12 March, responded to Schuschnigg's desperate appeal for support with the blunt telegram: 'His Majesty's Government is unable to guarantee protection.' This refusal forced Schuschnigg to resign from office immediately.

German troops entered Austria the next morning. Their rapturous reception led the Führer to follow them into Linz before nightfall. On Monday afternoon (14 March) his cavalcade entered Vienna, where church bells rang out triumphantly on orders from the Archbishop, Cardinal Innitzer. Celebrations by hysterical crowds continued throughout the night, with Hitler lapping up the adulation of the young in a city where he was once destitute. The German authorities made photographs of his welcome readily available to the foreign press and we could see in our papers swastika banners draped over the city's architectural treasures. We knew nothing of the cleverly contrived civil disobedience by loyal Austrians, young and old. Eight months elapsed before a new weekly, *Picture Post*, printed smuggled pictures of the abject humiliation inflicted on Vienna's Jewish population. It was then that we saw with disgust middle-aged and elderly men and women taunted as they scrubbed pavements, under the mocking eyes of their Nazi masters.

NINE

'A Quarrel in a Far Away Country'

On the evening Hitler was welcomed in Vienna we were surprised to hear on the wireless a special appeal by the Home Secretary, Sir Samuel Hoare, calling for 'at least a million men and women' to undertake voluntary 'work that in an emergency would be exciting and dangerous'. Momentarily it seemed as if the government acknowledged that Hitler was embarking on a new policy. Unknown to us, a few days later the prime minister met TUC leaders and won assurances that their members would not oppose changes in the engineering industry: henceforth in an emergency manufacturers of cars could switch to production of aircraft parts or planes themselves. Strange masts appeared on a spur of Suffolk coast. Radar was with us, though we knew nothing of it. We saw the masts, and wondered.

Even so, the threat of war was not taken seriously by most of the Cabinet or by the general public. Hoare's fluted voice was too refined to make him a mass recruiting sergeant and there was little response to his broadcast appeal. Lord Woolton, the head of John Lewis Stores, banned the sale of German goods in the chain's shops, but such protests were rare. Although sorry for Austria our attention turned to matters of less gravity. Dad's *Daily Express* speculated on the Welshman Tommy Farr's chances of becoming world boxing champion and we looked forward to Saturday's commentary on the England v. Scotland clash at Twickenham, which would decide the Five Nations rugby championship. To my dismay Scotland won but I had to admit that over the wireless it sounded like a good match.

So life continued through the spring and summer of 1938. 'Emergencies' came and went without war following and I was soon turning away from newspaper maps of Germany's new borders to the sports pages. The Australian cricketers arrived a month after the *Anschluss*, with Bradman on his third tour. For England, Hutton's batting promised to challenge the Australian's world record score and indeed in the final Test at the Oval he surpassed it. Alfred Hitchcock's light-hearted thriller *The Lady Vanishes*, shown in cinemas later that year, captured the reluctance with which we accepted a half-belief in the imminence of war.

'Look at Czechoslovakia!' the Paris taxi driver had urged us on 3 September; we duly did so from time to time all the spring and summer. Czechoslovakia was the most fragile fragment of the Habsburg Monarchy given independence by the peacemakers in 1919-20. Four Slav peoples had settled there: 7 million Czechs, 2 million

Slovaks, 450,000 Ruthenes (basically Ukrainians) and some 50,000 Poles. The population also included 700,000 Hungarians and, crucially, between 3.5 and 4 million *Volksdeutsche*. Most of these German speakers were in the Sudetenland, an industrialised region that had long served as a mountainous natural frontier with Germany. After the *Anschluss* many Sudeten Germans sought inclusion in Hitler's Reich.

I had dipped into much of John Gunther's *Inside Europe* by now and knew something of the background to international affairs, at least across the Continent. But I was too young to realise how apparently non-political events responded to a hidden diplomacy. At the end of May I was shocked by pictures of England's footballers giving a Hitler salute in the Berlin Olympic stadium before an international friendly match. We now know the team's reluctant gesture came in response to a plea from the British ambassador who wished to placate the Führer at a time of mounting tension in the Sudetenland. This was appeasement in action. It may have postponed the crisis which the ambassador feared. But a determined England team relieved their feelings by thrashing the vaunted German side 6–0.

Another newspaper picture has also stuck in my mind. Viscount Runciman was photographed on the boat train to Dover reading Elizabeth Wiskemann's newly published *Czechs and Germans* with earnest intensity. Lord Runciman, a survivor from Asquith's pre-war government, was on his way to Czechoslovakia as Chamberlain's 'unofficial mediator', accompanied by a team of Foreign Office advisers. They arrived in Prague on 3 August.

Runciman made an unfortunate start: he met spokesmen for the Sudeten German Party ahead of members of the government. Reporters at his first press conference thought him pompous and curt. Many remained hostile throughout his visit. Their judgments are reflected in several studies of the Munich crisis.

Konrad Henlein, leader of the Sudeten German Party, had visited London, where his apparent moderation impressed several leading figures, even Churchill. Runciman did not meet Henlein in person until 18 August; he found him patient and helpful in contrast to Beneš, the widely respected president, who was 'devious and dilatory'. After travelling around 'this accursed country' – his words in a confidential report – Runciman recommended a system of 'cantonal self-government'. He felt confident his findings would give Chamberlain a basis for negotiations to defuse the mounting tension.

Hitler would have none of it. Life for the German people in the Sudetenland 'is intolerable… Czechoslovakia is a monstrous creation… Beneš is a liar,' he yelled at Nazi legions marshalled beneath his rostrum for the party's Nuremberg Rally on 12 September. Although none of us understood German we caught the sound of him on our Ekco about eight o'clock that evening, screaming so violently that Bruce, our dog, sat up with ears erect, and growled. Later in the week I watched a newsreel. Hitler's face was screwed up, his body shook and words tumbled out in a torrent of wrath; *Must be off his head*, I thought. The rhetoric incited German fanatics to smash Czech and Jewish shops in a wave of mob violence, particularly destructive in the famous spa that Czechs called Karlovy Vary and Germans Karlsbad. Beneš mobilised the army, manned the powerful defensive line around the borders and imposed martial law.

Three days later Chamberlain made the most courageous journey of his life. At the age of 69 he set out in turbulent weather on his first long flight, resolved to talk to Hitler man to man. The novelty of airborne summit diplomacy made me eager to catch the *News* each evening. The two leaders met at the Berghof, high above Berchtesgaden. Chamberlain assured Hitler that, in principle, Britain would facilitate the transference of the Sudetenland to Germany, preferably after a plebiscite. He returned to London looking well satisfied.

On 18 September Daladier, the French prime minister, came to London for consultation with Chamberlain. Unlike Britain, France had treaty obligations to Czechoslovakia and he thought the British attitude too subservient to Hitler. With testy irony, Chamberlain pointed out that neither British troops nor aircraft could reach Prague. Eventually the French agreed to follow Chamberlain if he could broker a settlement that would include a collective guarantee of Czechoslovakia's revised frontiers.

Back he went to Germany again on 21 September, this time bound for Godesberg, on the Rhine, south of Cologne. He was soon disillusioned. Hitler was not interested in any compromise. He presented Chamberlain with a memorandum demanding the immediate cession of all the Sudetenland and the satisfaction of Hungarian and Polish claims for frontier revision. A grim-faced prime minister flew home to London where by now anti-aircraft guns, searchlights and barrage balloon launchers were being sited across the kingdom and the distribution of 34 million gas masks had begun.

On 27 September our papers reported a speech given by Hitler in Berlin's Sportpalast: 'Before us stands the last problem that must be solved and will be solved,' he said. 'It is the last territorial claim which I have to make in Europe but it is the claim from which I will not recede… My patience now is exhausted.'

Confidently we awaited a broadcast response that evening from the prime minister. I expected a calm riposte, a reluctant but defiant call to arms. Instead I heard Chamberlain say, 'How horrible, fantastic, incredible it is that we should be digging trenches and trying on gas masks here because of a quarrel in a faraway country between people of whom we know nothing.' I could hardly believe my ears. 'Faraway', when Karlovy Vary was nearer Westminster than some Scottish constituencies? 'Know nothing' of the land of Dvorak, Tomas Masaryk and Karel Čapek? Even I had heard of Čapek's robots and read a delightful essay by him on bicycling. The broadcast damned Chamberlain in my eyes as a philistine Little Englander. Yet probably most listeners that evening agreed with him, except perhaps in London's northern heights and in several universities.

We did not know that throughout these tense days Chamberlain used a personal emissary, Sir Horace Wilson, an experienced trade union troubleshooter, skilled in ways of appeasement, to work for a compromise. Chamberlain for his part warned Beneš that the only way to save Czechoslovakia from total destruction was to accept Hitler's demands. At the same time Mussolini, aware that the Italian army was in no state to fight a general war, came forward as a mediator. On 28 September, my 12th birthday, the wireless brought news of a dramatic scene in the Commons, when Chamberlain broke off a speech to tell Members he had just received an invitation to fly to Munich and confer with Hitler, Daladier and Mussolini in order to resolve the crisis. So great was the relief that MPs on both sides of the House rose and cheered the prime minister. Three successors – Churchill, Attlee and Macmillan – stayed silent. The diarist Harold Nicolson was among a small group who remained seated.

Chamberlain flew to Munich the next morning. The Big Four spent little time on details: a Czechoslovak envoy in a neighbouring room was not even consulted, though Chamberlain sought to persuade his companions to ask him to join them. The final agreement provided for the immediate transference of the Sudetenland to Germany and for a four-power guarantee of the rump of Czechoslovakia against an unprovoked attack once the claims of the Hungarians and Poles were settled.

A rapturous reception awaited the prime minister in England. At teatime on Friday, 30 September, his plane touched down at Heston, an aerodrome on land now covered by a motorway service station. The whole Cabinet and many other MPs were there to hail 'the nation's saviour'. He was escorted to a battery of microphones, an unprecedented sight in Britain. World radio stations tuned in. A young Richard Dimbleby set the scene for the BBC. Chamberlain held up a sheet of paper; it bore, he told us, 'Herr Hitler's signature and my own' and carried a momentous pledge: 'The desire of our two peoples is never to go to war with one another again. We are resolved that the method of consultation shall be the method adopted to deal with any other questions that may concern our two countries... and thus to ensure the peace of Europe. I believe it is peace for our time,' Chamberlain proclaimed.

As darkness fell, the prime minister's car headed back into London. He was welcomed by a jubilant crowd gathered outside Buckingham Palace and he and Mrs Chamberlain were invited to join the royal family on the palace balcony. Cheers rang out. They came again when the Chamberlains arrived in Downing Street. A companion in the car recalled how in 1878 an earlier prime minister, Beaconsfield (Disraeli), spoke of bringing back 'Peace with Honour' from the Congress of Berlin, and for a third of a century the turbulent Balkans were spared major war. From a first floor window at No. 10 a weary Chamberlain waved to the crowd below. Beaconsfield's words came to mind. 'Peace with Honour,' they heard him call. It was a flash of inspiration soon to be called into question.

The mood of exhilaration had gripped us too as we listened in to the broadcast from Heston. Bruce, stretched out on the carpet beside us, did not approve: 'That yelling a fortnight ago was enough to make a dog growl and now this; something strange must be happening. The young master needs to relax; a game is the answer,' he apparently reasoned. Confidently he dropped his indoor ball on my lap. I let it fall to the floor. He tried again with a rubber bone, always good for a tug. I brushed it aside. There was a pause. He went out of the room, seeking something to catch our eyes. A sluicing sound emanating from the kitchen cut across Dimbleby's reverent words. Bruce reappeared, triumphantly wagging his stumpy tail. Behind him came the contents of his basket: two thinning cushions, chewed around the edges; a forgotten collar with cracked leather; and a long discarded towel smeared with paw prints from the park. He laid them in obeisance before the wireless set. We could ignore him no longer and burst into relaxed laughter. Bruce's persistence and scant reward seemed a parody of Chamberlain's hollow endeavours.

TEN

Umbrella Year

'No conqueror returning from a victory on the battlefield has come home adorned with nobler laurels than Mr Chamberlain from Munich yesterday,' Saturday's leading article in *The Times* pontificated. But this post-Heston euphoria was soon dissolved. One Cabinet minister, Duff Cooper, resigned as First Lord of the Admiralty that very morning and there was a heated parliamentary debate in the following week. 'We have sustained a defeat without a war,' Churchill declared, and for the Labour Opposition Clement Attlee spoke of a 'gallant civilised and democratic people betrayed and handed over to a ruthless despotism'. On both sides of the Channel the very word 'Munich' became and remains a term of moral reproach in days of diplomatic tension.

For homework from Bancroft's one night in October I had to write an essay on 'My Country, Right or Wrong'. I interpreted the title as a question and wrote four pages, mainly an attack on the 'faraway country' Little Englander aspects of appeasement. I received starred full marks for it, which meant I had to show it to the headmaster, who clearly approved of it. But, as in many families, our feelings were mixed. My parents remained thankful we had been spared war. Dad's *Daily Express* assured readers day after day 'There Will Be No War This Year Or Next'. The *News Chronicle* reported the steady day by day advance of German troops into the Sudetenland. I thought the news reports wretchedly dismal.

Fortunately, we had a newcomer for arresting reading – if you could find a copy to buy. On 1 October the much advertised weekly *Picture Post* went on sale. Dad looked out for it when he left the office at midday. Not a copy was to be seen at Chancery Lane or Liverpool Street or outside Ilford station. Across the whole of southern England the public had gobbled up a print-run of a quarter of a million in under four hours. No doubt eighty glossy pages for a penny seemed too good a bargain to miss, while two flamenco dancers in full flight on the cover made a happy contrast to the weary wing-collared Chamberlain pictured in the dailies. Yet, though *Picture Post* hit the bookstalls with a froth of frivolity, Stefan Lorant, the editor, was a serious journalist. Gollancz published his *I Was Hitler's Prisoner*, extracts from a diary, as early as 1935. At heart he was a radical socialist. Here at last was a magazine to counter the pro-Hitler inclinations of *The Illustrated London News*. For the next six years we rarely missed a copy.

Picture Post's greatest service during those last 11 months of peace was to keep its growing number of readers aware of the latent menace from Germany and to expose the real nature of Nazi rule. The ninth number, sold on 26 November, included smuggled pictures of Jew-baiting in the streets of Vienna immediately after the *Anschluss*; it also carried on-going reports of a new wave of persecution sweeping across 'Greater Germany'. For the first time I came across the word 'pogrom', a term originally applied to the harsh anti-Jewish laws of Tsarist Russia.

On 28 October Hitler ordered the expulsion from the Reich of all Polish Jews. Herschel Grynszpan, a 17-year-old Polish Jew studying in Paris, received a letter from his father which gave an account of his family's plight. In anger Grynszpan went to the German embassy in Paris and shot dead the third counsellor, Ernst vom Rath. Hitler took vengeance on the whole Jewish community, who were 'fined' one billion marks for the crime. More dramatically, Nazi Party members were given free rein to destroy Jewish property. For 15 hours on 10 November 1938 Jewish homes, shops and places of worship were pillaged or destroyed. During *Kristallnacht* (The Night of Shattered Glass) 112 synagogues went up in flames. So too did many shops, their contents looted or piled on bonfires in the streets. Over the following days 20,000 more Jews were sent to concentration camps. Public opinion across the democratic world was shocked. On 11 November, the 20th anniversary of Armistice Day, *The Times* condemned the 'blackguardly assaults upon defenceless and innocent people' as 'a disgrace' to Germany. This unexpected rebuke from an editor who rarely criticised Hitler heightened the sense of outrage at home and abroad. Stefan Lorant, however, anticipated that public indignation would be short-lived. By delaying *Picture Post*'s broadside until the end of the month he ensured *Kristallnacht* did not slip from memory as an isolated event.

Among many people, including several of our friends, there remained a measure of respect, even affection, for Chamberlain. His rolled umbrella had looked incongruous when he stepped down from the plane on his first flight to Germany but in the closing months of the year it set a fashion. An umbrella suddenly became an accessory as essential for a well-dressed City gent as a bowler hat or kid gloves. Chamberlain himself encouraged the craze: he is said to have kept the original umbrella unrolled inside its neat cover while relying on two 'working' brollies for rainy days. An umbrella inspired songwriters – provided the lyricist could add an extra syllable to the word. 'You're a fine fellah, with your black um-ber-el-la' is a song best forgotten. Not so 'The Umbrella Man'. In this instance there was no mention of Chamberlain by name. Instead, a lilting refrain echoed the call of an itinerant umbrella repairer pedalling the streets: 'Any umberellas, any umberellas to mend today?' To some bands it was a slow foxtrot, to others a waltz; it became very popular. Umbrellas were still in demand at Christmas. I was told you could buy one in Paris, if you asked for 'Un Chamberlain'.

In the New Year there was a need for working brollies. Heavy rain poured down on Mother and me as we battled against a strong wind to reach Broadcasting House in the second week of January. Earlier that day Chamberlain and Halifax had their umbrellas open when they flew to Rome on a mission which sought to improve relations with fascist Italy. The visit was not a success: Britain had recognised Victor Emmanuel III as Emperor of Ethiopia in the previous April but Chamberlain was unwilling to accept further Italian expansion, either in Africa or around the Mediterranean. The Italian press turned sour. When, at the end of the visit the prime minister and the Duce were photographed inspecting a Guard of Honour in bright sunshine, the Rome papers stressed the contrast between the resplendent soldier dictator and the ageing 'umbrella carrier' from England at his side.

On his return to London, Chamberlain was confronted by a totally unexpected problem. On 16 January the IRA embarked on the first terrorist campaign in Britain for 15 years. Relatively small devices, often planted in pillar boxes, exploded in London, Birmingham, Alnwick and Manchester. First reports of the bombings surprised all of us but there were no signs of additional security. The attacks continued intermittently for seven months, particularly in the Midlands. Five people were killed in Coventry by an IRA bomb only six days before the outbreak of war.

By mid-March, however, central Europe was back in the headlines. After Munich the structure of Czecho-Slovakia was drastically changed: both Slovakia and Ruthenia were given full autonomy but disputes over federal funding between the central government in Prague and the two nominal dependencies culminated in Czech troops taking control of Ruthenia and then occupying Bratislava, the Slovak capital. Hitler was given an opportunity to intervene. Czecho-Slovakia was falling apart, he claimed, and on 15 March he formally took the improvised state under his protection. We first heard the news on the wireless at six o'clock that evening. It was a year and a day since we had listened to Hitler's triumphant reception in Vienna.

At first Chamberlain insisted Britain had no reason to intervene. Czecho-Slovakia 'was always regarded by us as being only of a transitory nature', he told Parliament on 16 March. But in a speech at Birmingham later in the week he deplored Hitler's decree that Czechs, and all other non-German-speaking nationals, would be treated as 'protected peoples' of the Reich, second-class citizens. A further ominous move soon followed: on 23 March Hitler struck for the first time in the Baltic seizing Memel, historically a German port as signed to Lithuania by the Versailles peacemakers. Germany also annexed a 100-mile strip of land along the River Niemen, a vital channel for Poland's trade and defence.

The Polish foreign minister, Colonel Józef Beck, was determined to avoid the isolation that ensnared Schuschnigg before the *Anschluss*. Poland and France were linked by a military alliance dating back to 1921. Beck now proposed to supplement this treaty with an Anglo-Polish agreement. His initiative was welcomed by Lord Halifax, who urged the prime minister to make a positive statement promising support to Poland. On 31 March Chamberlain accordingly announced in the

Commons that, if Polish independence was threatened, 'His Majesty's Government would feel bound to lend the Polish Government all the support in their power.' Was appeasement at an end we wondered? Beck came post haste to London to clarify the situation. He arrived on 4 April.

Mother and I were on the pavement opposite 10 Downing Street that Tuesday and we saw Beck and Halifax driven into the Foreign Office forecourt. Beck's face bore a cold smile of smug superiority. He knew he was spokesman for the only army in Eastern Europe that seemed capable of holding the balance between Nazi Germany and Soviet Russia. His hosts flattered him with the full red carpet treatment, including a special train down to Portsmouth to hear the guns of the Royal Navy in action. Chamberlain gave him what he most desired. On 8 April, as the visit came to an end, it was announced that Britain and Poland would conclude a mutual assistance treaty, with details to be settled later in the year. This pronouncement confirmed a decisive shift in British policy.

Yet I remember that, as a family, we took less interest in the Poles than in breaking news full of drama. On 7 April the Italian navy and army invaded Albania, chasing out of Tirana King Zog and his Hungarian-born queen, who had given birth to their first child earlier that week. The popular press ran stories, occasionally correct, highlighting their plight as they made their way through snow-capped mountain valleys to safety in Queen Geraldine's native land. There was also speculation over the political implications of the Italian move. Zog had been virtually a puppet on the Duce's string ever since his kingdom was proclaimed in 1928; even Albania's national bank was in Rome. Had Mussolini annexed the country as a prelude to expansion in the Balkans? Was Europe going to see a crablike advance by Germans in the north and Italians in the south? Halifax instructed ambassadors in Turkey, Romania, Greece and Yugoslavia to discover if these countries sought British support in facing the new threat.

An internal crisis in Yugoslavia ruled out any response from Belgrade but as early as 13 April Greece and Romania asked for similar guarantees to the offer welcomed by Poland a fortnight previously. Five days later Hitler delivered a speech, as vituperative as his outburst at Nuremberg in September. Now his wrath was loose on Poland: the German-Polish Non-Aggression Pact of 1934 was null and void, he thundered. As April ended, Europe it seemed was rushing headlong into war. Britain reintroduced conscription after a gap of 19 years: a National Service Act provided for the call-up of men aged 20 for six months in the armed forces.

A long stand-off followed, however. Germany was not yet ready for a campaign in the West. Throughout the early summer labourers toiled at digging and erecting the 'Siegfried Line', known to the Germans as the West Wall. This system of fortification was neither so deep nor so complex as France's Maginot Line but as it ran from the northern frontier with Holland down to Switzerland it required the completion of strategic *autobahns* to provide speedy communication. The Luftwaffe and the naval chiefs also needed time to complete plans and preparations.

Here in London we were relieved at the apparent relaxation of tension and I was suddenly turning to different pages of my atlas to follow the King and Queen's visit to Canada and America as reported on the wireless each evening. But people's tempers were on a short fuse that spring, presumably strained by the political tumult. I recall angry exchanges over barking dogs, bus queue jumping, and my father's garden rubbish bonfires. 'There you go, you're a smoked kipper, that's what you are,' came a call from an irate lady up the road. Privately we were much amused.

One sudden switch in the public mood I saw for myself. On 20 May Ilford's cricket festival matched Essex and Yorkshire. The visitors won the toss and put Essex in under a threatening sky; they were all out for 114 soon after lunch. As Yorkshire's innings began, the clouds lifted a little, and in the first over the great Herbert Sutcliffe drove the ball into the deep outfield with Rolls-Royce majesty. Hutton then took guard, to face Nichols. The crowd went silent, then we gasped – and the record-breaking batsman of nine months ago was on his way back to the pavilion, out first ball. There was generous sympathetic clapping as he disappeared into the dressing room. We settled down, looking forward to an exciting afternoon. The next Yorkshireman came in, faced one ball and appealed against the light. The umpires at once took the players off the field.

Howls of derision arose from a section of the crowd. Spectators old enough to know better rushed to the foot of the pavilion steps shouting 'Yorkshire cowards' and booing any white rose member spotted in the enclosure. After about ten minutes, the Essex skipper, Captain Stephenson, emerged from the pavilion. Imperiously he held up his hand and the protests died down. 'It is shameful of you to treat our guests like this,' he said, 'sheer bad manners… There'll be no more play today.' Meekly we drifted away.

Such behaviour made headlines in the popular Sunday papers. No one could recall anything like it in a championship match but Monday's papers hardly mentioned the trouble. The next year's *Wisden* merely said some spectators 'remonstrated in protest'. But when that edition of the Almanack went on sale, we had been at war for nine months; the comment came as an echo from a distant world.

On Tuesday Yorkshire had a seven wicket win, to my dismay. That evening, however, Dad sprang a surprise which lifted my spirits. He had been given complimentary tickets for the maiden voyage of the *Royal Daffodil* from London to Ostend, with an overnight stay in Belgium. I could think of nothing more enjoyable ahead of end-of-the-year school exams.

Well before eight on Saturday morning, 27 May, Dad and I arrived at Tower Pier. The *Royal Daffodil* looked so beautiful that I gasped. She was spotlessly white and 'dressed overall', with small flags fluttering from her sparse rigging. To my delight, Tower Bridge opened for her and we sailed downriver with tugs and far bigger vessels hooting in salute to welcome the newcomer. Her name honoured Liverpool's *Daffodil*, the little ship that had played a vital role in the Zeebrugge raid of April 1918, but I felt as if I was aboard a ship royal in her own right. Although she was crowded, the buffet restaurant was spacious and we had no difficulty in finding deckchairs in the sun. We picked up more passengers from Southend's mile-long pier and enjoyed a smooth crossing on a fine afternoon, rare in umbrella year. At Ostend, ships' sirens welcomed us and we berthed close to what remained of *Vindictive*, the cruiser that had sought 'to twist the dragon's tail' at Zeebrugge on St George's Day 1918 but was sunk as a blockship at Ostend in a second raid a few days later.

I would have liked to have taken the coastal tram down to Zeebrugge and Heist on the Sunday morning but Dad doubted if we had time for the double journey. We strolled along Ostend's long promenade. Dad bought an English paper and we sat down at a cafe near the quay. The news was sobering: Berlin pronouncements made much of Polish restrictions on German rights in the 'free city' of Danzig. A Belgian at a neighbouring table started talking to Dad, in excellent English. He told us how in 1917-18 he had fought in the waterlogged trenches at Dixmude, west of Ypres. Then he saw Dad's paper, with the news from Berlin in it. Leaning forward he tapped the table with a finger and said in a proud, confidential tone, 'It won't happen again. We've fine forts along the canals behind our frontier. If they come next time, they'll never get through.'

Thoughtfully we boarded the *Royal Daffodil* for the return crossing. I hoped the Belgian veteran was right. Dad was sceptical: he feared that his new friend was too optimistic, more so than the French with their faith in the Maginot Line. For the moment however I was content to enjoy the voyage home. I remember a slowly sinking sun which caught the diamond sparkle of the bow waves as we headed for the Thames. Six years elapsed before I next had the joy of seeing again sparkling waters in a calm sea from the deck of a ship.

ELEVEN

Happy Days

After the sunny break in Ostend, life in England seemed dreary again. We noticed the *Daily Express* had stopped assuring readers there would be no war, and hardly a day went by without a government pamphlet full of advice coming through the letter box with the morning post. Dad decided not to risk another trip to the Continent. Instead he booked a holiday in Devon for the last fortnight in August. Meanwhile we would see as much of England as peace allowed. We made a rail and coach excursion to Stratford-upon-Avon, Kenilworth and Coventry and friends took us by car to Canterbury. I am glad that before the bombs fell I had this opportunity to admire two great cathedrals and walk through narrow mediaeval streets unscathed by war down the centuries.

At 11.00 a.m. on Saturday, 12 August, we left Waterloo on the Atlantic Coast Express (ACE), the Southern Railway's rival to the Great Western's Cornish Riviera. The SR route was new to me and I was thrilled to see racing cars hurtling round the steeply banked circuit at Brooklands. Dad told me, correctly in those days, that the only mosque in England was at Woking, but he did not say it was a low-lying building near the station; I looked in vain through the carriage window for a towering minaret.

At Sidmouth Junction, near Honiton, the rear coaches, including ours, were shunted on to a parallel line, leaving the ACE to take a circuitous route through north Devon, eventually reaching Cornwall's Atlantic coast at Bude and Padstow. Our half made for Newton Poppleford, shedding coaches for Sidmouth there. On we went down the Otter Valley to Budleigh Salterton and Littleham; 'Liddle-um', the porter called out in warm and welcoming Devon-ese. About half-past three we arrived at Exmouth, where the SR had recently completed an imposing station. Across the Exe estuary we caught a first glimpse of Lyme Bay and the sea.

I have always liked Exmouth, it has a seafaring past going back to the Hundred Years' War, but it was also a holiday resort with a beach which, at low tide, was as sandy as any I knew in England. We had often visited friends and relatives in and around the town but never stayed there. Now Dad had booked us in at Fernside, a bed and breakfast guest house tucked away behind Exmouth's historic terrace, The Beacon. For a fortnight we were without a wireless. Now and then a murmur from the parlour made me wonder if news was coming through about which we ought to know but I was not worried. Dad took the *Daily Express* with him to the beach each weekday and it was optimistic once more: an Anglo-French naval and military mission was in Moscow to persuade Russia to cooperate with Poland. That seemed fine to me; quite enough to deter Hitler.

Only a few weeks later I found it hard to understand how I could have felt so detached from events. But these were happy days. All I sought was good firm sand and like-minded youngsters who would play beach cricket while the tide was out. In the trunk sent ahead by Carter Paterson, the invaluable carrier service, were a cricket bat, four stumps, bails and a few tennis balls. I was welcomed by a group whose natural leader was Neville, from Bristol. For a week we had great fun each morning. The fielding must have been good, for only one ball was lost in the sea, and that was because of my stupid vanity in wearing long trousers. 'Must've bandy legs,' the wicketkeeper speculated, loudly. Neville was teased because of his Christian name; 'Where's yer umbrella then?' came the call when he dropped a catch.

The holiday became more of a family gathering than I had anticipated. Uncle Bill regularly came back to his birthplace in late summer and was already staying with one of his cousins. Mother's sister, Aunt Margaret, and her elderly husband, Uncle Walter, were in a boarding house not far from us. There was also a Palmer link: Dad's brother Albert lived at Exwick, and we saw a lot of my cousins John and Joyce. I was so fond of Joyce that one afternoon I deigned to shed the male prejudice expected of me and sat beside her in the Manor Gardens listening to an all-girl band playing popular tunes. Daringly we held hands, for a moment or two. Such was calf love then.

On the second Monday Mother and Dad and I caught

a bus to Sidmouth. After a walk through the town they settled in deckchairs while I went along the esplanade towards the mouth of the River Sid. I had spotted an ice-cream man ladling out his own creations, three mixed-flavour cornets resting on an edible base. They stood up like roses in a bowl and looked just as colourful. Their taste was delicious. As I started back along the esplanade, my chin, nose and cheeks plastered with melting cream,I saw coming towards me a man whose picture I knew well. It was often in the papers. Generally he was shown in Norfolk jacket and knickerbockers but today he wore a grey suit, not unlike my father's. The beard, however, made Bernard Shaw instantly recognisable. He smiled at the spectacle I presented and would, I think, have spoken to me, but I looked away, too shy and cream-embarrassed to acknowledge him. What a fool I was! At least I could have said how much I had enjoyed *Pygmalion*.

Next morning, 22 August, Dad and I set off for the beach as usual while Mother and Aunt Margaret went shopping. We caught up with Uncle Walter opposite the old lifeboat house. I thought he seemed downcast. So apparently did an itinerant beach photographer from Paignton, for he called out, 'Cheer up Grandpa! They're not here yet.' Dad and I laughed as he clicked the camera. Uncle Walter managed a wan smile. He had read the paper under his arm; Dad had not opened his *Express*.

I joined my friends but by now tidal hours had changed and we could not find anywhere firm enough to keep stumps upright. Hitting the ball about in loose sand above the high water mark was unrewarding. It was hard to get a footing and we soon gave up the effort. We would come down again on Friday, when the tide might be better. Some boys went swimming. Rather disconsolately, I carried stumps and bat back to Dad's chair. That was the last I saw of Neville and his friends for, though we were slow to realise it, Europe's crisis had caught up with us.

By now Dad had opened his paper and the news left him as glum as Uncle Walter. Late on Monday evening the German Foreign Ministry informed the world that Ribbentrop was flying to Moscow to conclude a non-aggression pact with the Soviet Union. Banner headlines across Europe's papers saw war as inevitable. Communists and Nazis, bitter ideological foes throughout the decade, were apparently ready to divide Poland between them. The pact was signed in the Kremlin on 23 August.

Public and personal affairs were thrown into confusion. The West Indies cricketers, having drawn the last Test at the Oval, cut short their tour, with most players heading for home. So too did the Anglo-French naval and military mission, in Russia, who had met the Soviet High Command as recently as Thursday. Parliament was recalled even before the pact was signed and telegrams sent to reservists and everyone committed to fulfilling agreed evacuation plans.

Aunt Margaret had been a supply teacher for several years. Her 50th birthday fell on 24 August. We celebrated it with a Devonshire cream tea in a cafe in Exmouth's Strand. When she and Uncle Walter arrived back at their lodgings a recall summons for scholars in Ilford awaited her. They were lucky to find seats on the train next morning. When it reached Newton Poppleford it was standing room only.

We stayed on until Saturday as planned, while Uncle Bill remained in Devon for several months. On Friday Carter Paterson collected our holiday trunk from Fernside. Remarkably it reached us in Clarence Avenue on Monday despite heavy traffic on the return journey. Dad had booked reserved return seats on ACE before we left home. The journey started well but my scrappy diary entry describes it as 'horrible'. There was so much extra railway traffic that we had to wait for over an hour at Sidmouth Junction for the coaches from Cornwall and north Devon. The train then crawled up the track for London with the engine repeatedly whistling as if claiming a priority as an express that no signalman could concede. I thought it a dismal wail in contrast to the GWR's deep, peremptory blast that I had so often heard from the Cornish Riviera. Out of the window I saw Brooklands again: no racing cars this time; only a few aeroplanes within the circuit perimeter and a lot of bustle around the engineering workshops.

At Waterloo there was chaos. It seemed totally different, a station in a strange land, and a terribly hot one at that. I felt dizzy and the platform began to heave up under me – probably an attack of vertigo. All Tube lines passing under the Thames were closed for urgent work on preventative measures to isolate any part of the network ruptured by a bomb. Fortunately Dad found a taxi rank and off we went to Liverpool Street. Never before had I been in a London cab; taxis were for Paris. As we turned into The Strand and headed for the City my spirits began to rise.

Liverpool Street Station was also hot and crowded but less menacing than alien Waterloo. I noticed that the boat train for Harwich looked packed. Germans, I thought, heading for The Hook or Zeebrugge overnight. What cheek, I felt possessively, to use steamers like the *Archangel* to get back to Hitler's barracks! We made do with a suburban stopper to Ilford and the bus to Gants Hill. As yet nothing had changed, but from the wireless news on the dear old Ekco we heard confirmation that on Friday evening the Anglo-Polish Alliance had been signed at last. An Emergency Powers Act had been rushed through Parliament which gave the full authority of the law to government directives for national defence. The juggernaut of war was again rolling relentlessly forward. This time it seemed no act of man could halt its progress.

TWELVE

'At War with Germany'

The last days of August and the first half of September 1939 were weeks of unprecedented social upheaval for youngsters across Britain, a time that remains unforgettable to all who survive from those days. For many the first memory will be the coming of telegrams and the sudden disappearance of a father or brother called up as a territorial or as a reservist in the navy and air force. Then other members of the family would be summoned away, as the machinery of evacuation began to turn. Advance parties of senior management went first, to be followed by employees of the larger private business concerns, civil servants and workers in smaller firms. At last, as August ended, came the full impact of 'Operation Pied Piper', the exodus that sent almost 2 million schoolchildren and their teachers out from cities threatened with bombing into an unfamiliar countryside in supposedly safe areas.

Some villages and market towns had been content to sleep through history for centuries and saw the evacuees as young invaders, with no manners and deplorable habits. Others made the children so welcome that the newcomers stayed happily throughout the war and beyond. In many instances they or their families still felt part of the community 70 years later. On 1 September 2009 a congregation of several thousand evacuees, their families and friends came together at St Paul's Cathedral for a commemorative service of thanksgiving.

I was a fortunate boy, spared the uncertainty of strange homes and surrogate parents. Yet nothing in my childhood stands so sharply etched in memory as this transition from peace to war, with its strange mixture of drama, pathos, anticlimax and near farce. Almost certainly at no other time did we as a family find ourselves so dependent on the wireless. When we had gone on holiday news bulletins went out at 6 p.m. and 9 p.m. but not earlier in the day. On our return there was one as early as half-past ten and another at one o'clock, which Mother and I never missed. During the following week the first reports came even earlier. To a news addict like me that was a welcome development: Dad took the *Daily Express* with him to work, leaving us without a paper in the house, for with Uncle Bill still in Devon there was no *News Chronicle*. Automatically I turned to the Ekco, to catch bulletin after bulletin.

The foreign news puzzled me. Much of it was about Danzig and the Polish Corridor, danger spots of which we had heard already, but now came references to towns like Bydgoszcz and Grudzlądz, tongue-twisters impossible to find on any map in the atlas. Home news sounded ominous, as briefly, at the height of the Munich Crisis, there was a spate of special announcements from the government, delivered slowly and portentously and followed by 'I shall repeat that announcement' or 'I shall read that message again'. Much of this information we knew already. There must have been some light entertainment in those remaining days of peace but I cannot remember it. Like much else, programmes were unpredictable.

My elders might have been apprehensive but I found the uncertainty rather exciting. The shocked sensation of being plunged into a different world that numbed me at Waterloo on the previous Saturday soon disappeared. My spirit was bolstered with the natural resilience of a boy of almost 13 who, having accepted life was changing, felt thrilled by the prospect. I was convinced no bomb would get me.

After spending Monday (28 August) at the office, my normally optimistic father conceded, 'Things are on the move.' He had heard of Sunday's flight of families from the wealthier suburbs, their heavily laden cars heading west, beyond the range of German bombers at that time. He often grabbed a quick lunch at a Lyons teashop near his office where he would chat with staff from the Prudential Assurance, whose redbrick headquarters stand almost beside Chancery Lane station. They were not there on this Monday; most had gone down to hotels at Torquay two days previously in a special train from Paddington, travelling at the same time we returned from Devon on the Waterloo Line. Reservists among Dad's colleagues had been called up, including the partner to whom he was directly responsible, a commander in the Royal Navy, and we knew of many teachers on stand-by for evacuation orders. There might be something to be said for heading out of London 'for the time being', my parents felt. My Perriam grandfather and grandmother were staying in a newly-built bungalow recently purchased by Aunts Amy and Elsie in Walpole Avenue, West Worthing, and it was decided on Tuesday evening that Mother and I should join them. There was a scramble to get things ready, with Mother improvising blackout curtains for Dad's use in our absence while I took Bruce for a last long ramble in the park. Then, after breakfast on Thursday, we went up to Victoria carrying a couple of small suitcases. No cricket bat and stumps sent in advance this time; gas masks were with us instead.

Paddington and Waterloo may have been crowded that morning but at Victoria the bustle along the old London, Brighton and South Coast platforms was reassuringly familiar. Not quite normal, of course, for many travellers were in uniform, most hurrying off platforms rather than setting out. The train was almost full but not packed. It left on time, the railway unions having called off a threatened strike because of the gravity of the international crisis.

We moved slowly at first; congestion at Clapham Junction we thought. As the train crawled across Grosvenor Bridge I looked out over the Thames. In 1939 the view was better than today, with no high buildings on either bank of the river. A few tethered barrage balloons floated in the light breeze, silver when the sun caught them, leaden in the shadow of a passing cloud. As yet there were not enough to pose any threat to low-flying aircraft, their main purpose. We had no idea that when fully inflated and securely tethered a balloon would be the length of a cricket pitch and twice the width of a standard railway carriage. They looked playfully amusing, dipping and diving like kites on a beach as their crews wrestled with the unfamiliar task of getting them airborne. One bloated blimp, launched from Lambeth Palace, seemed to have a will of its own for, as I watched, the nose dipped and then shot up again, as if honouring Archbishop Lang with a deferential bob of respect.

It was a journey I knew well; we had been down to the Sussex coast many times in the previous six or seven years. As the train picked up speed old landmarks flashed by the carriage window. First were the Oval's gasholders, though with no match day flags fluttering; the ground had been commandeered, forcing Surrey to move their final home game against Lancashire to Old Trafford. Then came the Crystal Palace water towers, not demolished until 1941, even though they must earlier have served as navigational aids to German bombers. Central Croydon was in the distance; eventually we passed Gatwick, in those days a small aerodrome. Until 1936 it had been a private club's flying field and was still without scheduled services. I had never seen a plane take off or land there. Nor did I on this Thursday, though there were several light aircraft on the runway, no doubt ready for Channel hopping to Le Touquet if required.

At Brighton, where we changed for the Chichester train, returning holidaymakers mingled with newcomers on the concourse and there were more servicemen than at Victoria. By the time we stepped down at Durrington station, west of central Worthing, the sky was grey, the line of South Downs behind us lost in rising mist. It was rather depressing. We should have stayed in Devon, I felt.

There had been no congestion on the roads of south London that we saw from the carriage window. Twenty-four hours later all would have been different. For during our journey came the expected broadcast announcement that mass evacuation of children from London and other threatened towns would begin the next morning. Boys and girls from state schools would board special trains long since reserved for them. Fourteen trainloads of children from south London debouched in Brighton Station that day, so a local paper reported. The operation made nonsense of normal weekday railway timetables but disruption of this kind had been anticipated. So, too, was the need to close roads temporarily to allow commandeered buses to get the children from their schools to the waiting carriages. The planning in London had been good.

All went smoothly for the elementary school in Manor Park at which Aunt Amy was teaching. Her girls were off to Felixstowe and, as they were on the right side of London for the Suffolk coast, buses soon sped them to the nearest LNER station. Different destinations had been chosen for schools in the same borough. The corresponding boys' school – attended by several of the girls' brothers – was allocated to Northamptonshire, with pupils and staff bussed up Whitechapel Road to reach the train awaiting them. Aunt Margaret found herself attached to a school new to her and only met colleagues and pupils for the first time as they made their way to Cheddar. Luckiest of Ilford's evacuees were those from the borough's eastern fringe. Along with several schools from Dagenham and Barking their buses turned towards the river and they were borne down the Thames aboard three familiar vessels, the *Golden Eagle* and *Crested Eagle* paddle steamers that normally made day trips to Southend and Clacton, and the more spacious *Royal Daffodil*, now bound for Lowestoft, not Ostend.

Down at Worthing we remained a family group, a trifle cramped in the bungalow but comfortable enough for me to look on the affair as an extended holiday. There was a smart new wireless set, with more knobs to turn than the Ekco. In the paper on Friday (1 September) I saw there was still one cricket championship match left undecided: Sussex v. Yorkshire at Hove. Why not take the bus into Brighton and see the outcome, I thought? Mother, however, was far from enthusiastic: 'Let's hear what's on the *News* first,' she said. We switched on the wireless for the 10.30 bulletin and heard what we feared. War had come to Europe. Early that morning Hitler's army, navy and air force attacked Poland without the formality of an ultimatum; Polish cities were being bombed and there was fighting in the centre of Danzig.

I should of course have thought sympathetically of Poland, where children of my age were caught without warning by Stuka dive bombers howling down on them. More than 50 years later I met a Holocaust survivor who, as a boy of 11, had been playing among the fields

143

when his village went up in flames behind him in five minutes of fury. As I recalled my response to the news that morning, I felt ashamed. But at the time my thoughts were narrowly selfish. Mother insisted there could be no question now of going to Hove: 'Not at times like these,' she said firmly. So, with a regret still felt 75 years later, I missed this final day of inter-war county cricket and the last first-class overs ever bowled by my Yorkshire idol, Hedley Verity. He took seven wickets for nine runs in 36 balls on an uncovered wicket drying from overnight rain. Sadly he died in July 1943, a wounded prisoner in Italy.

Like so many mornings that September, Saturday began sunny. Mother suggested we might take the bus into Brighton after all, with my grandfather accompanying us. I was puzzled why we could make the journey denied me the previous day, but I have always liked Brighton and was ready to enjoy the trip. Yet it was a strange outing: odd to walk along Marine Parade towards Rottingdean with gas masks over the shoulders; odd that so few people were down on the shingly beach. About four o'clock, two flights of Fairey Battle bombers flew over the town and out towards France. I had read a lot about these 'fast modern light bombing aeroplanes' in the papers. When in May 1940 the great attack came in the West, they were found wanting in speed and manoeuvrability and the Germans took a heavy toll on the Battles as they vainly sought to remedy deficiencies in the Ardennes defences. But all that lay eight months ahead. We watched them fly out to sea with pride and a certain sadness in the heart that sobered my excitement.

144

Hardly had the sound of their engines died away than the first afternoon papers went on sale at the approach to Palace Pier. 'Warsaw Bombed', ran a placard: 'Half-time scores,' the vendor standing next to it called out, unconcernedly. The sky was clouding over and we headed home again. Back in the bungalow there was an urgent job to complete; we needed to make certain the curtains were thick enough to keep any light from seeping out. As we waited for the no. 31 bus, a rumble of thunder came from the Downs, ahead of storms bringing fitful flashes of light to London and much of the south on this first night of official blackout.

The sun was bright again before breakfast on Sunday, with the air invigorating after the thunder of the small hours. The date was 3 September, 12 months to the day since the Russian émigré taxi driver in Paris had alerted us to the mounting threat to Czechoslovakia. A glance at *The Observer* showed there now seemed little chance of avoiding war if Britain remained true to her treaty obligations to Poland.

The breakfast *News* told us the prime minister would broadcast at eleven. Mother busied herself in the kitchen preparing the Sunday roast; grandfather pottered in the garden and I think I joined him. Just before eleven we gathered around the wireless and waited. There was an awful lot of waiting on events that Sunday.

Eleven o'clock came and went with no announcement. Gramophone records filled up the interlude, as so often in the following week. Nothing vocal, nothing solemn, nothing aggressively patriotic; a Gilbert and Sullivan overture, I seem to recall, something cheerful to lift the gloom. At last, about ten past eleven, the announcer introduced 'The Right Honourable Mr Neville Chamberlain' and the reedy voice that promised 'peace for our time' a year ago brought us up to date. The British ambassador, he said, had delivered a final note to the Germans saying that unless they gave an undertaking by 11.00 a.m. that they were prepared at once to withdraw their troops from Poland, 'a state of war would exist between us'. After the shortest of pauses, he continued, 'I have to tell you now that no such undertaking has been received and that consequently this country is at war with Germany.'

There followed a generalised condemnation of Hitler's record of pledges cast aside. It was a simple speech; no rallying call rang out. A weary, ageing statesman barely concealed his inner sorrow. Instead of a peroration came a prayer: 'Now may God bless you all. May He defend the right. It is evil things we shall be fighting against – brute force, bad faith, injustice, oppression and persecution; against them I am sure that the right will prevail.' We were deeply moved, conscious this was a grave hour for the nation as a whole. A recording of 'God Save the King' came over the air. We all stood, as we had after King George V's Christmas message each year.

A few minutes later air raid sirens ululated across southern England, the rise and fall of their wail continuing for two minutes. The time of the alert varied: in Worthing we heard the banshee notes earlier than our friends in Ilford, where the sirens officially sounded at 11.28. Up in London, so we were told later, a few people ventured into the street, looked into a cloudless sky and saw nothing there apart from barrage balloons. Nevertheless they were shooed back indoors by air raid wardens shouting 'Take cover'. Almost all recollections of that alert share one common feature: the omnipresence of gas masks. Some were being worn 'just as a precaution', with lucky toddlers in Mickey Mouse masks they had been given to make it seem a game. More often the mask was carried, ready to put on as soon as wardens began twirling their metal rattles, the recognised warning of imminent gas attack. But in Ilford there was at least one person with no gas mask to hand: Dad had just stepped into a hot bath and saw no reason to leave it.

Down at Worthing we were good and conformed, sitting in the lounge four gas masks at our side, a coffee table between us with a *Radio Times* on it, listing programmes for sound and television that were never to be aired: all broadcasts were now restricted to a single channel and the television service had shut down at midday on Friday, not to return for seven years. Once again we waited; once again nothing happened. In a remarkably short time came the one minute continuous single note that we knew was the All Clear. The first alert of the war, long dreaded, had proved an anticlimax.

At teatime the *News* admitted the whole affair was a false alarm: a single unidentified plane had approached the Kent coast, apparently piloted by a roisterer back from a good weekend at Le Touquet. An alternative story, equally probable but never officially confirmed, said that a French light bomber had trespassed into British air space. Early next morning similar confusion over identification had tragic consequences when two Hurricanes from North Weald were shot down by Spitfires from Hornchurch above Barking Creek and a pilot was killed. Strict censorship kept this grave error secret until after the war.

Sunday lunch tasted good; there had been no interruption to the gas supply, another danger of which we had been warned. We kept the wireless on for much of the afternoon, listening mostly to gramophone records. A news bulletin reported fierce Polish resistance to the invaders and bombs falling on towns with unspellable names that meant nothing to us and on Warsaw, a name that did. The list of public announcements grew longer and longer. The most depressing stated that the government had closed all theatres and cinemas and had banned sports meetings, indoor or outdoor. Banned, too, was any gathering of large numbers of people, though church congregations were exempt.

One item, broadcast in mid-afternoon, aroused particular interest: Winston Churchill, out of cabinet office for the past ten years, had accepted an invitation from Chamberlain to return to the government as First Lord of the Admiralty, the post he held when the Great War began. Mother was pleased and so was I. A press campaign to 'bring Churchill back', persistent since early in July, had won support from *Picture Post,* the *Daily Express* and *News Chronicle,* acting in rare harmony. Grandfather was less happy at the news. He remembered those seven months,

Exmouth. My father, my uncle Walter and me. Taken by a beach photographer on the day news broke of the Nazi/Soviet pact in August 1939. See page 128.

EMPIRE DAY 1933

I am pretending to play the violin, as we dance around to celebrate Empire Day in the Valentine's School, Guildford. See page 27.

The unknown man at the Gare Du Nord Paris in 1936. See page 87.

FAVOURITE TOY

With my toy yacht in Valentine's Park, 1934.

The front of the house in which I was born in the first floor room upstairs. The photograph was taken in 1932.

AN EAST END WEDDING

My father and mother's wedding in September 1910, Hampton Road in Forest Gate, when the visitors seemed to have competed with big hats.

The author in the Luxembourg gardens, Paris, in 1953

A Dutch celebration in 1933. I am with my grandfather, mother and auntie Bessie at Middelburg

a mere 24 years back in time, when Churchill's tenure of the Admiralty ended with the Dardanelles expedition and slaughter on the Gallipoli peninsula. Churchill was egocentric and impetuous, he thought.

At six o'clock King George VI 'broadcasted a message to the Empire', as he wrote in his diary. He spoke simply, with no trace of the nervous stammer of earlier years. 'War can be no longer confined to the battlefield,' he warned us; but in what sounded like an echo of Chamberlain earlier in the day, he stressed his confidence that despite the 'dark days ahead... with God's help we shall prevail'.

There were no cheering crowds outside Buckingham Palace as there had been when war was declared in 1914. Across the country the mood was sombre and apprehensive. Mother suggested she and I should go to evensong at the parish church in Goring, barely a mile to the west. I objected at first, on what I regarded as patriotic grounds. Knowing virtually no German and being totally unacquainted with the language's intrusive umlauts, I associated the place name with Hermann Göring, commander of the Luftwaffe, Germany's air force. But we duly went along to Goring-by-Sea and found St Mary's Church almost full. For the first but certainly not the last time during the war, I was struck by the fitting relevance of Cranmer's Third Collect: 'Lighten our darkness we beseech Thee O Lord; and by Thy great mercy defend us from all the perils and dangers of this night.' It was a moment that brought lasting strength to my wobbling faith. We were home again before the blackout descended at a quarter past eight and total darkness enveloped the roads around us.

THIRTEEN

'A Dark, Cold Winter'

For many months people had anticipated that, if war came, it would begin with a massive air assault. The Luftwaffe would drop high explosive and incendiary bombs and we would cover faces with gas masks. The reality was highly different. Although naval bases in Scotland were attacked in mid-October, the first bombs did not fall on English soil until 10 May 1940 and another seven weeks elapsed before the opening of the great air offensive that became the Battle of Britain. We had been at war for 353 days before the first bomb fell on inner London.

In Sussex the war seemed as remote as the recent conflict in Spain. Only once did it come close. Shortly before dusk on 7 September I joined a knot of people at the end of Worthing's King George V Avenue who were looking out over the Channel. A plane was silhouetted against the sinking sun as it repeatedly dived down on the waves. 'There must be a German sub out there,' someone said. That seems highly likely, for we now know that the first transatlantic convoy left the Thames estuary on that Thursday and was heading down the Channel, escorted by destroyers. The pilot of the plane was evidently making certain no enemy submarine lurked offshore, waiting to lay mines or attack the convoy under cover of night. Already German U-boats had accounted for four British merchant ships and one French vessel around the coast.

With little happening in the West, there seemed no point in staying in Sussex. Like many other families we returned home at the end of the second week. There were no signs of war until the train approached Coulsdon and we saw ahead of us the balloon barrage spread across the sky. A fortnight ago the blimps seemed a playful joke; now, raised to their full height of 5,000 feet and in great depth, they looked impressive. Within our range of vision there must have been over a hundred, stretching far back in a seemingly endless forest of silver-topped cables. So long as the barrage was up, the cables ruled out dive bombing or low-level machine-gunning. We were heartened by this shield of protection, London's aerial Maginot Line.

Back in Ilford we found people behaved as if nothing had changed. There was no formal rationing, though we were issued with ration books early in October. No trenches were dug in Valentine's Park, as in Kensington and Westminster, but some recreation areas became allotments, while cabbages and potatoes were planted in many flower beds. It was another year before the famous 'Dig For Victory' posters exhorted us to greater efforts.

Several neighbours had been digging hard already

that year, installing 'Andersons' in their back gardens. These domestic air raid shelters – named after the Home Secretary, Sir John Anderson – comprised six curved steel sheets bolted at the top to form an arch and sunk 4 feet into the London clay. Some Andersons had a concrete floor. All were protected by at least 15 inches of earth on their roof. Dad was against Andersons: bad for rheumatism, he said; 'Worst comes to the worst' we could get under our good solid extendable dining table. We filled sandbags to form an outside barrier halfway up the dining-room door and crisscrossed the windows and the panes of our small conservatory with strips of brown paper to prevent glass shattering down on us. In 1942 we received a steel table shelter named after Herbert Morrison, Anderson's successor as Home Secretary. Morrisons were similar in size to the dining table but strengthened by wire mesh sides and a steel mattress foundation.

Sunday, 17 September, the day after our return, brought bad news: the Russians were sending troops into Poland; a stab in the back to which the Poles could offer only token resistance. By Thursday Nazi and Soviet officers were exchanging toasts of friendship in the citadel at Brest-Litovsk. To our newspapers the cheap Russian oil would be virtually on tap to Germany while Britain was dependent on tankers running the gauntlet of U-boats. Petrol rationing duly came, eight days after the Russian-German link was completed in Poland.

Rationing seemed to make scant difference to private motoring, and the government looked for a sharper deterrent. The price at the pumps was raised to a record level. From 14 November a gallon of petrol cost one shilling and nine pence, more than a £1 a litre by 2014 values. Many buses were taken off the road; there was no longer a line of taxis at Ilford Station and by Christmas there were few private cars on the streets.

The immediate danger to life and limb came not from bombs but from the blackout. It began each evening thirty minutes after sunset and lasted until half an hour before sunrise. We 'did the blackout' in less than ten minutes but it took far longer in large, detached houses. Once curtains were pulled, someone stepped outside to make certain no chink of light seeped out and on returning had to take care not to ruffle edging around the door. During the first three weeks no torches were allowed in streets and no lights on cars and bicycles or in trains and buses. At the end of September these restrictions were slightly relaxed: a torch might be used if pointed towards the ground and with the bulb masked by tissue paper to ensure light was diffused rather than beamed in one direction. Traffic lights were partially covered, showing no more than small plus signs of red, amber or green. Crossing the road remained dangerous: a former master at Bancroft's was fatally struck by a 145 bus; and in April 1940 the veteran Liberal historian H.A.L. Fisher was hit by a lorry in Chelsea and died a week later. British Summer Time should have ended on 8 October but was extended until the third week of November to delay blackout by an extra hour of daylight. 'Glimmer lights' were permitted in shopping streets before Christmas. By then, blackout began at four thirty but all shops had to close at six.

On 19 December Mother and I went up to the West End in search of Christmas presents, reaching Piccadilly Circus as the light began to fade. It was a strange sight: Eros had been evacuated to a place of safety and traffic was so slight that buses and cars swung speedily round the island where his empty plinth stood. The huge advertising signs – 'Bovril', 'Schweppes Tonic Water', 'Guinness is Good for You' – were still in position but there were no electric bulbs in them. Before going down to the Central Line at Oxford Circus I glanced along upper Regent Street, remembering the *Children's Hour* visit, 11 months previously. Broadcasting House was only faintly visible, the gleaming white stonework camouflaged grey, like a battleship berthed beside All Souls, Langham Place.

We rarely went out during those first months of blackout. We turned to the wireless for entertainment. *Band Waggon* returned on 16 September; *Monday Night at Seven* became *Monday Night at Eight* but kept the same ingredients as before the war. Saturday evenings still offered us *In Town Tonight* as well as *Band Waggon*. And on 19 September *It's That Man Again* slipped into the Tuesday slot.

Tommy Handley, the lynch-pin, was a veteran from 2LO days – he was in the light opera *Young England* broadcast on the day I was born. Although *ITMA* became the most loved wartime programme, it received little advance publicity. Three cautiously inoffensive scripts had been aired in the summer. I heard one and thought it unfunny; so apparently did other listeners. The new version was innovative in style and sharper in text. Ted Kavanagh, the New Zealander script writer was no respecter of persons, nor indeed was Handley himself.

Dad, Mother and I tuned in from the start. Like many listeners we remained puzzled: here was a comedy series that seemed surrealistic at times. But we soon came to appreciate the gentle satire, mocking all-pervading wartime bureaucracy. There were enough tales of administrative confusion circulating for us to accept a Ministry of Aggravation and Mysteries next door to a rival department of government, the Office of Twerps. No earlier programme had so many catchphrases: the excessively polite exchange of two colleagues – 'After you, Claud,' Cecil would say; 'No, after you, Cecil,' Claud would reply; and there was the deep-sea diver, who appeared in the most unlikely places, imploring Handley, 'Don't forget the diver,' before giving the lugubrious warning, 'Going down now, sir.' Best loved was charwoman Mrs Mopp's 'Can I do you now, sir?' on entry and her exit line, 'TTFN' or 'Ta-ta for now'. No listeners took offence at funny foreigners like Dino Galvani's Senior So-So or Jack Train's Ali-oop, the black-market pedlar from somewhere east of the Suez ('I go – I come back'). Some characters – including Mrs Mopp – did not appear until later but Funf, Jack Train's inept German spy, stamped his non-personality on *ITMA* from the start. We would hear a telephone lifted, followed by 'Dees ist Funf speaking', and a muddled message of misinformation in a Germanic stage whisper invariably sent to the wrong place.

In a Funf-mocking world it was impossible to take spy allegations seriously and the government thought it advisable to circulate light-hearted reminders of unseen enemy faces in familiar places. The cartoonist Fougasse (Cyril Kenneth Bird) designed a poster depicting two women gossiping on a bus, with Hitler and Göring eavesdropping behind them. This cartoon is the best remembered in a series of a dozen Fougasse posters, all carrying the warning 'Careless Talk Costs Lives'.

Careless listening, too, could become dangerous. From mid-September many habitual knob-twiddlers were attracted by the pseudo-aristocratic, supercilious voice of an Englishman who read the news from Berlin. Wild guesses were made at his identity. A maverick son of a peer? A renegade officer from a senior regiment, court-martialled a few years earlier? He was in fact William Joyce, an unsuccessful BUF candidate in the LCC elections of 1937 who crossed to Germany in late August and offered his services to Goebbels' Ministry of Propaganda. On 18 September, long before Joyce's anonymity was pierced, Jonah Barrington of the *Daily Express* called him 'Lord Haw-Haw', and the name stuck.

I only heard him occasionally: Dad thought listening to the broadcasts unpatriotic. But thousands *did* tune in to Radio Hamburg to hear him at 9.15 each evening. They listened to other German broadcasts in English too. Early in October *The Times* began printing a daily schedule of programmes from Germany to oblige its readers, a strange service to offer a month into the war. By then it was clear to people more perceptive than the editor of *The Times* that Haw-Haw had to be taken seriously. Letters of protest and questions in Parliament over the publicity given to German programmes led *The Times* to end the practice before Christmas. In Berlin, Goebbels was delighted at the furore: 'He is causing talk, and that is already half the battle', he wrote in his diary for 5 January 1940. During that month one in six adult listeners tuned in regularly to Radio Hamburg, but Goebbels exaggerated Haw-Haw's significance. The novelty of hearing what the other side had to say for itself wore off by March.

One feature of peacetime listening was sorely missed: there were no weather forecasts between the outbreak of war and VE day. Reference to current weather conditions was also banned, most noticeably in sports reports. It was hard to know what to wear before setting out in the morning. The autumn retained a mellow warmth longer than usual but frequently foggy days and a grey Christmas with pavements slippery from hard frost. Snow swept in from the east early in the new year. After a brief thaw, the cold returned and a thin layer of ice covered parts of the Thames. I cannot recall mild days bringing even a glimmer of sunshine until Easter. We grumbled at the absence of forecasts but accepted the official explanation: to let the enemy know a clear moonlit night lay ahead or a region was blanketed in cloud would help the Luftwaffe choose targets for bomber raids.

Not that raiding aircraft posed a threat to London that winter. The sirens did, however, wail out on 20

November, just as we were settling down to *Monday Night at Eight*, and to our surprise we heard distant gunfire; an All Clear came soon afterwards. The papers said a single German plane had ventured up the Thames Estuary but had turned back when caught by searchlights and exposed to anti-aircraft fire. That, we smugly felt, was as it should be. Guns, lights and balloons would keep the capital inviolate from attack.

The lone intruder's flight possessed a significance we never suspected. The plane dropped magnetic mines which blocked the approaches to the Thames' sea lane. Next morning a British steamship and a Japanese vessel were sunk in waters over which it had flown. Mines dropped by parachute. They lay on the seabed until a vessel's magnetic field activated an electro-magnetic detonator. Fortunately by Christmas progress had been made in 'de-gaussing', the fitting of vessels with protective coils that neutralised any magnetic field.

Once Poland was defeated, the land war simmered but never came to the boil. I bought a 'war map' from a local stationer, with French, British and German flags, to be pinned in as the battle lines changed. But where should I begin? We knew the British Expeditionary Force had crossed the Channel safely but not where it was deployed. A French communiqué claimed troops were advancing on Saarbrücken; hopefully I pinned a tricolour over the town. With even greater optimism I stuck a Union Jack over the Ruhr because the RAF had dropped leaflets on the region. I hung the map on the bedroom wall, stood back and waited on events.

Apart from occasional shelling and patrol activity beyond the Maginot Line the Western Front remained quiet. Naval actions provided the greatest news. On 24 November we heard with pride and sorrow how, north of the Faeroes on the previous day, HMS *Rawalpindi*, a converted P&O steamer with little gun power, had gone down in a successful bid to alert merchant ships to the first sortie of the German battleships *Scharnhorst* and *Gneisenau*. Captain Kennedy, commander of the *Rawalpindi*, was likened to Sir Richard Grenville of the *Revenge*, whose challenge of the Spanish galleons in 1591 is celebrated in Tennyson's dramatic poem.

Three weeks later came the Battle of the River Plate, the first naval action the public could follow on the wireless as the news came in. Twelve days before war began the pocket battleship *Admiral Graf Spee*, commanded by Captain Hans von Langsdorff, slipped out of Wilhelmshaven and headed for the South Atlantic. There, and in the Indian Ocean, Langsdorff prowled on British merchant shipping for eight weeks, sinking a dozen vessels. Their crews were taken into custody aboard *Graf Spee* and well treated or transferred to the supply ship, *Altmark*, with which Langsdorff kept a rendezvous in October. Eight British and French hunting groups scoured the oceans for the *Graf Spee*. It was Commodore Harwood, commanding Force H at the Falklands, who calculated that Langsdorff would strike next against vessels heading out of the River Plate. Only three of Force H's ships were at sea: the light cruiser HMS *Ajax* flying the commodore's broad pennant as command ship; the heavier cruiser HMS *Exeter*; and

HMNZS *Achilles*, a similar ship to *Ajax*, manned by New Zealanders.

Early on Wednesday, 13 December, Harwood was 100 miles off the mouth of the Plate when, in bright summer sunshine, the *Graf Spee* was sighted. With six 11-inch and eight 5.9-inch radar-assisted guns she was a formidable adversary, for the *Exeter* had only six 8-inch guns and *Ajax* and *Achilles* eight 6-inch guns each. At 6.15 the battleship opened fire, the first salvo straddling *Exeter*. Harwood had ordered the two lighter cruisers to cross *Graf Spee*'s bows and attack with guns and torpedoes from port while *Exeter* brought her under fire from starboard. An intense battle raged for an hour and a half: *Exeter* lost 64 men and was almost crippled; aboard the two light cruisers ten men were killed and five of *Ajax's* eight guns put out of action. But *Graf Spee* was hit more than 50 times and so badly damaged that Langsdorff feared she was unseaworthy. He ordered a westward course into the Plate estuary and headed for Montevideo, hoping neutral Uruguay would allow him to berth for sufficient time to complete repairs.

The news broke in the BBC's early evening bulletin, ten hours after the guns fell silent. The nation was elated and Churchill made certain the mood was sustained. A wireless signal of congratulation from the First Lord of the Admiralty informed Commodore Harwood he was promoted to Admiral and knighted. The *Graf Spee* was familiar to us: she had been Germany's courtesy visitor at the naval reviews of 1935 and 1937. For three cruisers to force such a prestigious warship to seek refuge in a neutral port was a striking victory.

Over the next four days I scanned the papers, trying to sift fact from rumour. A report from Rio de Janeiro – which was in fact misinformation put out to confound the enemy – said the aircraft carrier HMS *Ark Royal* and the battle-cruiser HMS *Renown* had taken on supplies before steaming for the Plate at full speed. Out came my atlas; would the *Graf Spee*'s crew be interned or creep out at night and make a dash for a home port? Might she head southwards, down Argentina's territorial waters, round Cape Horn and cross the Pacific to a friendly Japan? It was all very exciting.

The climax came during Sunday's nine o'clock *News*. There was a rustling of paper as new information was handed to the announcer; the *Graf Spee* had landed most of her crew and was sailing out into the River Plate, he told us. At 10.40, when she was six miles out of Montevideo, we heard that she had dropped anchor and lowered the swastika naval ensign. There would be no renewal of the battle. A launch sped downriver and across to Buenos Aires, for the crew could expect more hospitable treatment from Argentina than Uruguay. Twenty minutes after the flag was lowered the *Graf Spee* blew up, scuttled by timed explosives placed at vital points in the empty ship. Langsdorff's decision to scuttle the ship may have saved the lives of several hundred British and German sailors but he was a traditionalist with a deep sense of honour. He had lost the fine ship entrusted to him. Three days after reaching Buenos Aires, he turned his revolver on himself.

This battle was Britain's first victory in the war and

the first good news the nation had received. It proclaimed mastery of the seas in the Nelson tradition. *Achilles* headed home across the Pacific to be welcomed in New Zealand. Churchill was at Devonport on 15 February to greet the crews of *Exeter* and *Ajax* in person. Eight days later they were accorded the rare honour of a victory parade through cheering crowds in London to a luncheon at the Guildhall. There he congratulated them on: 'A brilliant sea fight that in a dark, cold winter warmed the cockles of the British heart.'

The first wartime Christmas came a fortnight after the battle. Our family was together as usual, with Uncle Bill back from Devon and Aunts Amy and Margaret returned to London with their schools. We enjoyed a small turkey and a traditional pudding, from which only a few richer ingredients like glacé cherries were missing. Fruit from overseas was already in short supply: no bananas; no nuts to crack; but we had dates, probably imported before war broke out. One box was distinctly mouldy. Wireless programmes followed the pre-war pattern: a 'Round the Empire' link-up ended with a broadcast by the King. In the evening we heard Gracie Fields. No novelty there; now, however, her broadcast came from France, for like many other stars of screen and stage she was entertaining the troops. 'Wish Me Luck as You Wave Me Goodbye', she sang.

The troops needed both luck and entertainment. They also needed assurance they were still in our thoughts. With deep snow covering the Western Front, there was little for them to do but wait and be ready for action when the thaw came. A near neighbour's son in the BEF chided his parents because he thought that they, like so many of us, were giving attention not to the 'lads in France' but to another war that in this coldest of winters was being waged astride the Arctic Circle.

On 30 November the Soviet Union had invaded Finland in a bid to strengthen Russia's hold over the eastern Baltic. The British public sympathised strongly with the Finns, the latest bully-boy victims, like the 'brave Belgians' of 1914. No one expected the war to last more than a few weeks. By 3 December photos of bombed Helsinki were in our papers. They looked familiar: Poland all over again, we assumed.

We were wrong. The Finns were well prepared for a winter war. Their veteran leader, Marshal Mannerheim, had supervised construction of a line of field works and concrete bunkers, not so formidable as France's Maginot Line but strong enough to check an incursion from Leningrad, only 18 miles from the frontier. Mannerheim could count on the best ski troops in the world. The invaders were hampered by short daylight hours and the impossibility of employing tanks and aircraft when the barometer dropped as low as minus 40° Celsius. It was from the BBC's war reporter Edward Ward that we heard for the first time of 'Molotov cocktails', bottles filled with petrol and rags that served as a fuse for improvised hand bombs hurled by white-clad infantry at tanks wallowing in slush.

So deep was sympathy with Finland that 2,000 serving British soldiers sought permission to enlist in the

Finnish Army, among them a keen skier from my father's office; he and others like him received an issue of white camouflaged clothing. Two regiments were retained in Britain for possible service in Scandinavia instead of crossing to France. In the first days of February there were rumours of an Anglo-French army passing through neutral Norway and Sweden to aid the Finns.

Intervention was however out of the question; neither Scandinavian kingdom would give transit rights to the Allies and no effective help could have reached Finland before the approach of spring. In mid-February the first signs of a thaw enabled the Red Army to launch another assault with tanks and a heavy artillery bombardment. With startling suddenness the Finns sued for peace. There was a delay of several weeks before a treaty was signed but on 13 March we read in our papers that the Winter War was over. We were deeply sorry for the Finns: some 26,000 soldiers and 960 civilians were killed in the conflict, a heavy toll for a country with a population of barely 4 million.

Churchill, the most belligerent member of Chamberlain's Cabinet, favoured intervention. He was, however, less concerned with curbing Russian expansion as with preventing iron ore from Gallivare in Sweden bolstering German heavy industry. German ships loaded the ore in the ice-free Norwegian port of Narvik and bore it through Norwegian waters to the Kattegat and then with impunity to Lubeck, the historic Hanse port on Germany's Baltic coast. Churchill wanted to order British warships into Norway's territorial waters if there was good reason to justify such action. On 13 February an unexpected source provided him with the opportunity he sought.

Early that Friday morning the observer in an RAF Coastal Command plane patrolling the eastern North Sea spotted off Bergen a ship that had eluded hunters for the past two months. She was the *Altmark,* the *Graf Spee*'s supply vessel, thought to be holding as prisoners seamen transferred to her from the pocket battleship. Churchill at once ordered Captain Philip Vian, commanding HMS *Cossack*, to lead his destroyer flotilla to intercept and board the *Altmark,* wherever she was found.

Vian sighted her approaching Jössing Fjord north of Stavanger. As the flotilla closed in on the German ship two Norwegian gunboats barred entry to the fjord: the *Altmark* had been searched and no prisoners found, the senior Norwegian officer assured Vian. A fraught stand-off followed until, at dusk, the *Altmark's* captain tried to ram the destroyer, only to run his ship aground. The *Cossack* came alongside; a boarding party armed with revolvers and cutlasses stormed the *Altmark*; and 299 seamen held captive below deck were freed. By midnight the *Cossack* and an accompanying destroyer were clear of the fjord and back on the open sea with the liberated seamen aboard. No iron ore ship was intercepted but pro-Nazi neutralists in Norway were reminded of a British naval presence beyond the western horizon.

Once the freed captives were in Britain, the Admiralty released news of the *Cossack*'s exploit. It was a scoop for that Sunday's newspapers and they printed detailed accounts of the clash of arms. What caught the public imagination was the shout, 'The Navy's here', heard below decks by the prisoners as Vian's officers pursued their search. The call made an excellent headline, providing a phrase of stern wartime reassurance to set beside the peacetime jollity of 'The fleet's lit up'. By chance the news broke on the Sunday that Churchill was at Devonport welcoming home the *Exeter* and the *Ajax*. He saw the rescue as a fitting epilogue to 'the action off the Plate' and in his speech at the Guildhall on 23 February he praised the Nelsonian spirit of the destroyer flotilla. The pride and confidence in the Royal Navy so many of us had felt in December was rekindled.

This buoyant mood continued through March. Life became easier once blackout hours shortened. British Summer Time was introduced on 25 February, four Sundays earlier than usual, and blackout starting time was changed from 30 to 45 minutes after sunset. By now we were growing accustomed to rationing. Mother first took ration books out with her in mid-January but only for sugar, butter and bacon or ham. We were allowed 12 ounces of sugar (336 grams) a week, four ounces of butter, and four ounces of bacon or ham. This was more than sufficient to sustain us. Late March brought meat rationing, with each person entitled to one shilling and six pence worth of meat a week, probably about 1 lb 6 ounces (600 grams) in weight.

There was little grumbling. After seven months in which Britain had suffered no reverses we approached the summer of 1940 optimistically, complacently perhaps. The prime minister exuded confidence. In a speech at

Birmingham on 5 April Chamberlain argued that Hitler's failure to strike in the West had let us build up our strength to confront his challenge wherever it came: 'One thing is certain,' he insisted; 'he's missed the bus.'

It was an unfortunate phrase, like that earlier four-worder, 'Peace in our time'. A few hours after he finished his speech, Whitehall received a clear warning from Stockholm of imminent action: a 'German descent on Narvik' was mentioned. 'Surely out of the question?' a diplomat who knew the length of Norway's coast commented in a marginal note. Over the weekend came more warnings from Swedish sources. They were ignored.

The British public had no inkling of any of these reports. When we switched on Tuesday's one o'clock *News* we heard with amazement that Germany had invaded Denmark and Norway before dawn. Copenhagen was already occupied; German naval forces had entered Oslo Fjord to threaten Norway's capital. The swastika flag flew over Narvik. That night Radio Hamburg mocked Chamberlain: Hitler had not missed the bus; he had taken a taxi instead. For once it seemed the wretched Haw-Haw might be right.

FOURTEEN

'They're in Paris'

Throughout April, Norway held our attention: we virtually ignored news from France. I had looked at the map on the bedroom wall during the *Cossack-Altmark* episode and spotted the name 'Bergen' but now I saw the map ran no farther north than Trondheim; the possibility of fjords within the Arctic Circle coming into a war zone must never have occurred to the cartographer. Surely, we thought, the Germans had over-stretched their supply lines. Confidently we awaited good news.

It came over the wireless as early as Sunday, 14 April. A flotilla of destroyers had entered Westfjord, leading up to Narvik before dawn the previous day. They were covered by the heavy guns of the dreadnought HMS *Warspite*. Eight German destroyers were sunk and the shore batteries silenced; not a single British ship was lost. The Norwegian army was offering strong resistance inland. To support them British troops landed at Namsos and Åndalsnes, intending to capture Trondheim by a pincer movement.

This optimism was premature. The hurriedly

improvised expeditionary force lacked the right weapons, suitable clothing and reliable maps. Moreover, the military commanders remained confused over their immediate objectives. Despite the continued bravery of the ill-equipped British troops , the initiative of destroyers off shore, and a small band of RAF pilots, the Namsos-Trondheim expedition was abandoned at the end of the month. Allied forces – British, French, Polish – remained farther north and on 28 May finally took Narvik. But the crisis on the Western Front forced them to pull out of Norway entirely on 8 June, after destroying Narvik's harbour facilities and much of the iron ore railway track down from Gallivare.

Criticism of the government intensified after the return of troops from Namsos with tales of confusion: shells of different calibre from the guns; lack of winter clothing. To veteran MPs the muddle was reminiscent of the blackest days of the Great War. A two-day debate in the Commons revealed deep splits. Chamberlain's government was falling apart. Who would succeed him and when? The Western Front was still far from our thoughts.

On the way to school on Friday, 10 May, I noticed outside a newsagent's shop in Woodford High Road a placard reading 'Belgium and Holland attacked'. There had been no mention of an invasion on the *News* 40 minutes earlier; just another rumour, I thought, and put it out of my mind. But not for long. At eleven o'clock, as Bancroft's mid-morning break ended, something unusual happened: Mr Jenkins was late for a French lesson. When he did bustle in, he told us he had heard on the Common Room wireless that the Germans were indeed in Holland and Belgium; the BEF had gone forward in response to appeals from both countries.

Gone was our lesson on irregular verbs. Instead, he told us of the legendary 'miracle of the Marne' in 1914, when the buses and taxis of Paris rushed out troops to save the city, and the chief of the German general staff collapsed in despair at his failure to gain a decisive victory. At this point Jenkins' flow of words stopped. 'I've forgotten his name,' he said ruefully. I put up my hand: 'Wasn't it Moltke, sir, the nephew of the Moltke of the 1870 war?' I suggested tentatively, hoping he would not think me a show-off. To my relief he was pleasantly surprised: 'Heavens!' he said. 'How do you know that?' I had no idea and could only mumble feebly, 'Oh, I read it somewhere.' From then until I left school four years later he recognised my enthusiasm for French history. I think he mentioned the incident to some colleagues, for in the dramatic weeks ahead no one objected if, as lunchtime ended, I lingered close to the Common Room window, trying to catch the latest news crackling from the wireless behind the masters' billiard table.

Fresh placards on the way home left no doubt the war was coming to the boil: 'Belgian towns bombed'; 'Lille and Lyons attacked'; 'Bombs hit Kent' (one stick fell between Canterbury and Dover); 'Swiss railways attacked' (a wild rumour). The balloons were up, forming a high protective barrage, as at the start of the war. On the Saturday I noticed shoppers with gas mask boxes on their shoulders, a rare sight since Christmas. But there were no air raid warnings. We had not heard the sirens in almost six months; 26 days went by before their wail alerted us for the first time in 1940.

The nine o'clock *News* on 10 May gave priority to a special broadcast. Sadly and wearily Chamberlain told the nation he had resigned: Churchill had formed a coalition that afternoon in which he would gladly serve. We knew nothing of the discussions over the succession that had continued for the best part of two days. Sir John Wheeler-Bennett's *King George VI* confirms the belief that the King would have preferred a government headed by his personal friend Lord Halifax. But neither Labour nor the Liberals would have joined such a government. Halifax himself, an unambitious realist, thought the task of wartime leadership beyond him.

On Monday, 13 May, Churchill told the Commons, 'I have nothing to offer but blood, toil, tears and sweat' and affirmed his determination to strive for 'victory, however long and hard the road may be'. The speech confirmed our belief that the nation's destiny was in the hands of a natural war leader. Yet the first call to action came over the wireless next morning not from the prime minister but from his war minister Anthony Eden. He appealed for men between the ages of 17 and 65 to join a new force, the Local Defence Volunteers (LDV), supplementing the army. A quarter of a million responded within 24 hours. By 23 July, when the LDV became 'Home Guard' at Churchill's instigation, the force numbered almost a million and a half.

Dad was among the early volunteers. On the way home on 14 May he went round to the police station on Ilford Hill and duly registered. Under his arm he was carrying the *Evening Standard,* which on that Tuesday included the famous David Low cartoon of a pugnacious Churchill rolling up his sleeves. The Labour leaders Attlee, Bevin and Morrison are at his side, leading a long column of MPs from every party: 'All behind you, Winston', ran the caption.

During the opening phase of the campaign news from the Front was scarce and official communiqués discreetly vague. Had I been older perhaps I would have spotted significant pointers, like the report on 14 May that King George had gone to Liverpool Street Station to receive Queen Wilhelmina of the Netherlands, or the apparently casual request broadcast next day for small-boat owners to register their vessels with the Admiralty. But at the time I was more concerned with finding the right places to stick pins on the map in my bedroom. Where was the front line, I wondered?

Twelve months ago our friend in Ostend based his assertion, 'If they come next time, they'll never get through', on the intricate system of forts and bridges constructed along the Albert Canal. Alas, it soon became clear the system had failed to halt the invaders. As dawn broke on 10 May, 100 hand-picked paratroopers landed from gliders close to Belgium's vaunted citadel at Eben Emael, considered more formidable than any of Maginot's forts. Explosive charges were dropped down apertures under the outer steel shell of the casements and even down the lift shafts. The Belgian garrison held out for 30 hours but their courage could do no more than delay the invaders.

Such details we did not know until long afterwards but the press and the wireless emphasised the unexpected role of airborne troops when a famous rumour reported parachutists disguised as nuns; I read in Dad's *Evening Standard* on 17 May that 'near Ostend' the invaders 'had transparent parachutes and sky-blue uniforms, hard to see in bright sunshine'. The novelty of assault from the sky determined many anti-invasion measures that summer. Early in June signposts were removed. Name boards on railway stations followed them, while place names on public buildings were blackened out or covered. Although we could not foresee it, on Sunday 9 June we heard bells summoning us to church for the last time. During the following week the government ruled they might be rung only to warn of airborne landings.

In a different category but also prompted by experience in Holland was the BBC's decision to check the spread of false wireless instructions by having announcers identify themselves. Soon we came to recognise the voices of Stuart Hibberd, Bruce Belfrage, Alvar Lidell, Frank Philips and Joseph Macleod, as well as pre-war commentators whom we knew by name already, like John Snagge and Freddy Grisewood. We felt they were friends we could trust. It would have been difficult to imitate them convincingly.

Preoccupation with airborne troops may have made us

slow to react to the more immediate danger from German tanks, the famous 'panzer' armoured divisions. Early on 12 May, the three divisions of General Guderian's crack XIX Corps emerged from the forests of the Belgian Ardennes which Gamelin, the French commander-in-chief, and his staff had long rated impenetrable by armoured vehicles. Three days' heavy fighting, in which the tanks were supported by Stuka dive bombers, enabled the Germans to outflank the Maginot Line and secure bridgeheads over the River Meuse and take Sedan with astonishing rapidity. A corridor 62 miles wide was opened up for an advance upon Paris and into the heart of France, or to the sea. French tanks, commanded by a Colonel de Gaulle, checked one column near Le Cateau but they could do no more than delay the Germans. Guderian's panzers pressed inexorably ahead, rumbling through Amiens, down to Abbeville. On the evening of 20 May a predominantly Austrian tank regiment reached the Channel coast at Le Crotoy, a small resort on the right bank of the Somme's narrow estuary. They had fought their way through 200 miles of France in eight days.

News that the panzers were on the coast came as a shock. The impact was, however, lessened by a burst of optimism in our papers. Gamelin was replaced as commander-in-chief by the 73-year-old General Weygand, Marshal Foch's chief of staff in the previous war. As he flew home from a command in Syria the papers speculated on the trap he was sure to spring on the invaders.

But was it already too late? The six o'clock News on 22 May was depressing. Paul Reynaud, the French prime minister, had told his countrymen, 'Only a miracle can save France.' Fortunately, by contrast, King George's Empire Day message the following evening was heartening, a rallying call for unity and courage; he called for a National Day of Prayer on this coming Sunday, 26 May.

On the Saturday afternoon of this weekend I heard the sound of battle for the first time. I was exercising Auntie Bessie's dog in the peace of Knighton Wood when, soon after five o'clock, I thought I heard a roll of thunder – no lightning, though, and no rain. The roll became a continuous rumble. I had read how the explosion of mines in the Ypres salient in 1917 was heard at Westminster and I assumed my ears had tuned in to the current battle being fought not many miles from Ypres. I stayed in Knighton Wood listening until the noise stopped abruptly. For many years I thought the rumble arose from the beaches of Dunkirk but Hugh Sebag-Montefiore's gripping narrative *Dunkirk* convinces me it came from Calais, where at that hour the Rifle Brigade was valiantly resisting a German assault on the town's citadel.

'Operation Dynamo', the evacuation from Dunkirk, did not begin until seven o'clock in the evening of Sunday's National Day of Prayer. It depended for success on holding a hurriedly fortified perimeter in the low-lying fields straddling the Franco-Belgium border; fortunately, throughout the nine days of Dynamo, the weather remained good and the sea calm. Reports of the evacuation were at first kept from us for there were doubts over how many troops could be brought home. Monday's nine o'clock *News* merely mentioned heavy fighting continuing in Belgium. We were therefore surprised and dismayed on hearing next morning that King Leopold of the Belgians had accepted German demands for the capitulation of his army. A spate of alarmist rumours in the wake of Leopold's apparent treachery induced the government to let the public know the evacuation was going well, though precise figures were not given. Before setting out for Bancroft's on Friday I saw the headline 'Tens of Thousands Safely Home' spread across Dad's *Daily Express*. The *News Chronicle* settled soberly for 'Thousands of BEF safely withdrawn from Trap'.

Thereafter we tended to minimise the gravity of the situation, although in fact 1 June became the most critical day of all, with bombing raids on the port and shipping off Dunkirk's two outer moles from dawn onwards. In Kent and Sussex trains were bringing weary survivors of the retreat up to London's termini at the rate of nine an hour by the afternoon, while other trains headed westwards to Southampton and beyond. Some 64,000 men landed in Kent alone during that day.

From carriage windows they looked out on a traditional English summer scene, little changed by war. Local cricket matches were in full sway. So, too, was one at Lord's to raise money for war-related charities. I remember hearing a broadcast commentary on the first wartime League Cup Final at Wembley, where West Ham United beat Blackburn Rovers 1–0 in a packed stadium. It is sadly ironic that one of the hospitals set aside for the Dunkirk wounded was on the outskirts of Blackburn.

By 3 June, 338,326 soldiers had been brought across the Channel, including some 120,000 Frenchmen. Yet the BEF had been forced to abandon more than 400 tanks and virtually all motor transport and heavy guns. Moreover, 34,000 British soldiers could not be rescued and passed into captivity; most were cut off in the outer perimeter, beyond the Belgian frontier.

One enduring memory of this summer is the mental sustenance we received from two contrasting masters of the spoken word: Winston Churchill, who always felt constrained in a studio; and the novelist and playwright J.B. Priestley, 'a comfortable pipe-and-slippers man' as he described himself. On Tuesday, 4 June, as the last ships left Dunkirk, Churchill rallied support in the Commons with the famous oration that affirmed, 'We shall go on to the end… We shall fight on the beaches. We shall fight in the fields and streets. We shall fight in the hills. We shall never surrender.' The speech reached a climax with a peroration that looked forward to the time when 'the New World with all its power and might sets forth to the rescue and liberation of the Old'.

Microphones were not yet installed in the Commons but the full speech was broadcast that evening and the cadence of these splendid words made our wireless ring with patriotic fervour. It never occurred to us that the speaker was anyone other than the prime minister. Yet on two occasions in the 1960s I heard the actor Norman Shelley say it was he who made the broadcast that evening as Churchill was too exhausted to come out to a studio and deliver the oration a second time within a few hours.

Whether we were listening to the prime minister himself or a skilful stand-by in no way diminishes the heartening impact of Churchill's rallying call in those critical days of the war.

Next evening we listened to the first of Priestley's 15-minute *Postscripts*, a series subsequently transmitted on Sundays. He skilfully combined a tribute to the 'little holiday steamers' that 'made an excursion to hell and came back glorious' with a prose threnody on the ones that were lost, like his favourite Isle of Wight ferry, the *Gracie Fields*.

Almost 850 ships took part in Operation Dynamo. They included destroyers – the British, French and Polish navies; cross-Channel steamers; *schlutys*, the all-purpose motor launches from Dutch canals; and most of the Ostend fishing fleet, as well as such French harbour craft as had survived the initial bombing of Dunkirk. But it was the armada of English 'little ships' that passed from obscurity into legend; motor boats from up river suburbia, the London Fire Brigade's tender *Massey Shaw*, coastal paddle steamers, lifeboats under naval command from as far as Frinton or locally from Ramsgate and Margate, cockle boats and even the last red-sailed Thames barges. Later on, as news seeped through, we grieved for ships personally known to us. Among them were the *Crested Eagle,* which plied the Essex coast and had taken Derek and me to Chatham Navy Day, and the LNER's *Prague*, aboard which in 1936 we returned from Zeebrugge. The Dieppe run's *Brighton,* converted into a hospital ship, was also sunk off the French coast, her speed unable to save her from Stuka bombers. Fortunately, calm seas enabled the small craft to rescue many survivors from these wrecks.

On the first anniversary of her maiden voyage the *Royal Daffodil* reached Dunkirk and over the following six days embarked a record 7,460 men. She made seven crossings to the moles and beaches but on 2 June was singled out for attack by six Stukas. One bomb penetrated two decks before exploding, leaving a hole beneath the water line. She was so well built that, miraculously, she proved able to reach Ramsgate. It was another year before she was back in service as a 'personnel carrier'. The *Canterbury*, too, had a lucky escape; she was hit in the raid that sank the *Crested Eagle* but was able to return to Dover. The *Maid of Orleans*, which took us to France in 1934, made six trips, relatively unscathed; nine years later I was pleased to cross from Folkestone to Boulogne in her again.

The Germans renewed their offensive on 5 June, striking south of the Somme, towards Rouen and Paris with 140 divisions. Less than a month earlier Gamelin could count on 94 French divisions and support from a BEF front-line force of ten divisions to meet the challenge of invasion but after Dunkirk, Weygand was left with only 49 French divisions and the British 51st Highland Division to counter the new threat. There were still 100,000 'lines of communication' troops from the BEF in Brittany and plans were broached for creating a second BEF to include newly landed Canadian troops, if Weygand could stabilise the front south of the Seine. But by 11 June all prospect of keeping a foothold was fast disappearing. On that Tuesday the 51st Highland Division was awaiting evacuation from St Valery-en-Caux when mist swept in from the sea after no more than 2,140 of the 8,500 Highlanders had embarked. Soon the high cliffs I had thought so impressive in 1938 trapped the mist. It became a thick fog and ended all hope of rescue. Next morning the remaining Highlanders surrendered to Major-General Erwin Rommel, commanding the 7th Panzer Division. Fog-free days at Le Havre and St Malo enabled over 15,000 troops to be evacuated during the week.

There was, too, at first an orderly evacuation of 27,000 soldiers and civilians in merchant ships from St Nazaire but it ended tragically on 17 June. Three bombs from a lone German plane hit the Cunard liner *Lancastria,* setting her on fire. She sank within 15 minutes, with the loss of over 3,400 lives – soldiers, airmen and several families of civilians working in France. Strict censorship kept the news out of the British press until 26 July when a spate of rumours emanating from returned survivors and American newspapers belatedly forced the Ministry of Information to confirm the loss of the ship. But the full extent of the disaster remained hidden from us until after the war and even now is rarely mentioned in general historical narratives. Yet when the *Lancastria* went down, over twice as many lives were lost as from the *Titanic* 28 years earlier, and slightly more than in America from the 9/11 terrorist assault 61 years later.

Much of our attention in the last days of May was given to the role of Germany's Axis partner, Italy. Throughout the winter Mussolini maintained a cautious neutrality but the initial German victories made us feel certain he would soon take Italy into the war, eager for a share in the spoils of victory. At Martineau and Reid's my father looked after the legal affairs of a popular Italian restaurateur whose family had lived in London for many years while keeping in close touch with relatives in Florence. Now he feared he would be interned as an enemy alien and was worried over the future treatment of his wife and children. To my father's surprise he passed over to him an 'incriminating' silk handkerchief depicting the Italian and German flags, one of many issued in 1938 to schoolchildren to wave during Hitler's visit to Mussolini. More alarmingly he then asked Dad to take care of an evil-looking small pistol, for which he had no licence.

Dad arrived home with the unexpected 'presents'. I was given the handkerchief and still possess it; the red, white, green and black colours are unfaded after 75 years. Dad clicked the trigger of the pistol to check it was not loaded and put it away in a drawer. Members of the LDV had been asked to hand in firearms they possessed; Dad took it with him next time he was on duty.

Sure enough, Mussolini announced Italy's entry into the war in a bombastic speech on 10 June and Italian men aged between 17 and 70 who had lived in England for less than 20 years were promptly interned, Dad's client among them. The Italian air force struck within hours of Mussolini's declaration of war, bombing British shipping and eventually Malta. At first French warships backed the Royal Navy's response in shelling maritime supply bases near Genoa but French interest in the war declined rapidly.

Time was running out for any second 'miracle of the Marne'. Weygand lost the will to fight during 12 June, the day the Highland Division surrendered at St Valery. That evening the whole of Greater Paris, from St Germain and Versailles eastwards to Meaux, was declared an open city which the invaders could enter with impunity. Soon after dawn on 14 June the first motorised German troop-carriers reached the empty boulevards. At an hour when Parisians normally begin their day's work a long column of field-grey infantry marched symbolically up the Champs-Élysées from the Place de la Concorde to the Arc de Triomphe.

The BBC news that morning confirmed that Paris was an open city but did not mention German troop movements. At lunchtime I again kept close to the Common Room window at Bancroft's, faintly hoping for good news. It did not come. Instead, Mr Herring emerged with a grim face; he turned to me and said gruffly, 'They're in Paris.' Then, on this day when the uncertainties of a terrible chapter of living history opened for France, he strolled heavily across the quadrangle grass to teach dead history from the agreed record of a familiar textbook.

I hurried to another classroom for a Latin lesson. What I was supposed to be studying I have no idea; my concentration had gone. All I remember is that the room was bathed in sunshine. My thoughts turned to the Rue de Fleurus and my mind's eye pictured that same sun reflected off the dome of the Pantheon, the shade of chestnut trees in the Luxembourg Gardens, and the pond on which it was unlikely any boy or girl would sail a little yacht this coming weekend. And I was close to tears.

FIFTEEN

Vapour Trails Across the Sky

Memories of high summer in 1940 evoke for me days of excitement and exultation. Hurricanes and Spitfires weave grey trails in blue skies, with German planes too far away to be named; I wait expectantly to identify them, a Penguin book of aircraft recognition close on hand. Messerschmitt 109 fighters, Heinkels, Junkers, Dorniers and Stukas, I prided myself on knowing them all in those days. The thought I might be killed never crossed my mind. I, and thousands like me, were privileged to watch slowly unfold a conflict unique in history. It was not a battle in which air power supported armies on the ground but a series of duels between men in machines which became a struggle for our survival. The Battle of Britain had no clear beginning and no precise end.

France officially went out of the war on 22 June when delegates from the government of Marshal Pétain accepted a German-imposed armistice. Briefly Hitler considered seeking a peace with Britain and there was a pause, broken by a German raid on Aldershot on 6 July, the first on a specific English target. A series of attacks on coastal convoys (called the *Kanalkampf* by the Germans) began four days later. This was preliminary sparring to assess the extent of Britain's radar system but it also provided knowledge of the manoeuvrability of opposing fighter aircraft.

Hitler issued his sixteenth directive of the war on 16 July. His choice of words was tentative. 'I have decided to prepare a landing operation against England and if necessary to carry it out,' he dictated. Plans began to be drawn up immediately for *Unternehmen Seelewe*, 'Operation Sealion': the German navy would mass 2,000 barges at nine ports from Zeebrugge down to Cherbourg and the Luftwaffe would be required to tow gliders and transport paratroopers for an airborne assault in Kent and Sussex. But Hitler stipulated that the invasion would not begin until the Luftwaffe had gained total mastery of the sky over the Channel and southern England.

At first the possibility of invasion made little change in our day-to-day life. Only a couple of alerts sent classes off to the shelters at school; that wretched experience became more common during the autumn. Although there was no 'Vis Day' at Bancroft's this year, the summer term ran its normal course. The war map looked bare on my bedroom wall. By now such flag pins as survived nine months of rough handling were back in their original box, with points blunted.

When I glanced at the map the fate of France was uppermost in my mind. Dad responded to a government appeal for photographs taken along the coast that was now in German hands. *The army is going back there*, I thought. Surviving albums have empty slots with captions in his handwriting: 'Edie and Alan on The Mole', says one; 'Sand yachts at Le Touquet', says another; 'Alan on Dieppe beach', a third. I hope Military Intelligence made use of our snaps. We never saw them again.

My map did not mark Vichy, the spa resort which served as an interim capital of occupied France, but it did show Oran, on the coast of Algeria, where on 3 July a powerful British naval force bombarded French warships at the naval base of Mers-el-Kébir to forestall its possible seizure by Germany. This sorry event, that took the lives of 1,300 of our recent ally's seamen, brought the Entente Cordiale to a tragic end.

Those of us who loved France and grieved for the harsh necessity of Oran put our hope for the future on General de Gaulle, who had flown to London from Bordeaux before the German net closed in and who appealed on the radio for his compatriots to join him in continuing the fight against the invaders. I was pleased when on 14 July, France's National Day, Mr Jenkins made us stand and sing the 'Marseillaise' at the start of our lesson. Like me, he admired General de Gaulle's courage and determination.

Later in the war I had a chance to show the general my respect. In April 1942 I was walking along Carlton House Terrace with my classmate Desmond Perry when we saw a group of French officers turn round the corner from the Duke of York's column with the tall figure of the general in their midst. We were across the road from the group as they reached no. 4, the Free French headquarters. Desmond and I raised our school caps, thinking he might perfunctorily acknowledge our gesture. Instead, he halted his group outside the sandbagged entrance, turned and gave a solemn salute, as if we were a guard of honour. Emotion stifled my shyness: 'Vive la France Libre,' I called across the road. The grave head nodded in recognition.

But in 1940 that brief encounter lay two years ahead. The Battle of Britain grew in intensity during what would normally have been summer holiday time. One BBC reporter, Charles Gardner, speaking from the Kent coast, described the combat in the skies with the heartiness of a cricket commentator – 'There goes one down, and here's another' – which Mother thought inappropriate. The background noise, with planes screaming in dives and what was presumably the rattle of machine guns, was more dramatic than his words. Soon these sounds would reach Ilford too, but not yet. South London and Essex east of a line from Hornchurch to Ongar were bombed earlier than us, with airfields the main target.

The most spectacular day was Thursday, 15 August. A raid began shortly before midday when I was with Bruce in the park. There had been alerts on the previous two days but the weather had been cloudy. On this particular morning the sky was clear and by the time I had reached home it was criss-crossed with vapour trails. I thought at first the trails were smoke from falling aircraft. So the sight continued until early evening, although no bombs or planes fell anywhere near us. Friends in Croydon were less fortunate; there the aerodrome was attacked before the sirens sounded and after one particularly heavy explosion a thick pall of smoke drifted over Purley, making our friends hurriedly put on their gas masks.

Friday's papers hailed a great British victory, with over a hundred planes brought down. Post-war reassessment has corrected the figures: 1,270 German fighters escorted 520 bombers; 75 were shot down, for the loss of 34 British aircraft. This was the highest number of enemy planes destroyed in any single day.

The daylight bombing continued next morning, with airfields as far inland as Oxfordshire singled out for attack. On Friday afternoon (16 August) Churchill went to the headquarters of the fighter group responsible for southern England at Uxbridge. In his *The Second World War* he describes how he anxiously watched plotters in the Operations Room moving symbols on a vast map to show RAF squadrons engaged in battle and the waves of incoming bombers identified from radar stations. At the moment that the Germans broke off the attack every serviceable plane in the fighter group was in the air. There were no reserves.

His Uxbridge visit was in Churchill's mind on the following Monday when he told the Commons, 'The gratitude of every home in our island... goes out to the

British airmen who, undaunted by odds, unwearied in their constant challenge and mortal danger, are turning the tide of the World War by their prowess and their devotion. Never in the field of human conflict was so much owed by so many to so few.'

These words are immortal and the tribute fully merited. Yet two miles from the Uxbridge Operations Room is a memorial to other brave heroes of the war in the sky. At Northolt a Polish eagle surmounts a plaque on which are inscribed the names of 2,165 Polish airmen who died while flying from RAF airfields around the world. Among them is Flight Sergeant Brzezowski, an ace Spitfire pilot killed on 15 September. Another Polish air ace Anton Gtowacki who shot down five German planes in a single day survived the war, living to see his country freed from communist rule. Some 70 Czechs and Slovaks fought alongside the Poles. Sergeant Josef Frantivsek shot down 17 Luftwaffe fighters or bombers, a higher number than any other Battle of Britain pilot, but died in a flying accident in October. Men from Australia, Canada, New Zealand and elsewhere in the empire fought in the battle. In 1940 we in Britain may have stood alone but we never fought alone.

The first bombs fell on central London five nights after Churchill's fine oration. On Sunday, 24 August, a raid was made on oil storage tanks at Thameshaven. By mistake one flight of planes bombed riverside facilities higher up the Thames. The RAF responded with small-scale attacks on Berlin on the Sunday night and the following Wednesday. Such 'tit-for-tat bombing' – as we called it at the time – became a regular feature of aerial warfare in Europe.

Two days later the Luftwaffe made its greatest attack so far on British airfields, particularly in Kent and Essex, with 800 planes taking part in the raids. Over Biggin Hill, a Spitfire base close to Churchill's country home at Chartwell, 17 of the German attackers were shot down. Only one British fighter was lost; the pilot parachuted to safety – and was back in the air before nightfall. Such was the spirit in which the Battle of Britain was fought.

The sirens sounded intermittently day and night during the first week of September. Some writers report instances of low morale in the East End and across the river. So far as I know, there were no signs of war weariness in Ilford. Excitement continued to bolster me up. As yet I had seen only the vapour trails of distant German planes. Surely, I thought, there must come a time when some would come close enough for me to put my aircraft recognition to the test? It seems an odd hope; but at heart I retained the simplistic 'ready for a fight' outlook of a boy of 13.

SIXTEEN

London's Burning

Saturday, 7 September, began as an idyllic summer's morning. The sky was cornflower blue, barrage balloons already silver with the sun at breakfast time.

All of us should have treated the day with caution; across the Channel preparations were well-advanced for an invasion. Although there had still been no deliberate attack on inner London we had little doubt the sirens would soon wail out again. But by noon the temperature was climbing into the 80s Fahrenheit; too fine to stay indoors.

There was an attractive programme of sport to watch. Peacetime idols were almost all in uniform by now but off-duty hours enabled scratch sides to be raised for cricket and the Football Association let clubs 'borrow' players. That afternoon West Ham was playing Tottenham while Arsenal entertained Fulham at White Hart Lane as its Highbury ground was an ARP depot. At Lord's, Middlesex were playing a war charities match against an invitation XI. The match card included such familiar names as Squadron Leader R.W. V. Robins and Sergeant D.C.S. Compton.

Some families were content to go out walking, cycling or visiting relatives. At no. 38 Dad busied himself in the garden. I remember cutting the grass but after lunch I badgered him to take me to Barking Park where his Home Guard company had recently provided relief sentries for an anti-aircraft battery. He had left a padded body belt in the park which he would need if the temperature dropped while he was on duty elsewhere this coming night.

When we arrived, I was a little disappointed. The guns pointed skywards but there was no sign of imminent activity. Dad collected his belt and we wandered about rather pointlessly before catching a trolley-bus back up Ilford Lane to Ley Street, where we had to change. It was twenty to five as we crossed the road to the station bus stop and the siren's banshee notes greeted us. Nothing surprising in that: there had been a similar alert at teatime the previous Saturday. Now, however, I noticed people on the pavement looking to the sky behind us. We turned round – and saw an unbelievable spectacle, ominously impressive.

Three miles away or more, in the sky above Dagenham and Rainham, a fleet of German bombers, some 150 Heinkels and Dorniers with a protective shield of Messerchmitt fighters, was heading upriver, flying so high that no Spitfire or Hurricane could reach them and scorning the balloon barrage below. On and on they flew with impeccable orderliness, in a diamond formation as perfectly positioned as guardsmen on parade. I had been waiting for a chance to identify German planes but never expected to see them on a scale like this. A second even larger wave of bombers further to the south came into view soon afterwards as we waited for the bus. There was no sound other than the rough roar of their engines, growing in intensity as the aerial armada made for London's docks.

The bus ride up Cranbrook Road was no different from any other, the conductor punching tickets unconcernedly, the driver pulling in at four scheduled stops. But when we reached home we found Mother highly agitated. She thought she had heard the crump of bombs exploding; yet it did not occur to us to reach for out gas masks as we would have 12 months previously, nor indeed did we take shelter. Dad and I stood at the top of the garden, with the sandbagged dining-room door behind us, mesmerised by the drama five or six miles away to the south-west.

The light was good and occasionally we saw the planes themselves, no longer closely regimented but swooping down on particular targets in V-formation, like silver arrow heads. Several spirals of smoke whisked up, until suddenly an all-embracing grey cloud spread out from the centre. It was as if a long row of haystacks had caught fire, though we could see no flames. Dad decided we had better go indoors. Where were those gas masks, he wondered? But there was no sound of air raid wardens twirling gas-alarm rattles, only the noise of fire-engines speeding along Eastern Avenue towards Wanstead and on to Stratford.

Then unexpectedly, soon after six, the sirens gave the All Clear: the bombers had turned south over Surrey and Kent, back to France and Belgium. The raid had lasted less than 90 minutes. That was that, we hoped. Tea was a little late. Dad changed into khaki and caught a 66 bus to his Home

Guard post, almost in Romford. At Upton Park, Spurs led 4-1 when the raid began, while Arsenal had gone 5-0 up against Fulham. Both matches were at once abandoned but many spectators were late home because of bomb damage close to the grounds. At Lord's, where Middlesex was in a strong position at the interruption, cricket was resumed. As *Wisden* records, the game had a 'strange and dramatic end': Middlesex took the last four wickets in only seven balls. No doubt the batsmen had other matters on their minds. A crimson sky in the east warned them of grimmer problems to face that night than the pace and swing bowling of Lance Corporal Laurie Gray.

In Clarence Avenue, Mother and I were slow to realise the gravity of the raid. A south-west wind carried the smoke cloud over central Ilford but only a few wafts of acrid fumes drifted up to Gants Hill. Then as dusk fell we saw the ring of fire over West Ham and beyond. South of the Thames planks of Scandinavian wood stacked on the quayside formed a beacon for the Surrey docks that continued to light the sky until dawn. Most bombs north of the river fell on Silvertown and the Isle of Dogs but there was a systematic attack on Beckton (the largest gasworks in Europe) and on the railways around it: fires were started at points along the District line from East Ham to Plaistow. Sulphurous fumes caused a near panic and there was fear of a great explosion. One early bomb was a direct hit on an Anderson shelter in a garden close to my parents' old home in Milton Avenue, East Ham, killing a family they knew well.

Two days previously my cousin Madeline became

eight years old. In peacetime, she would have had a birthday party that Saturday at their house in Windsor Road, south Ilford. Not this year, however: her father – Uncle Warren – had re-enlisted and was with a searchlight unit at Abridge; her 15-year-old sister Jean was out with school friends. As a consolation Madeline's mother, Aunt Beattie, took her to collect presents from her grandparents at Plaistow. They were about to go home when the raid began.

As soon as the All Clear sounded they began the return journey, passing bombed houses where rescuers were still digging in the debris and avoiding roads where fire crews were at work or where police feared there were unexploded bombs (UXBs). There was no power for trams or trolleys but remarkably they reached Ilford by a roundabout route involving three bus changes. As they neared home they saw Jean sitting on the low stone wall in front of the house, head in hands, shoulders heaving in misery. She looked up and, through the dim light, saw them emerge, walking hand in hand, as so often when Madeline was collected from school. Jean leapt up and waved them away. 'Don't come near me,' she screamed. 'Go away; you're ghosts. I know you're ghosts.' After her mother calmed her down, Jean explained she had hurried home from her friend's house when the All Clear sounded, saw the fires over West Ham and was told by a passer-by, 'It's terrible, luv, Beckton's gone up; they're all dead, right up to Plaistow, they are.' While she sat on the wall, she prayed her father would soon come from Abridge to comfort her.

The sirens sounded again about five minutes past eight that evening. A different type of raid followed. This time almost 250 Junkers-88 medium bombers came, flying in small formations, and the bombardment continued for more than eight hours, most of which Mother and I spent on a mattress under the dining table. A few bombs fell in Westminster and Chelsea but the main objective remained the docks, on both sides of the river. Silvertown, where 13,000 people had their homes, was virtually wiped from the map. Police and wardens believed there were as many as 100 UXBs in the district, although some suspect cracks in pavements or mole-like holes in gardens were caused by splinters from anti-aircraft shells. Bombs ruptured the Northern Outfall Sewer near Beckton, contaminating water supplies over a large area. Once again Plaistow was heavily hit; Madeline and Jean's grandparents, having escaped damage in the earlier raid, were less fortunate in the night attack; later on Sunday they reached Windsor Road, unharmed but homeless. Other families found temporary shelter in church halls, schools and at least two cinemas; a swimming pool served as a morgue. Officially, 436 Londoners perished in this first night of the Blitz and over 1,500 were gravely injured but the toll of deaths from the raid mounted during the following week.

In Canning Town several hundred families were crammed into South Hallsville School after Saturday's bombing, awaiting evacuation to safer areas in the outer suburbs. They were still there on Monday evening, expecting the imminent arrival of a convoy of buses. A dreadful error sent the buses to Camden Town rather than to Canning Town. When the convoy set out again, the bombers were back and the buses were delayed by new fires and diversions. They arrived too late. The school received a direct hit at 3.50 on Tuesday morning and the roof caved in. No one knows how many died; 75 bodies were buried but a survivor I met many years later thought several hundred a more likely figure. Although details of the tragedy were kept secret, on Wednesday *The Times* gave a graphic description of the devastation left by bombing at 'an East End school' and of the search for bodies or survivors. Rumours abounded across the eastern suburbs, as they did frequently throughout the eight months of the Blitz, but after Jean's experience we discounted many of them.

When the All Clear came at 4.30 on Sunday morning I went up to my bedroom and slept well into the day. I do not know what time Dad arrived home but I do remember he seemed subdued when we sat down for a late Sunday dinner. He was obviously very tired but he may too have had reason to think invasion imminent. At 8.07 on Saturday evening – just as the second air raid began – General Sir Alan Brooke, commander-in-chief of the Home Forces, ordered the code-word 'Cromwell' to be sent to all military units under his command; it was the signal for regular troops and Home Guard to be ready to repel German landings from sea or air. In a few areas outside London overzealous Home Guard commanders had church bells rung to muster their men, believing an invasion had begun.

A second night of bombing began at 7.45 on the

Sunday. We tuned in as usual to Priestley's *Postscript*. He recalled how '25 years ago... young men were mown down by the million'... while civilians remained 'sitting at ease' in England until 'the telegrams arrived', bringing dreadful news to countless families. 'We are much better off now,' he insisted. 'We're not really civilians anymore.' He likened us to a mixed 'gallant corps'. 'It's possible that distant generations will find inspiration, when their time of trouble comes, in the report in their history books of our conduct at this hour.' The broadcast was given in the person-to-person style we always found heartening. By now I had become a Priestley fan, enjoying the escapism of *The Good Companions* between raids.

More than 200 bombers targeted London that night, at first concentrating on targets in the West End: Sir Alan Brooke noted in his diary that he 'counted over 60 bombs fall in [the] vicinity in one hour'. But the eastern suburbs were not spared: during a lull Dad and I slipped into the garden and found ourselves once more looking out towards a horizon of flame. The low guttural drone of a new wave of bombers arrived. Back we went under the dining table. It became rather cramped.

By Wednesday the noise of battle was thunderous; anti-aircraft batteries were now fully deployed and maintained a constant barrage. Weary East Enders for the first time defied the law and brought pillows and blankets down to the platforms of the Central Line Tube stations and refused to be moved out again. At Clarence Avenue Bruce crept out of his basket and sought to nestle up to us, for the only time in the war. Uncle Bill, aged

87 and almost stone deaf, was in his bedroom as usual, having slept undisturbed through the first four nights of bombing, but when Mother brought him his morning cup of tea he greeted her with an anxious, 'I thought I heard a little popping in the night, Edie?' Not that the intrusive awakening changed his habits. For the rest of the war he never slept anywhere other than in his own bed.

Mother, ever restless, would frequently slip out from our 'shelter'. On one September night – I am not sure of the precise date – she hurried briefly back into the room to wake us. 'What did she say?' Dad asked me. 'She said the house is on fire,' I replied sleepily, nestling back unconcernedly in the improvised bed. Dad's reaction was different. He sat up suddenly, almost giving himself concussion as his head struck the underside of the tabletop. In fact, Mother had told us the garage showrooms in Eastern Avenue were blazing. Fortunately the fire was extinguished before it reached the petrol pumps.

There was a daylight raid in the late morning of 13 September, a drizzly and cloudy Friday, and during it three bombs fell on Buckingham Palace. One destroyed the private chapel; the others made craters in the quadrangle close to rooms the King and Queen were using. The narrowness of the royal escape was kept secret but news that the palace had been bombed was released for Saturday's papers. The subsequent British Movietone News film was shown widely in America and made excellent propaganda, intensifying the mounting sympathy for 'the folks across the sea'.

These daylight attacks continued for the first fortnight

of the Blitz, with the Messerschmitts providing cover for bombers, as in the initial raid. We had no rest day or night on Sunday, 15 September; 950 planes crossed the Channel from 35 airfields. Our spirits were lifted when Monday's papers reported 185 had been destroyed, 'a record score'. In reality the total German loss was 56 bombers and fighters and the RAF's was 23 planes. The record 'score' was therefore the 75 planes shot down on 15 August. Yet even before the war ended 15 September was commemorated as Battle of Britain Day and so it remains. It was certainly a decisive moment in the war, for two days later Hitler decided the losses were so great that the invasion of England must be indefinitely postponed; the British would be brought to their knees by terror bombing of cities.

While the Blitz was still a novelty, *Punch* tempted providence with a cartoon showing an immaculately dressed BBC announcer reading the evening bulletin: '... And here is another bit of news that has just come through,' he says; beside him embedded in the floor was a huge UXB. Alas, three weeks later reality struck. On Tuesday, 15 October, we were listening to Bruce Belfrage reading the nine o'clock *News* when there was a distinct thump and a pause, with a worried whisper of 'Are you all right?', before Belfrage continued, imperturbably. Broadcasting House had received a direct hit from a 50-pound bomb that penetrated the fifth floor and killed seven employees. The *News* studio had been moved down to the sub-basement, which was not damaged.

That night became the worst London had suffered,

with the Luftwaffe dropping high-explosive bombs, incendiaries and parachute mines. A bomb fell in Whitehall, close to the Cenotaph, and a mine exploded in the branches of a tree in St James's Park, blowing out the remaining windows of Buckingham Palace facing The Mall and damaging the frontage of many historic houses in Piccadilly. By a macabre coincidence the total number of fatal casualties, 410, was identical with the number of raiding planes. Almost a thousand fires were started and 900 people gravely injured.

Fortunately the bombing ceased about half-past two. I managed a few hours' sleep before catching the usual bus to Bancroft's. Dad and Aunt Elsie had big problems making their ways to town because UXBs left many roads closed and bombs had fallen close to the railway track. The sirens sounded just before half-past eight that evening but this time the All Clear came at one in the morning and I enjoyed another hour in a comfortable bed. Dad and Aunt Elsie again had difficult journeys and on this morning my 145 bus was late but we all reached our destinations in Gray's Inn, Whitehall or Woodford Green at a reasonable time.

This 'business as usual' attitude became a tacitly accepted point of honour. I do not recall a single occasion when our newspapers failed to be delivered, though sometimes they came later than usual. Like many other boys and girls across the suburbs, I occasionally set off for school before the All Clear had sounded. If a boy failed to come to school it was because he was genuinely ill, or had lost his home, his family – or his life.

On Monday, 7 October, I was worried because my friend Ted Ellis was absent from morning assembly and I was told bombs had fallen close to his home. He lived in Forest Edge, about half a mile south of Bancroft's, overlooking the railway out to North Weald, where a highly successful Hurricane squadron was stationed. At lunchtime I heard that Ted and his family were safe but had had a narrow escape. Their house – built only just before the war – was wrecked by a bomb with a delayed action fuse that fell in the front garden. Fortunately they were in their Anderson at the back when it exploded and were shaken but unharmed. I remember reflecting that if such a bomb fell on our house the dear old dining table would not give us much protection.

The bombing continued for 56 consecutive nights before murky weather over France brought a respite. Derek Tatnall and I became accustomed to picking up pieces of shrapnel in the back garden, while at Bancroft's scouring parties moved slowly across rugby pitches before games were played on them. The only encouraging war news was of General Wavell's victories against the Italians along the Egyptian-Libyan border and the repulse inflicted on Italian troops Mussolini had ordered to invade Greece from Albania. But these welcome successes were too distant to influence the on-going Blitz. We had heavy bombing again on Wednesday, 6 November; a short, sharp raid in the small hours of Thursday; another pause until a raid in bright moonlight on the following Tuesday, 12 November; and an extremely heavy attack, with clusters of incendiary bombs on 15-16 November, the night following the appalling raid to obliterate Coventry, which left considerably more than a thousand civilians dead.

The Luftwaffe gave the code-name 'Moonlight Sonata' to the attack on Coventry, an introduction to a methodical programme which brought nights of non-stop bombing to other major cities: Birmingham on 20 November; Liverpool and Southampton on 29-30 November; Bristol on 2 December; and Manchester three nights before Christmas. Censorship hid the identity of most targets. Wireless bulletins simply said a 'town in the north-west' or 'the Midlands' had been attacked. There were, too, frequent references to 'coastal towns in the north-east', leaving us to wonder if the target was Newcastle, Middlesbrough or Scarborough, whereas it was more likely to be non-coastal Hull, a river port raided so often that 90% of its houses were destroyed or left badly damaged.

Attacks on London declined in intensity by early December, partly because of frequent fog coming in from the Thames estuary. There was a raid on 23 December but a respite over Christmas itself. The family gathered at 339 Eastern Avenue as usual and we discovered some pre-war decorations at the back of a cupboard. But it was roast chicken rather than turkey to eat, though Mother had found a tin of treacle and improvised a Christmas pudding that included sliced carrot, as recommended by the Ministry of Food. I was happy with books as presents, including General de Gaulle's *The Army of the Future*, and Priestley's *Postscripts*, which was rushed into print by Heinemann barely seven weeks after his increasingly left-wing slant brought an abrupt end to the series. I still cherish this little book, with the text of all 19 broadcasts packed into a hundred pages. Nothing evokes so vividly the hopes, fears and challenges of 1940, the most dramatic 12 months of my life.

The year had not yet run its course. In a letter to *The Times*, dated 27 December, R.D. Blumenfeld, editor of the *Daily Express* during the Great War, described how at that moment he could hear carol singers in his village rendering 'Hark the Herald Angels' to an accompaniment 'of sirens and AA guns… while we see the fireworks over London 50 miles away'. In reality the Friday 'firework' display was comparatively restrained. It should however have served as a warning that the peace of Christmas was over. Instead, London opted for a relaxed weekend. Banks, offices, warehouses and city churches remained locked and bolted, even though the tidal Thames would be at its lowest ebb on Sunday evening, intensifying the difficulties confronting firemen if they sought to throw powerful jets from their pumps on to the centre of a blaze.

The bombers came back in force that Sunday. By midnight almost 1,500 fires were burning at the heart of the City. Eight Wren churches were destroyed. St Paul's was hit by some two dozen incendiary bombs and saved from destruction only by the speed of efficiently trained firewatchers. The Guildhall roof was set on fire and caved in, with flames consuming statues of the legendary giants

Gog and Magog that had been carried in processions and pageants in earlier centuries. A square half mile from Old Street through Moorgate to Cannon Street became a field of flame, as fire swept through office buildings and threatened the Bank of England. South of the Mansion House alleys down which the Great Fire passed in 1666 became torches bringing destruction to waterside warehouses. A total of 163 deaths was mercifully low, largely because the huge area was almost deserted on a Sunday night. Sixteen firemen were killed and more than 250 taken to hospital with broken bones or burns. The courage of the firefighters saved London from the firestorms that devastated Hamburg in July 1943, Dresden in February 1945 and Tokyo five months later.

From Clarence Avenue we saw again ever changing spurts of flame in the Western sky. Next day we heard that among the burning buildings in Aldersgate was a block where Mother worked before her marriage and while Dad was overseas in the war. The following night brought another raid, smaller in intensity. When, in the morning, Dad made his way to Raymond Buildings he found Martineau and Reid's three floors in ruins, wrecked by a bomb or parachute mine that fell close to Theobald's Road. For 36 years Martineau and Reid had been 'the office' for him. Now there was nothing he could do except help move sealed deposits from the vaults to the firm's temporary accommodation in High Holborn. He arrived home that evening exhausted; for three weeks he was excused Home Guard duties. It was a sombre New Year's Eve for both my parents.

There was a raid on Saturday, 5 January, and a more serious one a week later when over 50 people were killed by a direct hit on the booking hall of the Bank Tube station. In general it was a quiet month, partly because of the weather; at the end of the third week there was a heavy fall of snow and another one early in February. My most vivid memory of March is of exciting news from the Balkans, a region that greatly interested me. A military coup at Belgrade in the small hours of 27 March deposed Prince Regent Paul, brought 17-year old King Peter II to the throne in his own right and installed a government hostile to the Axis. I heard of the coup on the eight o'clock *News* and went off to Bancroft's elated. Hitler was furious: he ordered 'the destruction of Yugoslavia militarily and as a national unit'. Early on 6 April Belgrade was heavily bombed by Stuka dive bombers. Germany also declared war on Greece, the panzer columns advancing so rapidly that by 9 April they had taken Salonika – much to my father's shock and dismay. The Yugoslavs gained successes against the Italians but German intervention ended resistance on 17 April. Peter II was evacuated to Cairo from Budva in Montenegro.

By then other matters were on our minds. The Blitz returned to London on Wednesday, 16 April, with an eight and a half hour raid in which 650 bombers, mainly Junkers 88s, flew low and illuminated their targets with chandelier flares. Mayfair, Holborn Circus and suburbs south of the Thames suffered most damage and casualties. The Junkers-88s were back again on the following Saturday night but once again Ilford came off lightly. Although in retrospect it seems absurd, I remember that my big concern was for a newly purchased bicycle – my first. I had drawn out a whole £8 from my savings book to pay for it and dreaded the possibility that my shiny 'Raleigh' bike might be destroyed before I had had a chance to ride it.

This Saturday raid was an ordeal for families living farther west than those who suffered on the Wednesday, particularly people in Lambeth, Chelsea and off Piccadilly. In all, during the two April raids more than 2,300 people were killed, over 3,000 seriously injured and 148,000 houses and other buildings destroyed or badly damaged. These are higher figures than from any two nights during the eight-week initial attacks of the autumn.

Fortunately, we in London then had a three-week respite, without a raid. From our relatives in the West Country we knew that the Luftwaffe was concentrating on the Plymouth area and on Bristol. At the turn of the month inner Plymouth, Devonport and Torpoint were attacked on four nights, with the centre of the city wrecked, the naval barracks hit and a waterside fire threatening to spread along the Cornish bank of the Tamar.

At the time we did not realise the intensity of this sustained bombardment, nor did we know of similar nights of bombing on Belfast or of a raid which concentrated on a small enclave in the centre of Londonderry.

For Londoners the worst of all air raids during the war was still to come. On Saturday, 10 May, the moon was full and the Thames at low ebb, propitious conditions for a raid to set London burning again. I had gone upstairs to bed and was sound asleep when the siren woke me and sent me hurrying down to the familiar dining-table shelter. The moonlight, seeping through our kitchen blackout, was so bright that I thought it must be almost dawn, rather than about one in the morning.

For some five hours 380 planes pounded the whole of London. When at five minutes to two the Houses of Parliament were hit by bombs that gutted the House of Commons and set fire to the roof of Westminster Hall, crews were already struggling to find water to save the British Museum and trying to contain a blaze that had engulfed Bethnal Green Road. Within the next few hours Westminster Abbey, a section of the Tower of London and the Royal Mint were all hit. Buildings shorn up in dockland after the main Blitz came tumbling down. The gas mains around Beckton were fractured and fires started south of the Thames. In all, the Luftwaffe killed 1,436 people, more than had perished at Coventry in the great raid six months previously.

I woke early, despite the broken night's sleep. We were surprised by a fresh alert at breakfast time but nothing happened and we soon heard the All Clear. Distant pockets of fire on both sides of the river were still throwing up smoke at midday. After lunch I took Bruce out for his customary Sunday afternoon run in Valentine's Park. Office papers, crisp at the edge like burnt toast, had been carried nine or ten miles by a strong south-west wind and fluttered across the cricket ground. The air was rank with the scent of charred invoices.

As darkness closed in we waited expectantly for

a siren call. It did not come then, nor in the days that followed. Birmingham was bombed on 16 May but in London weeks went by without a raid. By mid-June we were ready to accept that the Blitz was over at last. More than 20,000 people had lost their lives and 350,000 homes were destroyed or severely damaged. Remarkably, 38 Clarence Avenue survived unscathed. But for how long, we wondered? By now Britain had been at war for 20 months. Another 48 were to elapse before the only smoke in the night sky came from bonfires around which a happy people swayed rhythmically and sang, as they greeted the return of peace to a divided Europe.

SEVENTEEN

War's Changing Fortunes

Sunday, 22 June 1941 was the hottest midsummer day we could remember. Sensible people headed for a swimming pool or found a shady spot for a deckchair. But not me; I was far too excited. The one o'clock *News* reported that before dawn on this shortest night of the year German troops had invaded the Soviet Union. The news staggered me. After a quick lunch I grabbed my bike, pedalled up to Chigwell Row and down deserted roads humming happily. I was in a strange mood, eager to savour alone my conviction that Hitler had blundered. Like Napoleon he was plunging into Russia at midsummer. I had read two books about the 1812 campaign and knew how the heat that assailed the *Grande Armée* after it had crossed the River Niemen was followed five months later by heavy snow and disaster. Why should Hitler fare better?

Few would have agreed with me. The Nazi-Soviet Pact of August 1939 and the Winter War against Finland had left Soviet Russia unpopular. There was widespread mistrust of communists. As recently as January the printing and circulation of the communist *Daily Worker* had been banned as 'subversive'. In 1918-19 Churchill had wished to strangle the Bolshevik republic at birth. How would he respond to this latest development? Anxiously we awaited his broadcast in the nine o'clock *News*.

'No one has been a more consistent opponent of Communism than I have for the last 25 years,' he admitted, 'I will unsay no word that I have spoken about it but all this fades away before the spectacle now unfolding. We shall give whatever help we can to Russia and the Russian people... Any man or state who fights on against Nazidom will have our aid. Any man or state who marches with Hitler is our foe,' he declared. This was straight talking. We now knew he had every intention of getting help to the new Eastern Front. The Soviet Union was our ally.

At first my hope of a re-run of 1812 seemed illusory. The 'spectacle now unfolding' proved far bigger than any earlier enterprise. Napoleon crossed the Niemen with 430,000 men, drawn from eight nations under his personal command and struck directly at Moscow. Hitler's 'Operation Barbarossa' committed 3.2 million German troops to a six-pronged advance along a thousand-mile Front. By October Leningrad was besieged while two crab-like pincers sought to close on Moscow but, as in 1812, 'General Winter' came to Russia's aid. Partisan groups penetrated behind enemy lines and by December snow and ice in the hills west of Moscow forced the Germans to break off their assault on the city.

Once it became clear Russia would continue the fight, the public mood in Britain veered round completely. There was particular sympathy for the starving people of Leningrad. In the Christmas holidays I saw a red hammer and sickle flag hanging down from the pediment of an art gallery in the West End and I enjoyed excerpts from Russian ballets danced at the People's Palace. For the first time I noticed on a wall the graffito 'Second Front Now'. The *Soviet Weekly*, a publication never seen before, went on sale at many bookstalls. I even spent good pocket money on a copy that included a free print of Stalin. With great forbearance, Mother let me mount it in the left alcove of our sitting room. Churchill beamed down from a framed photo in the right alcove.

Admiration for Russia was widespread and continued until the final weeks of the war. People gave generously to a charity under the active patronage of Mrs Churchill which sent gifts to relieve the suffering of victims in this grim conflict. Some local councils welcomed our new ally with gestures of solidarity. In London the Labour council of Finsbury commissioned the distinguished Georgian-born architect Berthold Lubetkin to create a bust of Lenin for insertion in the wall of the house in Holford Square where he and his wife had lived when he was studying in the British Museum. The memorial bust was to be unveiled by the Soviet ambassador, Ivan Maisky, on 23 April 1942. It was a fitting Anglo-Soviet date, St George's Day and the 72nd anniversary of Lenin's birth. So determined was I to be there that I rang the Soviet Embassy on Grandfather's phone to check the time of the ceremony.

The square was packed and the light fading when I reached Finsbury but red flags and bunting brightened the dreary grey of the house fronts. Maisky, a popular and respected figure, was cheered as he joined the mayoral party on an improvised stage. His short oration, in faultless English, extolled Lenin as 'the perfect embodiment of all that is of most value in my country'. He then stepped down and formally unveiled the bust. The stirring notes of the 'Internationale' boomed out, made slightly discordant by loudspeakers. It was a Red evening of celebration. *The Times,* which had printed a photograph of Lubetkin's beautiful memorial ahead of the ceremony, ignored the event itself. Ironically there was no *Daily Worker* to report it; the ban on the paper was not lifted for another six weeks.

By now America was in the war. We had first heard of the Japanese attack on Pearl Harbor in a newsflash during the nine o'clock bulletin on 7 December. Congress declared war on Japan the next day: Germany and Italy went to war as Japan's allies against the USA on 11 December. We were relieved to gain such a powerful partner but our initial elation soon turned to dismay: Japanese aircraft sank the battleship HMS *Prince of Wales* and the battle-cruiser HMS *Repulse* as early as 10 December, leaving Britain with no capital ships in the Indian Ocean. Grimmer news followed over the next 11 weeks. Hong Kong fell to Japanese invaders on Christmas Day. On 15 February 1942 more than 70,000 British and Commonwealth troops and airmen were forced to surrender in Singapore: 'The worst disaster and largest capitulation in British history', Churchill later wrote in *The Second World War*, though of course he made no such admission during the war. Publicly he remained resolute in his determination to defeat Japan.

On 13 February came the 'Channel Dash', a humiliation close to home which deepened our dismay. The German battleships *Scharnhorst* and *Gneisenau* and the heavy cruiser *Prinz Eugen* sailed from Brest up the Channel and along the North Sea's continental shore with apparent impunity, destroying ten aircraft which sought to torpedo them. Both battleships had been severely damaged by British mines but we could not know of this success at the time.

Yet in 1942 the fortunes of war changed more swiftly than in any other year. A fortnight after the Channel Dash our spirits were lifted by the first British paratrooper assault. The objective was a radar station on the cliffs at Bruneval, north-east of Le Havre. The base was destroyed and innovative radar equipment brought back to Britain. Then on 28 March came an audacious raid on St Nazaire, the most ambitious amphibious operation yet undertaken by the navy and commandos. It involved a three-day voyage from Falmouth and up the Loire to destroy the only dry dock capable of servicing and repairing the battleship *Tirpitz* if she needed shelter after emerging from a Norwegian fjord to attack convoys in the Atlantic or bringing military aid to Russia through Arctic waters. The raid achieved its purpose through a glorious display of courage and endurance. The cost, however, was heavy. Almost 700 British seamen and soldiers took part in the raid; 169 were killed and 215 taken prisoner. Five Victoria Crosses were awarded for valour during the raid. Among commando VC recipients was Lt-Colonel A.C. Newman, an Old Bancroftian well known to us as judge of the school's pre-war boxing competitions.

But in late summer an even larger operation brought disaster. On 19 August an attempt was made by British commandos and a predominantly Canadian landing force to seize and temporarily hold the port of Dieppe. It was four years, almost to the day, since we had stayed there, and as I heard of the raid, a clear image of the seafront came to mind: the castle in the west; the long green *plage*; the narrow entrance to the harbour; the belt of loose shingle at the water's edge; and cliffs to the east, looking down on the cramped streets of the town. What could justify a raid on such a natural bastion, I wondered?

We heard later that of 4,963 Canadians taking part in the raid, 907 were killed in action. The only success was achieved six miles west of the castle, where Lord Lovat's no. 4 British Commandos made two landings beneath Varangeville and scaled the cliffs to destroy the coastal battery there. In the central area tanks assigned to support the infantry suffered heavy losses. Twenty-nine of the latest Churchill tanks made the crossing in special landing craft; two sank in deep water; 12 were stranded because their traction failed to grip the loose, slippery shingle. The remaining 15 were destroyed by anti-tank devices in the low wall at the head of the beach or across the former green *plage*. Aboard the landing craft and escorts 345 seamen were killed and a destroyer was sunk.

The RAF lost 96 aircraft and 70 airmen. In all, 3,623 men were killed, gravely wounded or taken prisoner in a battle waged for less than six hours. Defenders of the raid argue that it proved the value of commando training, while revealing tactical weaknesses righted by D-Day. But did it require the sacrifice of so many lives and the waste of fine equipment in such an ill-conceived venture?

Despite my concern, by now I had become more escapist than earlier in the war. This was the summer I first read *Pride and Prejudice* and belatedly discovered Poirot, Peter Wimsey, and the happy lunacy of Caryl Brahms and S.J. Simon's novels. On the wireless we had more choice. *The Brains Trust* came on the Forces Programme as early as January in 1941 and ran non-stop for 19 months. It allowed Cyril Joad, Julian Huxley, Commander Campbell and a host of lucid guests to insert a slot of didactic reasoning into Sunday afternoon listening. Joad's 'It all depends what you mean by…?' became as familiar a catchphrase as Mrs Mopp's 'Can I do you now, Sir?'

Four days before Christmas 1941 we heard the first instalment of the most controversial series of the war – in Sunday's *Children's Hour*, of all unlikely places! Dorothy L. Sayers' *The Man Born To Be King* cycle of 12 plays presenting in modern speech the gospel record of Christ's incarnation and resurrection. The puritan taboos that so often blight our worship attacked the programme: she assigned human emotions of joy and grief to familiar biblical characters; they spoke everyday words, considered irreverent. One extremist group even insisted that the fall of Singapore had come as a sign of God's wrath with a nation of blasphemers. I recall two special pleasures: the firm, incisive tone of Robert Speaight's Jesus; and Sayers' skill in bringing drama to parables that often seem remote from modern life.

I was broadening my mind in another way too. When the Air Training Corps was created in February 1941 Bancroft's was one of the first schools to take part in the venture and I became a cadet as soon as I reached the entry age, in March 1942. This enabled me, a few weeks later, to go to the annual camp, which that spring was at RAF Waterbeach, six miles north of Cambridge. It was a non-operational station for Stirlings, the biggest four-engined bomber in service. Aircrew who had flown Blenheims or Wellingtons were re-trained at Waterbeach to familiarise themselves with the huge monsters.

We arrived there on Saturday 6 April and after lunch the following day I took a bus into Cambridge. The sleeping beauty of The Backs enchanted me. I followed the river to Grantchester, the village with the old vicarage that Rupert Brooke's poem had made famous. By now the church clock stood long past three; too late to see if there was honey still for tea. A picnic party sat beside a punt, enjoying the early April sunshine. I envied them: the ATC tunic and trousers stifled me on the walk back. 'With luck, I will see Cambridge from the air later in the week', I wrote on a card home; the prospect worried Mother.

Cadets from another school went airborne on Monday. Our turn came on Tuesday afternoon. We waited on the tarmac for a Stirling to taxi from the dispersal point.

Then, as it began to move forward, we saw to our horror a second plane heading at speed along the runway and about to cross its path. There was a hollow crash. Senselessly we broke ranks and started to run towards the stricken planes. A sharp order halted us. By now black smoke billowed across the village. One plane revolved on its axis, with revved up engines screaming on a high-pitched note. The other Stirling looked like a blackbird hit in low flight by a passing car and left fluttering a crumpled wing. The crew of a fire tender prevented flames engulfing both aircraft but some airmen must already have perished.

We continued the training routine for the rest of the week. Although there were no more flights for cadets, we did at least have a guided tour of a Stirling, brought into the hangar for servicing. Soon after the Bancroft's term began, I entered a nationwide ATC competition open to all squadrons for essays on their year's camp. I included an account of the fatal accident and was surprised to receive a runners-up book token prize.

The air war intensified in this spring of 1942. British attacks on historic German towns, including Lübeck, Rostock and Cologne, induced the Luftwaffe to retaliate with raids on five English cities. All were marked with three stars in Baedeker's travel guide, showing they were picturesque places rich in history: collectively these retaliatory attacks are remembered as the 'Baedeker Raids'. Oxford and Cambridge were spared but great damage was inflicted in several raids on Exeter, Bath, Canterbury and Norwich, while in a single raid on York the mediaeval Guildhall was destroyed. More than 6,000 people died in the 11 attacks which began on St George's Day a few hours after I had been at London's 'Red evening' in Holford Square. We were particularly sad to hear from friends in Devon that much of central Exeter had been flattened. Fortunately, all the cathedrals or abbey churches in the five cities remained standing when the war came to an end.

Five months later news from North Africa lifted winter's gloom. On 23 October the second battle of Alamein began, with a thunderous artillery barrage that enabled Montgomery's 8th Army to press forward in pursuit of Rommel's German and Italian army as it fell back westwards across Libya. Then on 8 November Anglo-American landings in Morocco and Algeria (Operation Torch) seemed to herald a triumph. Cautiously Churchill conceded that these events marked 'perhaps the end of the beginning of the war'; he authorised the ringing of church bells on 15 November to celebrate this first major Allied land victory.

Our personal joy over this change of fortune was, however, suddenly dampened, for my father, by now 56, suffered a heart attack while hurrying to catch a bus in Leadenhall Street and was rushed across the river to Guy's Hospital. Mother was very worried at first but within a few days he was taking an interest in all that happened in his ward. I went up to Guy's the second Sunday he was there and found him in good spirits. There had been an air raid alert a few nights previously and patients had been moved down to shelters. 'That's the porter who pushed my bed,' Dad remarked, as a tall, well-dressed man went by. 'They say he's an Austrian professor; seems a nice chap.' I gave the disappearing figure a cursory glance. Even had I been told he was Ludwig Wittgenstein, the name of the century's greatest innovative philosopher would have meant nothing to me. Wittgenstein served as a porter at Guy's for two years. His biographers emphasise he loathed the Nazis but as an officer of the old Imperial army he could not bring himself to bear arms against his compatriots.

Dad came home from Guy's in mid-December, with orders to rest and cut down his activities. Although he lived another 28 years, he never regained his old vigour. Reluctantly he left the Home Guard, while I did the heavy work in the garden.

Everyone had expected the North African campaign to have finished by Christmas but Rommel's crack troops maintained stiff resistance in Tunisia well into the New Year. Yet, though no British or American armies had crossed to Continental Europe, news of Russian successes came over the wireless day after day and in London we were optimistic. Christmas in 1942 was far happier than its predecessors. Surely, we thought, by now the worst was over?

EIGHTEEN
Long Days of Summer

A glorious sound rang out across the country on the last Sunday of May in 1943. We had heard bells celebrating Alamein in November but now their peal could welcome us to church again, Sunday after Sunday. The tide of war was flowing towards victory. Gone was all risk of invasion. The last Germans in North Africa had surrendered a fortnight earlier; the Russians were regrouping after throwing back Hitler's armies from Stalingrad; and the Royal Navy had mastered the U-boat threat in the Atlantic.

Soon afterwards Mother, Dad and I spent a few days at Worthing for the first time in three years and one evening I set off for a ramble over the South Downs, taking buses to Chanctonbury Ring. From there I could trace the rise and fall of the cliffs along a great stretch of coast. It was hard to believe that beyond the horizon, 65 miles away, were similar cliffs bristling with enemy guns. Next day I wrote a few hundred words on the sheer exhilaration of of Sussex by the sea on an evening late in spring; I posted my paean of delight to the county's magazine. It appeared in the next issue.

We did not go away in August that year and much of my summer holiday was spent wandering around London. I would jot down on a note-pad names shown on plaques where famous people had lived and try to discover more about any who intrigued me when next I went to the library. But there were plenty of other pursuits to follow too. Double British Summer Time brought long evenings. It was fun to play tennis at 10 p.m. in July, knowing the blackout would not begin for another hour. Local authorities promoted 'Holidays at Home', giving us new pleasures, like good Shakespeare in Regent's Park, for example, or go to Victoria Park and watch a 24-year-old Margot Fonteyn dance with Robert Helpmann as her partner. Tickets cost no more than sixpence.

My circle of friends widened during this summer. In an attempt to bridge class barriers and foster a sense of community Ernest Bevin, the Minister of Labour and National Service, required 14-18-year-olds to register with a youth club. I joined the one attached to Eastern Avenue Methodist Church which met for social evenings on Saturdays and as a discussion group on Tuesdays. The 22 members all came from similar white collar social backgrounds, hardly Bevin's intention. Yet the club did at least curb gender divisions. Five girls and one boy came from co-educational Wanstead County High, but the rest from single-sex schools, including Bancroft's.

Apart from occasional days with cousins, I had not mixed with girls since I was six. Now, on my first Tuesday visit, I spotted a girl in a light blue frock with polka dots. She was petite and pretty, with an engaging quizzical smile. I could see from her reactions that she was intelligent too. *Phew! Can this be love?* I wondered, as we walked the quarter of a mile back to her home.

I suspect Rita thought me a big joke at first; too possessive, she once complained. As a Wanstead High pupil she was at ease with boys, and she had a brother serving with the Royal Signals. Yet our friendship blossomed, though she was more than two years younger than I; it was a very innocent romance. My ego was boosted when her mother, Mrs Grabham, said 'I know she'll be in safe hands' when she joined me for a trip up to London. In the autumn we went to local cinemas and a matinee at Shaftesbury Avenue. No air raid alert curbed our activities.

The war caught up with us on a wet Tuesday in November. We were walking back to Rita's home. No siren had sounded but I suddenly heard the guttural note of a German plane and, seconds later, the swish of falling bombs. At once I pushed Rita down and straddled her protectively. The bombs exploded well away from us on open ground... I helped Rita up. Her hand was covered in mud. So too were her first pair of fashionable nylon stockings, a recent present from her brother. She was furious, too angry for tears. *That's that*, I thought gloomily as I trudged home. Happily I was wrong: by the weekend Rita had forgiven me. Did she have a second pair of nylons? It seemed wise not to enquire.

Twelve days later came my closest sighting of a German plane. I was on the way to the park, giving Bruce his Sunday ramble. The sky was overcast and all was quiet until I heard a familiar gargling sound coming nearer. I looked up and saw a Messerschmitt 109 emerge from a gap in the clouds, flying slowly and so low that I caught a glimpse of the pilot, silhouetted in his cockpit. No bombs fell and in less than a minute the plane was wrapped in cloud. A single siren belatedly wailed, followed almost immediately by an All Clear. Bruce got his afternoon run without further interruption.

It was an odd episode. I wondered if, though the plane bore German markings, it was a crashed Messerschmitt restored by British mechanics and flown by an RAF pilot. This would explain why I had only heard a single siren and why the 'alert' had been so brief. On the other hand, the plane could have been on photographic reconnaissance. The bombs dropped 12 days earlier suggested the Germans were interested in our part of Ilford; and with good reason. We discovered after the war that subterranean rumbling we heard from time to time came from work on aircraft parts and electronic equipment by the Plessey Company, who used the twin tunnels of the unopened Central Line extension from Newbury Park to Leytonstone. We never realised that for at least a couple of years we slept each night above a factory.

The year ended with freezing fog and slippery pavements; there were no alerts over Christmas and, when the first bombs of 1944 came on 21 January, they took us by surprise. Fifteen raids followed in the next three months; none lasted into the small hours. No high explosive bombs fell near us. Even on a night when a shower of incendiaries straddled north Ilford, no serious fires were started. The worst bombing came south of the Thames and around St James's Square, where high explosives flattened Georgian mansions that had escaped destruction earlier in the war. Yet though the raids were short, I felt wearier next morning than during the Blitz.

I had entered the sixth form in September 1943, with every intention of leaving Bancroft's at the end of the school year. My ambition was to go up to Oxford, ideally with a scholarship in English or History, but I knew this would be difficult in three terms and so I prepared an alternative plan. After two years in the ATC I could seek a place on a naval short course, by which potential officers had six months in a University Naval Division; for half their time in academic study, the rest in nautical training. After satisfying a board of officers, who grilled me on naval affairs past and present, I was accepted for the October intake at Oxford. So far so good.

It was however a difficult time for Bancroft's. Mr Wells' tragic death left the school without a headmaster for two terms. My housemaster, Mr Peet, bridged the gap ably, while still teaching Chemistry. I was encouraged by Messrs Wheeler, Jenkins and Francombe. Unfortunately as head of History we had an inexperienced newcomer. His range of knowledge was limited and he could not keep order. We would arrive for a lesson and find the poor man shaking and with his thoughts confused, after failing to tame a junior class. There was however one advantage for me: I was not shackled by a prescribed syllabus and I made good use of the fine libraries at Bancroft's and Ilford. I could range widely, choosing topics that interested me and steadily ploughing my own furrow. But was I following the right track? The Christmas break from routine left me worried.

Help came from an unexpected source. My father's cousin Percy Warren was tenant farmer for the Vyvyan family at Merthen, in Cornwall. Early in the new year two of his daughters – twins teaching in London – came to tea. Never before had I met any of the Warrens and I was deeply interested in everything the twins told us about Merthen, past and present. I was eager to go there as soon as possible. At Ilford's main library I came across A.L. Rowse's *Tudor Cornwall*. There, on p. 155, was a reference to 'William Reskymer's [home]… at Merthen, the delightful Tudor house above the Helford River that still stands'. Soon afterwards my aunts bought a copy of Rowse's *A Cornish Childhood* and lent it to me. Here I read about Cornwall in the early years of the twentieth century and of how a grocer's son from St Austell won an Oxford scholarship. On one occasion he went over to Fowey to seek guidance from 'Q', the poet, scholar and novelist Sir Arthur Quiller-Couch. Why not follow the young Rowse's example, I thought? I wrote to him at Oxford, mentioning Merthen and telling him about my way of preparing for the university.

To my surprise, he replied within a few days. It was an encouraging letter. He listed a dozen books that I might find useful. Ten I knew already; the other two I did not tackle until five years later. He urged me to keep a diary, analysing my thoughts and feelings rather than merely chronicling events. As an apparent afterthought, he invited me to visit him if I came up to Oxford. The letter did not so much help me directly but it boosted my confidence and self-esteem, not least because it began 'Dear Mr Palmer'. No one had accorded me that status before.

By Easter we knew the war must soon reach a climax. Time and time again we had switched on the *News* and been taken by surprise. Nothing, however, was so puzzling as the breakfast bulletin on Tuesday, 6 June. 'A new phase of the Allied air offensive has begun', we were told. People living within 25 miles of the enemy-held coast were advised to go inland, carrying as little as possible with them and avoiding railways or main roads. The announcer added that a German broadcast reported airborne landings near the mouth of the Seine, with the German navy in action against landing craft in the same area; Le Havre, Calais and Dunkirk were being heavily bombed. 'Well,' I said to myself, 'whatever is happening, this isn't another Dieppe.' And off I went on the 8.20 bus, thinking not of France but of the afternoon's cricket. I would captain my house for the first time.

Shame on me! I was out first ball and deserved it. We played on a hurriedly mown and rolled pitch. A mid-school youngster sent down a leg-break which shot in sharply off a squashed dandelion patch and skittled my stumps. We lost the match and I went home cursing all dandelions. Only when I reached Clarence Avenue did I wonder what was happening across the Channel.

Mother had listened to the wireless for much of the day and quickly brought me up to date. At midday

John Snagge announced officially 'D-Day has come'. At nine o'clock I heard the King's broadcast to the nation. He spoke firmly and with a clarity that showed his inner confidence. The bulletin following the royal broadcast left us in no doubt of the day's historic significance. It reported Churchill's two statements to Parliament in which he spoke with the military knowledge and verbal imagery only he could master. We heard of the 24-hour postponement caused by bad weather; of airborne troops coming by gliders and parachutes on a scale never thought possible in previous operations; of how more than 4,000 warships from the navies of seven Western Allies concentrated 460 guns on shelling enemy-shore batteries before providing protective cover for some 2,000 landing craft. The flow of record statistics continued throughout the bulletin: 11,000 planes in the sky above Normandy; at night the lights of 'an aerial armada' 200 miles in depth flying low over the waves from the English shore to the French beaches and on inland to support advancing troops by bombing the German supply chain. Fighting continued in Caen, we were told; losses had 'been smaller, far smaller than we had apprehended'; but he warned us heavy fighting must be expected in the weeks ahead; so far, however, all was satisfactory. That was enough for me. I went to bed thrilled to be living with history. By my reckoning Allied troops must be less than 150 miles from Paris.

A week after D-Day the Germans launched their first 'revenge' onslaught against London. On Tuesday 13 June Dad and hundreds like him found their train to town diverted to Fenchurch Street. A German plane had come down in Bow, with an apparently full bomb load which exploded when it hit Grove Road station, cutting the Liverpool Street line. I was puzzled, for though I was woken by the sirens about 4.30 I heard no sound of bombs or gunfire. Rumours soon spread: it was a pilotless plane, people said. Two nights later 73 explosive aircraft fell on Greater London, with Croydon, Lambeth and the northern heights the worst hit areas. We were under bombardment by the *Vergeltungswaffe-1* weapon. We knew it as a V-1, a flying bomb, a buzz bomb or, more commonly, a doodlebug.

The flying bombs were launched from sites in France, Belgium and Holland that were eventually captured by the advancing armies but not before they had taken a heavy toll of lives. More than 2,000 V-1s reached Greater London, killing 2,420 people. In Kent, Sussex and Hampshire another 1,650 died. The worst tragedy came on the first Sunday, 18 June, when the Guards Chapel in Birdcage Walk received a direct hit during matins, killing 119 worshippers outright and gravely injuring 102 others, several of them fatally. At lunchtime on 30 June more than a hundred people died after a flying bomb fell at the junction of Kingsway and Aldwych.

These V-1s headed in at almost 400mph, flying as low as 2,000 feet and came down when their primitive jet engine cut out for lack of fuel. People in the vicinity had only a few seconds to dive for cover before it exploded. Resort was made to watchers who could spot an incoming V-1 through field glasses and sound a whistle or hooter to give as long as a minute's warning. At Bancroft's our new headmaster, Sydney Adams, devised his own system, with a rota for school monitors operating from the turret of the school tower. If a V-1 was sighted, the monitor would ring the school bell urgently and classwork would stop while boys and masters crouched under desks or tables. When it had exploded or was seen heading elsewhere the watchman would ring the bell again as an All Clear.

My first spell up the tower came in the second week. For half an hour nothing happened. Then I focussed the field glasses on a distant speck, rang the bell and followed a doodlebug as it sped along the Roding Valley. It plunged down on the western fringe of Ilford, throwing up smoke or loose earth from Roding Lane South, where my classmate Denis Quilley's family lived. I adjusted the glasses and realised it had fallen on an open slope well away from Denis's home. Relieved, I lowered the glasses. From down below, a hand-cupped Oxonian-elocuted voice reached me. 'Palmer! Palmer! Hasn't the thing gone off yet? For heaven's sake ring the bell.' For some reason the name Palmer did not appear on subsequent rota.

Once the 'matriculation' and 'higher' examinations ended there was no good reason for seeing out the full term; we broke up a fortnight early. During my last journey to school I ducked between the upstairs seats as a V-1 passed over the bus a short way from the school. I did not finally shake Bancroft's dust off my shoes for a few more days, however. Mr Adams allowed me to use the library while I was reading for Oxford, where I would sit for a History scholarship at Oriel College in September.

Meanwhile, why linger in London? We had already been invited to Merthen for a holiday in late August. It was now agreed I should go down earlier. Off I went to Paddington on 1 August, with a case full of books and notes. Uncle Percy met me with a car at the last station before Falmouth. We drove towards Constantine, where the tall granite church tower dominates village, copses and fields alike. Eventually we turned into a drive and I assumed Merthen was around the corner. How little did I know Cornish lanes! There was another mile to cover before the lane suddenly opened out to form a stone courtyard.

As I stepped down from the car, a little shaken, birds in the trees trilled a welcoming rhapsody. Facing me stood a long two-storey manor house, set well clear of encroaching woods. I was given a room over the entrance porch. A stone beneath the window bore the Reskymer arms and the date 1573, years before watchers on the Lizard, a dozen miles away, first sighted the billowing sails of the Spanish Armada. I could think of no better room in which to let my thoughts fall back to a Tudor past. No ghost disturbed my sleep. I rather wish one had.

My intention was to settle down with books and notes each morning and go walkabout in the afternoon but the lure of Merthen Woods enticed me away immediately after breakfast. I found a steep path running down to the river. Epping Forest and Knighton Wood made me familiar with fine trees but never had I seen beeches or oaks to match this hundred-acre mantle of green spread along the north shore of Helford River. Several brooks cut through the woodland and the path became slippery. I nearly lost my balance but a last scramble took me down to a quay, the Merthen Groyne. There I found a boathouse, well padlocked. Circling seagulls screeched. Otherwise all was tranquil. I felt at peace, and for several minutes sat on a tree stump, content to listen to the lazy lap of a river rippled by a westerly wind.

Next afternoon I went back to the Groyne with two guests staying at the manor, who had a key to the boathouse. Over the following days they taught me river lore. Off we would go downstream, Polwheveral Creek to port and the thatched roofs of Helford village to starboard in the distance; Helford Passage lay dead ahead. For three blissful weeks I was down on the river every fine afternoon, sharing oars with Dad once my parents joined me at Merthen. Surprisingly there were no disasters, not even on a day when the strong current at Gweek threatened to sweep the boat out as Dad was stepping ashore. He clung desperately to one mooring ring as I slipped a rope through another and pulled hard. All this went well beyond the 'light relaxation' prescribed by Guy's Hospital back in December but it did not seem to harm him.

Aunt Alma, Uncle Percy's wife, allowed me to use her parlour for reading and working. A wireless stood in one corner and I listened to it regularly. First reports from across the Channel were disturbing: the Germans held on tenaciously to Falaise. But the middle of the month brought heartening news. The Canadian divisions in Montgomery's 21st Army Group cleared the Falaise Gap at last on 15 August, although two days' street-fighting followed before the town was finally taken. That evening we heard that an American and Free French invasion force had landed on the Riviera between Toulon and Nice and was thrusting northwards with astonishing speed. France was again uppermost in my thoughts. I switched my reading to accounts of the hunger days that followed Napoleon's landing on that coast in 1815 after his escape from Elba and ended with the final Allied victory at Waterloo.

News of an uprising in the heart of Paris reached us on 19 August. Initial reports were sketchy; it was hard to know what was happening but when I came back from the river on 24 August I heard that Free French troops were in the southern suburbs. By next evening General de Gaulle, who crossed to Normandy in a French cruiser on 14 June, was in the city centre. Sniper fire continued as he addressed a welcoming crowd outside Resistance headquarters. Those of us who loved France rejoiced that the tricolour flag flew again over the city. While we were still at Merthen news came of another capital freed from the enemy: on 2 September the Germans pulled out of Brussels.

We left Merthen and returned to London on 5 September. There had been a sustained flying bomb assault two nights after I went down to Cornwall but by the end of August far fewer doodlebugs were reaching the Kent coast, let alone inner London. Colonel Duncan Sandys, Churchill's son-in-law and chairman of a Cabinet committee for defence against revenge bombardment, assured the press on 7 September that the V-1 menace was gone. German propaganda broadcasts had threatened that more devastating weapons would bring terror to English cities; sheer scaremongering, Sandys declared dismissively.

Early next day a gasometer blew up in Chiswick, or so we were encouraged to believe. Later in the morning Mother and I heard a distant boom while shopping in Ilford High Road; a gas explosion at Epping apparently. By the end of the week it was clear that London was under bombardment by heavy supersonic rockets, V-2s.

At the same time the Germans perfected ways of carrying flying bombs 'piggy-back' on conventional aircraft capable of launching them from high altitudes and thereby extending their range of attack. One flying bomb even reached Oldham but at least they now came so infrequently that sirens could warn of their approach.

V-2 rockets had three times the destructive potential of flying bombs. Occasionally, if they fell on a relatively 'soft' target, their propulsion speed delayed the explosion by a split second, creating a deep, broad crater and limiting the surface damage, as at Chiswick and Epping on the first day of the bombardment. Paradoxically a V-1 was more terrifying than a V-2: the engine of a buzz-bomb would cut out, leaving you wondering for a few seconds if it would hit you. But the supersonic speed of a V-2 gave no warning of approach: if you heard the thunderous roar of a rocket, the ghastly weapon had already wrought its havoc, and you were safe.

Yet as summer's sunshine made way for a wet and windy autumn, I was in high spirits; my dreams were of Merthen and I was looking forward to seeing Oxford for the first time. There was a spate of bad news in the third week of September when Montgomery's advancing army could not reach Arnhem in time to save airborne troops, who had seized a vital bridge over the Rhine, from encirclement and captivity. But despite this setback, V-1s and V-2s, people were optimistic. The Western Allies were stronger and better poised for victory than six months back. Everyone felt sure this fifth winter of war must be the last.

NINETEEN

Gown and Bellbottoms

I was back at Paddington's Platform 1 on the last Monday in September, ready to catch the train for Oxford and take the Oriel scholarship example. No doubt as an examinee I should have been nervous but at heart I was as happy as a holiday maker. Failure would not be disastrous, for I was sure of at least six months at the university, thanks to the naval cadet scheme. It was good to get away from embattled London and head for the 'beautiful city' that Matthew Arnold had found 'so venerable, lovely and unravaged' 60 years ago.

The train stopped some way short of Oxford station and I looked out eagerly through the carriage window; where were the enchanting spires and towers? To my left stretched several acres of cemetery, the gravestones streaked with the green moss of time. To my right, less than half a mile away, loomed the full majesty of two gasometers. This was hardly the vista of Arnold's purple phrases.

I was surprised but not disillusioned. Oxford in the autumn of 1944 was delightful, totally unscarred by the war, a haven of peace in a storm-tossed world. No bombs had fallen on the city, no V-2 rockets reached the county and no doodlebugs came within earshot, the nearest cutting out over open country south-west of the Chiltern Hills. The outer walls of colleges, libraries and churches looked as they must have done through the 20s and 30s. The grass in the quadrangles was rolled and trimmed, even around fire points and the edge of emergency sunken water tanks. Clocks chimed hours and quarters with their customary disregard for each other's timekeeping or for Greenwich's scientific accuracy. The absence of motor traffic imposed by petrol rationing revealed the crescent beauty of 'The High' in all its classical elegance. As I walked into Oriel's Front Quad and saw the lettering '*Regnante Carolo*' inscribed on the parapet above the hall porch I felt a thrill of continuity with the past, dating back to the early reign of Charles I, before civil war split the nation. I was enchanted. Matthew Arnold – once an Oriel don – was right after all.

Next morning we candidates sat at the long tables of the hall and the examination began. In format it too was almost unchanged from pre-war years. A three-hour essay came first, with a choice between a sententious aphorism and a single word topic. I opted for 'Exile' and began jotting down names that came into my head from the plaques I had seen in London streets or people encountered in French and Latin lessons as well as in general reading. Ovid was there for his days beside the Black Sea; so was Lenin from one London square and Chile's liberator San Martin from another. I included Huguenots bringing

237

their skills to England when Louis XIV revoked the Edict of Nantes, and refugees fleeing from the Jacobins. I sorted this ragbag into a little order, added some topical references and wrote the essay hurriedly, aware that Merton College clock was ringing the quarters far too often. But it was finished in time, with a few minutes to spare. Soon I was enjoying the light lunch brought to us on those same tables in the hall by elderly 'scouts' (college servants).

In the afternoon we had a conventional English History paper, rather an anticlimax after the pre-lunch fun. Next morning came the general paper, which was taken by potential classicists as well as historians. It posed discussable questions over a wide range of subjects. I remember tackling Pope's 'For forms of government let fools contest, What e'er is best administered is best' and, more happily, the nature of patriotic poetry. We also took a paper on European History. Finally we had to offer prose 'unseens' from foreign languages: I could only manage Latin and French.

Between papers came interviews: a few polite exchanges with the Vice-Provost and a more serious discussion with J.W. Gough and W.A. Pantin, both of whom had been History tutors before the war and continued to teach and lecture for many years after it. They were particularly interested in my Exile essay, asking me about my sources of information, and they seemed intrigued by distinctions I made in the general paper between boastful patriotic verse and a true love of country as shown, for example, in Browning's *Home Thoughts from*

Abroad and Joachim du Bellay's sonnet *Heureux qui, comme Ulysse...* with its longing for his native Anjou. I returned to Clarence Avenue on Friday smugly pleased – until the distant thunderclap of a V-2 rocket came as a sober reminder of a war still to be won.

A letter arrived from Oriel as early as next morning, to our surprise: I had been elected to the Open History Scholarship. Hectic days followed, for at the end of the week I was to return to Oxford and go into residence, but I was back on Platform 1 on Friday afternoon for the familiar journey. The train again stopped short of Oxford station, indulging that mischievous whim to dampen high expectation with intimation of mortality. But the head porter at Oriel welcomed me warmly and I was assigned two pleasant rooms on the first floor of a mid-Victorian building at the corner of Merton Street and Magpie Lane. Here the scout who had fathered me during the examination offered congratulations and told me that by chance he had a second-hand scholar's gown that I could purchase without surrendering precious clothing coupons; I snapped up the offer.

In the rooms above me was John Locke, from Watford Grammar School. We had chummed up during the examination, even going to the theatre in George Street to celebrate my eighteenth birthday. He too would train as a naval cadet and had won a scholarship endowed for those with a close West Country family background. I was not surprised to hear that the scout just happened to come across another scholar's gown to sell him.

We soon discovered that buildings around us were

not as untouched by war as I had thought. At the far end of Merton Street the Examination Schools had been converted into a hospital for wounded soldiers from the advancing armies. St Hugh's, one of Oxford's five women's colleges, also became a military hospital, specialising in head injuries. Oriel's St Mary's Quad housed hush-hush intelligence workers, forcing the college to seek outside accommodation; John and I were in rooms leased from Corpus Christi.

As Oriel was without a resident chaplain there were no chapel services on the first Sunday of this Michaelmas term and so we went to choral evensong at the cathedral. The choir sang beautifully but the canon who shuffled out to read the first lesson looked unpromising: a mumbler of gloom and admonition, I feared. How wrong I was! The moo of a cow desperate for milking echoed down the nave: '*Woe* to the *bloody* city; it is all full of lies and robbery'. Although the prophet Nahum was castigating Nineveh some 3,000 years ago, Canon Claude Jenkins thundered the words with the wrath of someone cheated out of money only yesterday. We were fortunate to have heard on this first weekend one of the university's legendary eccentrics. Sixty-five-year-old Canon Jenkins – Regius Professor of Ecclesiastical History since 1934 – littered the staircase to his rooms with cast aside tomes and is said to have preached a sermon with an alarm clock suspended from a cord around his neck, bouncing over his surplice like a pectoral cross.

Next evening all naval cadets were summoned to the School of Geography in Mansfield Road to be addressed by our commanding officer, Lt-Commander Dundas-Grant. The University Naval Division (UND), he explained, had headquarters in Christ Church boathouse, at the confluence of the Isis (Thames) and Cherwell; use was also made of the picturesque barges of two other colleges permanently moored near the boathouse. We would be issued with our uniforms there next morning: bellbottom trousers, traditional collars with lanyards, and cap-ribbons stamped U.N.D. rather than H.M.S. Each week we would spend two days in training as well as report for a weekly pre-breakfast session at the Alfred Street gymnasium. Later would come a route march, and tests to ensure we could swim 50 yards and run a mile in five minutes. For rugby, hockey or football we played in teams of our respective colleges.

Commander Dundas-Grant was an Etonian with wide-ranging interests. He had rooms in Magdalen where his friendship with C.S. Lewis flourished so well that with the return of peace he became one of the group of literary friends known as the Inklings. His contacts ensured a stream of writers and intellectuals helped broaden our minds in Tuesday evening talks at Mansfield Road.

Our academic lectures in term were intended for naval and air squadron cadets but as they appeared on the university list a few outsiders joined us. Among the lecturers in this first term was C.T. Atkinson, an elderly military historian at Exeter College who had written the history of the 7th Division, in which he had served in Flanders: he could speak with sympathy of the rank and file in the English Civil Wars. His misogyny was notorious and no women came to hear him. That was perhaps fortunate for them, as his lecturing style could be anti-social: on one particularly wet morning he had a cold and most of his words were delivered over his shoulder, while holding a succession of filthy handkerchiefs to dry in front of a gas fire. I thought Atkinson a crusty radical Tory but I was glad he would respond to questions well past his allotted hour. He had a sharp tongue, however, and mischievously one Friday I asked him what he thought of G.M. Trevelyan's recently published *English Social History*. His nose twitched with the disdain an Oxford Tory reserved for Cambridge Whigs. 'An inflated version of his great-uncle's second chapter,' he replied dismissively. It was flattering he assumed I would recognise the reference to Macaulay's *History of England*, published almost a hundred years back in time; Trevelyan's grandmother was Macaulay's sister.

A.J.P. Taylor's radicalism was far from Tory. I had heard him many times giving talks on our wireless. Now I could attend his lectures on German History at Magdalen College hall every Wednesday. They always started promptly at 10.05 and continued for exactly 50 minutes without any glancing at a note. He was more cautious than in later years, when he became a TV celebrity. The phrase 'by and large' would follow a sweeping generalisation; fourteen in a single lecture, a friend counted. He always looked carefully casual with bow tie and corduroy trousers.

Lectures opened with a 'Gentlemen' salutation until on the third Wednesday he acknowledged the persistence of a young lady from St Hugh's. To her evident delight he began his lecture with 'Madam and Gentlemen', a practice he followed until the end of the series. Madam never missed a word.

Dundas-Grant had urged cadets to take a full part in university life and so one evening in the second week of term I went to a much publicised meeting of the Conservative Club. The chair was taken by an undergraduate from Somerville College, 'M.H. Roberts' an order paper said. She was a chubby, pretty blonde. I thought her attractive until she opened the meeting by berating college representatives for failing to round up newcomers. The main business was to discuss the new Beveridge Plan, proposed in *Full Employment in a Free Society*, the famous second report of the outgoing Master of University College. It would, she insisted, destroy personal initiative and family responsibility. I was shocked. To me the plan provided a blueprint for a stable, protective, 'from cradle to grave' post-war society. I realise now that it was a privilege to have seen the Iron Lady in action a few days before her nineteenth birthday but her politics could never have been mine, either then or when, as Margaret Thatcher, she cast aside her party's consensus Conservatism to sharpen the Tory image with a new look and hard granite face. I decided next week to see what the Liberals had to offer.

A great deal, I soon discovered: politics was taken seriously but never earnestly. The club's liveliness owed much to the wit and intelligence of the chairman, Alan Gibson, who already possessed the gifts that made him a sharp-eyed cricket commentator and entertaining sports writer. He was also President-elect of the Oxford Union Society. When I noticed that a guest speaker was A.L. Rowse, the Cornish scholar who had answered my *cri de coeur* so sympathetically earlier in the year, I joined the Union, and went along to the debate, mainly to hear Rowse's contribution to it.

He was then approaching his forty-first birthday. A recurrent stomach ulcer and poor eyesight had exempted him from military service though he looked and sounded remarkably fit. It was the first time he had spoken at the Union and he coyly craved to be received 'as a promising maiden'. I introduced myself to him after the debate and he invited me to look in on him at All Souls after dinner one evening in the following week.

It was an enjoyable get-together. He talked about books and music and places around Oxford that 'you simply must see'. I told him I had cycled to Woodstock and Blenheim the previous Sunday. 'Did you notice the rooms in the arch of the bridge over the lake?' he asked. 'Do go out to Rycote, and of course you've seen Iffley church?' I said how much I enjoyed Arthur Bryant's evocation of Trafalgar England in *The Years of Endurance*. 'Yes,' Rowse reflected, 'yes. Dear Arthur wanted to dedicate the book to Churchill but he declined, remembering [Bryant's] sympathy for Germany during Munich, so Arthur dedicated it to me instead.' Rowse gave me a copy of his newly published *Poems Chiefly Cornish* and initialled it.

I was never conscious, then or later, of his homosexual inclinations. He suggested we should go to a concert the next Saturday at the Town Hall but I explained that my parents were visiting Oxford for the first time that weekend and I had bought tickets for the Playhouse. 'Ah,' he at once replied, 'would they like to meet *me* while they are here?' Perhaps his kindness was an instance of the solipsism to which his biographer Richard Ollard gives so much attention in *A Man of Contradictions* but I jumped at the offer: I was to bring them to his rooms mid-morning on the Sunday.

Mother and Dad were delighted by his attentiveness. He showed us around All Souls including the chapel and the Codrington Library, pointing out architectural features, notably the reredos, where the line of sculpted saints is 'interrupted' and stands out more sharply than at New College. He took us up to little known second-storey rooms overlooking the corner of Catte Street where T.E. Lawrence, a Research Fellow in 1919-20, wrote the first draft of *The Seven Pillars of Wisdom*. Dad was especially interested as he had met Lawrence briefly at Ismailia in 1916; Rowse mentioned the 'genuine respect' the Fellows felt for Lawrence as a scholar. Inevitably talk turned to Cornwall, not only Merthen but the far west around St Buryan, where some of my Warren ancestors are buried. Dad had stayed there with relatives many times as a boy and Rowse wrote about the monastic community at St Buryan in *Tudor Cornwall*.

When I saw my parents off at the station a few hours later I noticed for the first time how strained they looked.

We had barely mentioned the war in our talks, apart from hoping it would soon be over. 'We've still got the rockets you know,' Dad gently reminded me. Yet neither he nor Mother said anything about his narrow escape when a rocket came down less than a quarter of a mile from him on his way home. In the six months I was at Oxford 35 V-2s fell on Ilford, more than on any other borough. Neighbouring Barking, Dagenham, and East and West Ham suffered almost as badly.

The pleasure of being up at the university made it easy to forget the world outside. A candlelit carol service in Oriel, in which I sang in the choir, tightened the cocoon around me. But almost as soon as I arrived home on ten days' Christmas leave reality impinged. I was speaking on my grandfather's phone to Desmond Perry in Forest Gate when there was a sudden boom. 'Gosh, did you hear that?' he said, and at that moment I heard it again, as the muffled, rolling sound wave reached Gants Hill, four miles away. A V-2 had fallen in Green Street, half a mile from Desmond's home. The rocket demolished St Stephen's church, where my parents were married. Fortunately no one was in the church that evening. Had the rocket fallen a few nights later, on Christmas Eve, the death toll would have been horrendous.

This sixth wartime Christmas was far from merry. There was no respite from rocket attacks and the weather was as cold as in 1939. The wireless news from the battle fronts was depressing: a German counter-offensive in the Ardennes threatened a breakthrough into Belgium; the Russian advance was checked by savage fighting around

Budapest; and a civil war erupted in Athens, two months after the city's liberation. Although partial relaxation of the blackout gave Ilford's streets artificial 'moonlight' they were still darker than at Oxford. Rita and I joined caroller friends, but we raised little money that year. People seemed reluctant to open the front door and let in the cold.

On New Year's Day I returned to an Oxford deep in snow. I had persuaded Oriel to let me study Contemporary History and for this period I was assigned to an external tutor, no less a person than A.J.P. Taylor. He taught his pupils at his home, Holywell Ford, on the edge of Magdalen deer park. I was told the house could be reached from Longwall Street. No doubt in clear weather I could easily have found my way there but the morning was misty and snow blanketed all signposts. I was glad to see coming towards me a man heavily muffled. He assured me I was heading in the right direction and we exchanged light-hearted remarks about the 1812 conditions. His English was fluent, his voice cultured, though he spoke with a slight impediment. He may well have been Count Mihály Károlyi, who for a few months after the Great War was president of a potentially democratic and socially reformed Hungary. Taylor held him in high regard and was a good friend to him in exile during the later years of the war. There could hardly have been a more fitting start to a term studying Europe's recent past.

Tutorials at Holywell Ford were unusual affairs. They were conducted in a study above a former mill-stream of the River Cherwell. Taylor would sit back in an armchair, pensively scowling as he listened to essays read to him by me or by a pupil from Pembroke College with whom I shared the tutorials. Above Taylor's left shoulder was a stuffed white owl in a glass case, and on his lap a favourite white cat, occasionally purring as he tickled her. Once she jumped down; the door had been flung open and a befeathered Native American burst in, only to be shooed away by his father.

A.J.P. Taylor was the most stimulating tutor I have known. Generally he would sit listening to our essays and follow them with a lively discussion but he could be sharp on occasions. A paragraph I read beginning, 'There were many factors...' prompted an anguished howl of 'No! No! Factors are for mathematics...' In one discussion I risked correcting him: 'Surely Chicherin not Trotsky was foreign commissar in 1920,' I suggested. Graciously he nodded his head.

Term at Oriel ended with 'Collections'; undergraduates appeared before the Fellows in hall to hear reports from their tutors. Anxiously I waited for Mr Gough to read a note sent by messenger from Magdalen. It was succinct: 'Mr Palmer writes a pretty essay,' it said. There was laughter all round. As in so many of Taylor's book reviews his meaning was ambiguous. Were these six words praise or criticism? I am still not sure.

The persistent bad weather restricted our bellbottom activities. Instead of drilling along the tow-path we had to square-bash resoundingly inside Christ Church boathouse itself, while classes in navigation continued on the first floor. Practice in Morse-code tapping and in sorting out the bends and hitches of ropes was given in one of the college barges by an extremely patient Yeoman of Signals who had fought at Jutland and was a boy seaman in days of sail. At times we envied air squadron cadets, who on clear days were learning to fly at Kidlington. We did at least have an opportunity to steer a small launch as far as Folly Bridge and back, taking care not to scrape the side of a college barge on our return.

Winter relaxed its grip early in March, in time for the route march through Wytham Woods and back to the Trout Inn at Godstow. I cycled out to Rycote, and on one Saturday John Locke and I pedalled over to Henley to see Oxford come second in the last wartime boat race. Then suddenly the two terms at Oxford came to an end. We were sent home on ten days' leave with a travel warrant for Waterloo to Portsmouth dated 4 April. It was time to hang up my gown in the bedroom wardrobe. As the train down from Liverpool Street passed Bethnal Green, arc lights shone on a rescue team searching for survivors in a block of flats struck by the last V-2 to fall on London. I was at home in Clarence Avenue when, on 29 March, a plane-launched doodlebug sent London's sirens ululating for the 1,224th, and final, time in the war.

TWENTY

Dancing on the Hoe

Back home in Clarence Avenue I reverted to old habits and got cross with myself if I missed the wireless *News*. By now it always sounded good. British and Canadian troops were advancing across the Rhine near Essen and the Americans had secured three bridgeheads 70 miles to the south. The Russians were well into Austria and had penetrated East Prussia in the north. I was not surprised to receive a letter saying my leave was extended by a fortnight. Presumably Portsmouth had more urgent concerns to handle. A sign of imminent victory, we hoped.

My father's sister, Hilda Heathcote, lived at Hothfield, near Ashford in Kent, where her husband was a tenant farmer. Although we kept in close touch in the 1930s when they farmed in Suffolk, I had not seen them for six years and I was pleased when, hearing of my extension of leave, she invited me down for a few days. Peter, her eldest son, was serving with the tanks and was in Germany by then. Three other cousins and Aunt Hilda herself worked on the land or in the milkshed.

Their war had been more exciting than mine. They

had seen crucial dogfights in the sky over their fields in 1940 and they were on the flight path of German planes emptying bomb bays as they headed back to Northern France from raids on London or the Midlands. More recently, they were in an area where over 1,000 doodlebugs were intercepted and destroyed, either by RAF fighters or by a concentrated belt of low-level anti-aircraft guns. All that was over now. Life was returning to normal. I was glad to be down on a farm again.

On 10 April, the third day of my visit, I borrowed Peter's bicycle and rode over to Canterbury. The city had suffered grievously from three Baedeker raids. There were bomb site gashes across the mediaeval streets I remembered from 1939 but the cathedral looked magnificent, with Chaucer's 'noblest tower in Christendom' triumphantly erect.

While I was walking through the cloisters I noticed a couple of women wandering around. One came up to me: 'Do you know where the tomb of Thomas à Becket is, please?' she asked. 'It was destroyed,' I replied. Before I could say 'by Henry VIII' she called across to her friend, 'It's no good looking, Mary. It's been bombed.' I did my best to place blame for the tomb's destruction on Henry's Erastian thoroughness but I am not sure the impromptu history lesson convinced them.

In Oxford the previous autumn – 26 October, to be precise – I was dismayed to see beside a newspaper stand in St Aldate's a stark placard – 'Archbishop Dies'. Both at York and Canterbury William Temple was a hero of mine, an outspoken critic of social injustice who, for much of the past year, had been urging the government to grant immediate asylum to persecuted Jews. He was enthroned at Canterbury in 1942, a few weeks before the worst Baedeker raid, and the burdens of the war years imposed a strain on his heart. Now the cathedral was preparing for the enthronement in eight days' time of his successor, the Bishop of London, Dr Fisher. I cycled back to Hothfield sad that William Temple was not still at Canterbury to see the spring flowers of peace coming into bloom. I am certain that with his understanding of the nation's social needs he would have rooted out many thorns among them.

When I returned home I typed my impressions of war-ravaged Canterbury into an article of some 500 words and sent it, unsolicited, to the *Evening Standard*. It appeared in the midday edition on 18 April, the eve of Dr Fisher's enthronement, but it was dropped from the rush-hour edition because of grim news from Germany, where three days previously British troops had discovered the horrors of Belsen concentration camp. I was on the train to Portsmouth when the article was printed and did not see it until two days later when my father enclosed it in a letter. A colleague at his office had passed the paper to him, with a 'Is that your boy?' In due course I received a cheque for eight guineas – more than £40 by 2015 values – my first literary fee.

At Portsmouth we joined UND cadets from Cambridge for a week aboard HMS *Foudroyant*, a 'wooden wall' frigate dating back to Trafalgar. For the first time we slept in hammocks.

We spent two mornings on the parade ground at HMS *Excellent*, the gunnery establishment on Whale Island, marching and square-bashing to shake off Oxonian sloth and tighten round shoulders. From the masthead of a cruiser I looked out over Nelson's *Victory* to the battleship named after him as she lay at anchor off Spithead. In 1937 she was there as flagship for the Coronation Review and I still associated her with Tommy Woodrooffe's 'the fleet's lit up' commentary, although during the war her 16-inch guns had thundered out many times in the Mediterranean and covered landings at Salerno and on the Normandy beaches. One afternoon we left Portsmouth and went by train to Devonport. For the first time I crossed the River Tamar into Cornwall on the Torpoint ferry and saw broken houses and empty spaces along the riverside, a legacy from five heavy air attacks in May 1941. HMS *Raleigh* was almost a mile south of the ferry, off the road to Antony and Looe. It had the customary cantonment of huts, an asphalt parade ground with a high ship's mast, and beside it a small cinema and even a bookshop. Our basic naval training, ashore and on the waters of the inlet known as the Hamoaze, was left to a patient and sympathetic petty officer, while our divisional commander, the fittingly bearded Lieutenant Neate, ensured we appeared shipshape. There was plenty of running water, essential not only for showers but for washing clothes. Spring turned very hot that year and from 1 May onwards we had to wear a clean white front every morning. One hut was set aside for 'education' and there we could catch up with wireless news from a fast-changing Europe. 'I doubt if we shall ever be in a more comfortable camp,' I wrote in a letter home. 'The countryside around it looks glorious in this weather.'

Each day of our second week at *Raleigh* brought dramatic news. On Monday 30 April came confirmation from Milan that Mussolini and his mistress had been shot by Italian partisans and their bodies hung upside down before a jeering crowd in the Piazzale Loreto, one of the city's smaller squares. In Berlin the Russians were said to have reached the Brandenburg Gate. Where was Hitler, we wondered? Had he flown out of the city to a mountain redoubt in Bavaria? Our speculation ended on 1 May, when a broadcast on German radio announced that 'the Führer had died fighting the enemy in Berlin' on the previous afternoon. He had appointed Grand Admiral Doenitz his successor. All German troops in Berlin surrendered to Marshal Zhukov on 2 May. The Russians reported, correctly, that Hitler had shot himself but we had to wait two years before Hugh Trevor-Roper's *The Last Days of Hitler* provided a detailed account of life, marriage and death in the bunker of the Reich Chancellery.

The war dragged on for more than a week after Hitler's death. We heard of German commanders surrendering independently in southern Austria, Italy and the Netherlands, reaching a climax with the surrender of all troops in northern Europe to Field Marshal Montgomery on Lüneburg Heath on 6 May. At last on 7 May came the news which we were waiting to hear. In the small hours of the morning Grand Admiral Doenitz and General Jodl had signed a document at Eisenhower's headquarters in Rheims surrendering all remaining German fighting forces on land, sea and air. The following day, 8 May, would be celebrated throughout Britain and Western Europe as Victory in Europe Day.

All training was suspended for two days. Unfortunately on VE day itself I was on duty watch and had to remain 'on board' officially. The broadcast of the morning's celebrations in Westminster relayed over the camp's tannoy and I was surprised that the day had started with rain in London as it was gloriously sunny in Devon and Cornwall. In the evening some of us found it easy to slip 'ashore' and join revellers in Torpoint. I felt that should Lt Neate spot us it would be with a Nelsonian blind eye.

Next afternoon I took a bus up to Tavistock and walked to a wooded point where a stream sparkles down from the moors to broaden the modest River Tavy almost imperceptibly. I enjoyed a cream tea sitting under the trees, thinking of Merthen and trying to decipher the 'Intruder sighted' emergency bird warnings which alone broke this perfect peace. But war's aftermath soon returned to my thoughts; on the ride back to Plymouth I half expected to see activity in the Hamoaze as there was a rumour that surrendered U-boats would be escorted up to Saltash. None materialised, however.

In Plymouth preparations were well advanced for a second night of celebration. Everything was centred on the Hoe, the historic promontory where Drake famously found time to finish a game of bowls before sailing out to face the challenge of the Spanish Armada. A pyre of wood, presumably from bomb sites or felled trees, was climbing higher, foot by foot, until I wondered if Hitler was to be burnt in effigy. Later in the evening I met John Locke, my friend from Oriel days, and we returned to the bonfire, now more like an Armada beacon than a heretic's stake. We joined dancers on the Hoe. Sometimes we linked together and moved forward and back in a long chain, as I have since seen Serbs and Greeks do with far more rhythm and natural musicality. An inevitable conga followed and then we watched couples happily jitterbugging. I would rather have joined friends in Ilford but this was a merry way to release our pent-up emotions of relief. There was much raucous singing, with 'Roll out the Barrel' a favourite. The local MP, Nancy Astor, ardently teetotal, looked down from her house high up on the Citadel. In a letter to Aunt Margaret on Saturday, 12 May, I wrote, 'I don't know what she thought of her constituents but it struck me her temperance efforts seem to have had little effect.' I then added with some irritation, 'Tomorrow some of us hoped to catch the bus to Looe but we have to march through Torpoint in a Victory Thanksgiving.'

I should not have written so peevishly, for ahead of me was a ceremony striking in its emotional simplicity. As we marched down the hill I suddenly thought of the honour bestowed on us. After only a few weeks in the navy we not-so-Able Seamen represented hundreds of sailors who had trained like us at *Raleigh* and sailed out to fight in seas and oceans around the globe but had never come back to a home port. We halted on what I assume was a cleared bomb site, looking out across the Tamar to Devonport. Would so compact an arena live up to the occasion, I wondered?

My doubts were soon dispelled. The Chairman of the District Council spoke splendidly. He recalled the communal spirit during the nights of bombing. Then, his voice rising to Laurence Olivier pitch, he praised 'our brave firemen who said, "Torpoint shall not burn" and saved us from destruction'. These words struck to the heart. I thought of the firefighters' bravery in the blazing streets of the London Blitz. Most of the war I had spent in a metropolis threatened with bombardment and it was salutary to hear how a small community faced a similar challenge from the skies, and survived. As we marched back up to *Raleigh* I felt privileged to have shared Torpoint's day of thanksgiving.

Four evenings later my favourite 'pipe and slipper man', J.B. Priestley, broadcast a *Journey into Daylight*, his postscript to the *Postscripts* that had bolstered our spirits in the dark days of 1940. 'We are,' he said, 'like people who have been travelling all night in a railway carriage and, at last, see a thin, grey daylight round the edge of the blinds, feel the speed of the train slackening, begin to move cramped legs, stretch ourselves and yawn.' There was nothing overtly political in his message but the broadcast echoed the mood around us. The experience of war had altered our character. 'We are a better people than we thought ourselves to be,' he concluded.

He might have added 'and a more critical people too'.

Perhaps there should have been a porter on the platform calling, 'All change here'. Voters would soon be going to the polls in the first General Election for ten years and there were signs they were 'fed up with the old gang'! Common Wealth, an independent left of centre party founded by Sir Richard Acland in 1943, had already won three by-elections, the most sensational at Chelmsford only a month before VE day when the government lost this rock solid Essex Tory seat by 6,400 votes. Bevin and Morrison encouraged Attlee to take Labour out of the wartime coalition, and on 23 May Churchill formed a caretaker government, pending a General Election.

Eighteen-year-olds were not enfranchised for another quarter of a century and so I did not have to decide which party to support but I followed the vote-chasing campaign closely in the papers or on the wireless. Churchill gave the first political broadcast on 4 June. 'A free parliament is odious to the socialist doctrinaire,' he told us. 'To silence expressions of public discontent,' he claimed, 'they would have to fall back on some form of Gestapo, no doubt very humanely directed in the first instance.' I could hardly believe that I was listening to such nonsense from the warrior leader I revered.

I did not hear any other party political broadcasts, for we still had naval training duties to fulfil, but at the end of the first week *Picture Post* included a four-page upbeat report of the Labour Party Conference at Blackpool by Maurice Edelman which made stimulating reading. He wrote of the optimism and vigour of young delegates fresh from battle. They included a Major Denis Healey who had flown home from Italy. In 'a passionate speech he declared, "the struggle for socialism in Europe has been hard, cruel, bitter and bloody... After paying this price, our comrades won't let go".' The conference let Labour make 'its plans for power', Edelman wrote; Bevin said he would seek understanding with Moscow; Morrison promised 'great changes in our time on home policy'. Accompanying photographs show a party confident of victory. Had I been enfranchised, I am sure that I would have voted Labour. On 3 July Churchill made a pugnacious speech at Walthamstow on the fringe of Attlee's constituency; he was booed and hissed. Two days later Britain went to the polls but the ballot boxes remained sealed for three weeks, to allow for the arrival of voting papers from the armed services overseas. Not until 25 July were the seals broken; the counting of votes began and continued well into the night. It soon became clear Labour had gained a landslide victory, winning 146 more seats than the combined Opposition. Churchill stood down, and on 27 July Clement Attlee became the first socialist prime minister in a government with an overall majority. I sensed that this marked the end of an era. The Europe I knew as a boy was gone. Few mourned its passing.

SOURCE REFERENCES

Fuller details of books cited below can be found in the Select Bibliography. The initials ODNB refer to entries in the *Oxford Dictionary of National Biography* (2004).

Chapter 1: What's in a Name?

This chapter relies heavily on *The Times*, especially for 28 September (including shipping details) and 1 October 1926. See also Cobham's *Australia and Back,* and for wireless development see Asa Briggs' *The Golden Age of Broadcasting*.

For more information about Reith personally see his autobiography *Into The Wind* and the biography by McIntyre.

Chapter 2: Across the Roding

I found Ilford's architectural and historical past extensively covered in *London: East Vol 5*, with Gants Hill, pp. 329-30, and central Ilford, pp. 335-50, including Valentine's Park and mansion, pp. 332, 344-47.

Top of bus knowledge of London has been taken from Krupskaya's *Memories of Lenin,* pp. 46-7.

For the the Ilford murders, I supplemented Rene Weiss's *Criminal Justice* with the later information in his entry on Edith Thompson in ODNB.

Chapter 3: Willingly to School

Most of this chapter is based on personal memorabilia, including the photograph of Empire Day 1933 at Valentine's School. For Madeleine Carroll, David Parkinson in ODNB, which includes an American reference to her in 1936 as 'The most beautiful woman in the world'. For Bancroft's School, see histories by Coult & Francombe and by Kevin Wing and the memoirs of Denis Quilley in *Happiness Indeed: An Actor's Life*.

For Sylvia Pankhurst's life and influence see the ODNB entry by Professor June Hannam.

Chapter 4: Children's Hours

For information on Reith see his *Into the Wind* and the McIntyre biography, *The Expense of Glory*.

For Derek McCulloch, see Ian Hartley's *Goodnight Children Everywhere* and the ODNB entry by Jeff Walden.

For Stephen King-Hall see the ODNB entry by E.R. Thompson, revised by M.C. Curthoys. I wrote an account of my visit to Broadcasting House soon afterwards and in

1970 discussed the Askeytoff incident with Arthur Askey at the Savage Club.

Asa Briggs' *The Golden Age of Wireless* places BBC programmes in their context, but he says little about Children's Hour.

Chapter 5: The King Riding By

The principal sources for this chapter are the official life of King George V by Harold Nicolson and Kenneth Rose's less formal biography. See also James Pope-Hennessey's *Queen Mary 1867-1953*, especially the diary entries, Philip Ziegler's *Edward VIII: The Official Biography* and Lockhart's biography of Archbishop Lang, which all have material on his last days.

The *New Statesman* of 23 January 1936 paid King George an unexpected tribute.

Chapter 6: Crown Imperial

The works by Pope-Hennessey, Ziegler and Lockhart cited above are relevant for the whole chapter.

Roy Hattersley's *The Locust Years* is good on the abdication crisis.

J.W. Wheeler-Bennett's official life of George VI includes entries from the King's diary.

For the Spithead commentary on the naval review, I have transcribed a recording of the commentary heard on the radio in 2010.

Chapter 7: Foreign Shores

Barrie Pitt's *Zeebrugge, St George's Day, 1918* is the fullest account yet published of the raid that so interested me as a schoolboy.

My work, *The Salient*, pp. 203-4, describes the impact of tourism on Ypres in the 1930s.

For Clemenceau's life and legacy see the biography by David Watson.

For King Peter II's tragic boyhood see his memoirs – *A King's Heritage*.

Wheeler-Bennett's *King George VI* gives an account of the royal visit to Paris in 1938.

Lord Charles Williams' *Pétain* includes disparaging private remarks on the visitors made by the marshal.

Chapter 8: The Crooked Cross

See Chamberlain's 1933 letter to *The Times* in *The First Cuckoo*, a collection of letters to the newspaper edited by Kenneth Gregory.

The first four chapters of Martin Gilbert's *A History of the Twentieth Century Volume 2* covers Hitler's consolidation of his dictatorship, with particular attention to Nazi treatment of Jews, p. 14. See also the first two chapters of Ian Kershaw *Hitler 1936-1945*.

The smiling face of Germany in 1936-37 merits a separate chapter in Robert Rhodes James' *'Chips': The Diaries of Sir Henry Channon*.

Dan Waller's *Field of Shadow* is mainly concerned with cricket in Berlin but also touches on other sporting links between England and Germany. There is a fuller study of German cricket in Synge and Cooper's *Tales From Far Pavilions*.

For Cable Street, see Hattersley's *The Locust Years*, Cross's *The Fascists in Britain* and my work, *The East End*, pp. 134-5.

For the Charlie Goodman at Cable Street see the compilation edited by Nick Lowles, p. 77.

On Spain, see the updated 2001 edition of Antony Beevor's *The Battle for Spain*. See also Raymond Carr's *The Spanish Tragedy*.

On Picasso, see the biography and critical assessment by Roland Penrose. Reference to the Guernica mural at Oxford, and Trevor-Roper's reaction to it is referenced in Adam Sisman's *Hugh Trevor-Roper* p. 85.

The following offer a detailed treatment of events, which culminated in the Anschluss: Macartney and Palmer's *Independent Eastern Europe: A History,* pp. 372-4, *The Lands Between,* pp. 228-30, Brooke-Shepherd's *Anschluss: The Rape of Austria,* G.E.R. Gedye's *Fallen Bastion* and Schusnigg's *Austrian Requiem*.

On Halifax, see Andrew Robert's *The Holy Fox: A Life of Lord Halifax*.

For Eden, see the second volume of his memoirs, *Facing the Dictators: The Eden Memoirs, Volume 2*.

Chapter 9: 'A Quarrel in a Faraway Country'.

See *Independent Eastern Europe* cited above; Andrew Robert's and my work *Lands Between,* pp. 232-6, cover most of the issues raised. See also Beneš' *Memoirs,* Elizabeth Wiskemann's *Czechs and Germans* and Gilbert's *A History of the Twentieth Century,* pp. 190-96.

The relevant days' entries in Shirer's *Berlin Diary* are informative on the hostility of journalists to the Runciman mission.

For Arthur Bryant's consistent support of Hitler see the closing chapter of Andrew Robert's *Eminent Churchillians.* Robert Self's *Nevillle Chamberlain* is a good defence of the prime minister while also throwing light on his personality.

Chapter 10: Umbrella Year

The post-Munich parliamentary debate is best followed in Hansard, with Churchill's speech in full, pp. 364-74. Extracts are printed in Gilbert's *Power of Words,* pp. 200-05. Tom Harrison's *Picture Post 1938-59* describes the founding of the weekly, its rising popularity and the skill of Lorant, as well as reprinting many pages of photographs and trenchant comment.

Events, which culminated in Kristallnacht, are outlined and illustrated in Harrison's *Picture Post* for 26 November supplement Gilbert's *Kristallnacht.*

Chamberlain's visit to Rome see D. Mack Smith's *Mussolini*.

The best general treatment of the 1939 crises is in D. Cameron Watt's *How War Came*. Robert Self's biography of Chamberlain shows the prime minister's persistent hostility to Russia. Beck's arrogance permeates his memoirs in *Dernier Rapport*. In my work *Northern Shores,* pp. 314-22, I outlined his policy, partly from German sources that I had also used for the German naval reaction to the Memel crisis.

In *The Holy Fox* Andrew Roberts traces Halifax's influence on the abandonment of appeasement.

For the royal visit to Canada and the United States, see Wheeler-Bennett's *King George VI*.

See *Wisden Cricketers' Almanack 1940,* p. 273, for details of the ill-tempered county cricket match. For the construction and maiden voyage of the *Royal Daffodil,* see *The Times* 23, 24, 26 May 1939 with photographs.

Chapter 11: Happy Days

On historic Exmouth, see Christopher Long's *Exmouth Through Time*.

For the Southern Railway in Devon, see T.W.E. Roche's *The Withered Arm*.

To see more on the political background, see D.C. Watt and Beck's memoirs, which are cited above, supplemented by Namier's *Diplomatic Prelude*.

For the Anglo-French mission to Moscow, see my

Northern Shores, pp. 322-24. Nigel Nicolson's editing of *Harold Nicolson: Letters and Diaries* provides a clear, day-by-day account of the transition from holiday making to Emergency Power legislation.

For the extent of the new powers, see A.J.P. Taylor's *English History 1914-1945*.

Chapter 12: 'At War with Germany'

See Watt and Robert Self, cited above. Andrew Roberts' *Holy Fox* and Wheeler-Bennett provide more detail on the King's reaction and broadcast. For Churchill's activities see his *The Second World War*. For the first alert see Philip Ziegler's *London at War*, pp. 36-9. Details of the last pre-war county cricket match, *Wisden 1940*.

Chapter 13: 'A Dark, Cold Winter'

For naval matters, see Correlli Barnett's *Engage the Enemy More Closely*, and Marder's *Winston is Back*.

The chapter heading is from Churchill's speech honouring crews from the cruisers *Ajax* and *Exeter*: see Gilbert's *Power of Words*, pp. 234-37, for more information.

On ITMA see Kavanagh's *Tommy Handley,* Asa Briggs' vol.2 *The War of Words* pp. 237-39. Asa Briggs gives details of many British programmes, including ITMA, and assesses the effect of German propaganda broadcasts.

For reaction in Berlin, see Goebbels' *Diaries.*

For the BEF in France, see Dranchev and Todman's edition of the *Alanbrooke Diaries*.

On the war in Finland, see Trotter's *The Winter War.*

In *Northern Shores,* pp. 336-37, I examine events in Scandinavian waters prior to the assault on Norway.

Chapter 14: 'They're in Paris'

For information on Norway see *The Campaign in Norway* by T.K. Derry.

Correlli Barnett's *Engage The Enemy More Closely* is highly critical of Churchill. Sir John Colville's diary *The Fringe of Power* records his transition from a Chamberlain admirer to a devoted Churchillian. Extensive passages from Churchill's 1940 speeches are in Gilbert's *Churchill: The Power of Words,* pp. 244-77. Priestley's broadcasts are in his *Postscripts*.

The best general account of the campaign in Belgium and France is in Alistair Horne's *To Lose a Battle,* and Sebag Montefiore's *Dunkirk: Fight to The Last Man* is indispensable. For individual participants, see Danchev and Todman's *Alanbrooke War Diaries*; Weygand's *Rappellé au Service*; Guderian's *Panzer Leader,* pp. 33-54; Hamilton's *Monty: The Making of a General.*

I found Alexander Werth's diary *The Last Days of Paris* very moving.

Chapter 15: Vapour Trails Across the Sky

Of books entitled *The Battle of Britain* I found Overy's account the most comprehensive and judicious, while Deighton's work is good on fighter tactics and the comparative performance of opposing aircraft. For German invasion plans and hopes see Richard Cox's *Operation Sealion*; Kershaw's biography of Hitler cited above; Shirer's diary.

For the British response see Churchill's *The Second World War*, vol. 2, supplemented by Gilbert's *The Power of Words*, with 'the few' speech, pp. 241-45; Danchev and Todman's *Alanbrooke Diaries*; Colville's *Fringes of Power*; Hamilton's *Monty: The Making of a General;* L. Mosley's *Backs to the Wall*.

Andrew Roberts in *The Holy Fox* examines apparent wavering over peace overtures. Barnett is critical of the naval actions at Oran and Mers-el-Kebir in *Engage the Enemy*. On de Gaulle, see the first volume of *War Memoirs: The Call to Honour.* The best biography of de Gaulle is by Lacouture; the English edition is co-edited by the translator, Patrick O'Brian. I found the brief biography by Julian Jackson also very useful.

For Pétain, see Charles Williams' biography.

Chapter 16: London's Burning

The books cited above for the Battle of Britain overlap with this chapter too. Constantine Fitzgibbon's *The Blitz* remains the best basic account, supplementing T. O' Brien's *Civil Defence* and Titmus' *Problems of Social Policy*. My reminiscence of the first daylight attack on London can be compared with accounts in Ziegler's *London at War*, pp. 113-4. For cricket at Lord's see Stephen Chalke's article 'We were Prisoners no Longer', Wisden Cricketers' Almanack, pp 54-6. I have again drawn on the Danchev and Todman edition of Field Marshal Alanbrooke's diary, Colville's *The Fringe of Power* and the second volume of Harold Nicolson's diary. Asa Briggs' third volume, *The War of Words,* includes accounts of the bombing of Broadcasting House. R.D. Blumenfeld's letter about carol singers is included in Kenneth Gregory's selection *The First Cuckoo.* For events in Yugoslavia see Peter II's *A King's Heritage*; Hoptner's *Yugoslavia in Crisis* and my *The Lands Between,* pp. 252-54.

Chapter 17: War's Changing Fortunes

Churchill's broadcast of 22 June 1941: Gilbert's *The Power of Words,* pp. 284-87. For the German campaign in Russia see Guderian's *Panzer Leader*; Werth's *Russia at War*; Erikson's *The Road to Stalingrad*. See also the books on besieged Leningrad by Alan Wykes and by Harrison Salisbury. In regards to British Russophilia, see Ziegler's *London at War,* pp. 223-25.

I have transcribed Maisky's words from a British Movietone News film of the ceremony in Holford Square.

On Lubetkin's life and works see the entry in ODNB.

For Churchill's reaction to Pearl Harbor and to subsequent events in South-East Asia and the Pacific, see Gilbert's *The Power of Words,* pp. 289-312, and his speech of 23 April 1942 to a secret session of Parliament, pp. 312-16. See the criticism of Churchill's persistent illusion that Singapore was impregnable in Frank Owen's *The Fall of Singapore* and Thompson's *The Battle for Singapore.* For the St Nazaire raid see Ken Ford's *St Nazaire 1942.* Robin Neillander's *The Dieppe Raid* is a moving account; Colonel Stacey's *The Canadian Army 1939-1945* contains a dispassionate assessment of the disaster (the author was Canada's official war historian).

On the Brains Trust and other BBC innovations see Asa Briggs' *The War of Words.* For a curious response to the Baedeker raids see Ziegler's *London at War,* pp. 207-08. To find out more about Alamein and its aftermath, see Nigel Hamilton's *Monty,* the closing chapters of vol. 1 and opening of vol. 2.

Chapter 18: Long Days of Summer

For the summer evening entertainment, see Palmer's *The East End,* pp. 145-6. Ziegler's *London at War,* pp. 273-76 on sporting activities in general. On pp. 263-67 Ziegler assesses the enervating raids of early 1944. For A.L. Rowse see his *A Cornish Childhood* and Richard Ollard's *A Man of Contradictions*, a biography that should be supplemented by Valerie Jacob's *Tregonissey to Trenarren*.

For the landings in Normandy see Gilbert's *D-Day* and his *Routledge Atlas of the Second World War*. I benefitted in 2014 from BBC broadcasts of contemporary News bulletins that stirred my memory and helped make sense of my scattered notes. On the V-1 bombardment see David Johnson's *V for Vengeance* and Ziegler's *London at War* (1995), pp. 282-94. On Merthen see Rowse's *Tudor Cornwall* p. 155 and the three works by Charles Henderson, which include the region around Merthen and which are models of scholarly social history at its best. For the campaign in France see Stacey's *Canadian Army*; Nigel Hamilton's *Monty, Master of the Battlefield*; De Gaulle's *War Memoirs: Unity*; Larry Collins and Dominique Lapierre's *Is Paris Burning?*

For the V-2 rocket bombardment see Johnson's *V for Vengeance* and Ziegler's *London at War*, pp. 295-97.

Chapter 19: Gown and Bellbottoms

Nina Bawden's contribution to Ann Thwaites' *My Oxford* gives a good account of university life in the last two years of the war. See Humphrey Carpenter's *The Inklings* on Dundas-Grant and G.M. Trevelyan's *An Autobiography* recalls his kinsman Macaulay.

For A.J.P. Taylor, see his *A Personal History* and Adam Sisman's biography. The first volume of Charles Moore's biography of Margaret Thatcher clarifies her undergraduate view of politics. Antony Gibson's memoir *Of Didcot and the Demon* preserves his father's natural wit.

For Rowse's character, Ollard's *A Man of Contradictions,* supplemented by Halliday's *A History of Cornwall* .

For the high number of rockets falling on Ilford, see Ziegler's *London at War,* p. 298.

Chapter 20: Dancing on the Hoe

Gilbert's *The Routledge Atlas of the Second World War* well illustrates the converging army advances from east and west; see also Erickson's *The Road to Berlin* for more information. For Archbishop Temple, the biography by Iremonger provides good information. For the East Cornwall background to *Raleigh* see Halliday's edition of *Carew's Survey of Cornwall in 1602* as well as his history of the county. For events leading up to VE day see Trevor-Roper's *The Last Days of Hitler*; final narrative chapters of Kershaw's *Hitler: 1936-1945 Nemesis* and Gilbert's *The Day the War Ended.*

For Lady Astor see the entry on her in ODNB by Martin Pugh. Priestley's 'Journey into Daylight' was reprinted in *The Listener's* 50th anniversary issue, 18 January 1979.

For internal political matters see Henry Pelling's *Britain in the Second World War* and Taylor's *English History 1914-1945.*

For Churchill's Gestapo broadcast see Gilbert's *Power of Words* pp. 360-62, followed by the ill-received Walthamstow speech, pp. 362-66.

For Labour's plans for power, see *Picture Post*, 9 June 1945, in Hopkinson's *Picture Post 1938-50.*

SELECT BIBLIOGRAPHY

Unless otherwise indicated, the books listed below were published in London. The bibliography only includes works I used while writing this present book .

Barnett, Correlli *Engage The Enemy More Closely: The Royal Navy in the Second World War*. (1991)

Beck, Josef *Dernier Rapport* (Neuchatel 1952

Benes, Edvard *Memoirs* (1954)

Beevor, Antony. *The Battle for Spain. The Spanish Civil war 1936-39* (revised ed, 2006)

Briggs, Asa, A History of Broadcasting in the United Kingdom
vol 2 *The Golden Age of Broadcasting* (1970)
vol 3 *The War of Words* (1974)

Brooke-Sheppard, Gordon *Anschluss, The Rape of Austria* (1964)

Bullock, Alan *Hitler and Stalin* ((1981)

Bawden,Nina *In My Own Time* (1994)

Calder, Angus *The People's War. Britain 1939-1945* (1969)

Carr, Raymond, *The Spanish Tragedy. The Civil War and its Consequences* (1994)

Carpenter, Humphrey. *The Inklings, C.S. Lewis ,J R Tolkien, and Their Friends* (1978)

Churchill, Winston S., *The Second World War* Six volumes (1952-69)

Cobham, Alan *Australia and back in a Month* (1927)

Collins, Larry and Doinique Lapierre *Is Paris Burning?* (1991)

Colvillville, John *The Fringe of Power* (revised edition 2004)

Coult D.E. and Francombe D.C.R. *'Bancroft's School 1737-1937* (1937)

Cox, Richard , *Operation Sealion* (1970)

Cross, Colin *The Fascists in Britain* (1961)

De Gaulle, Charles *The Army of the Future* 1940).

    War Memoirs: Call to Honour 1940-1942 (1955)

    War Memoirs; Unity 1942-1944 (1959)

Deighton, Len *The Battle of Britain* (1980)

Derry, T. K. *The Campaign in Norway* (1982)

Eden, Anthony *Memoirs* vol. 2 *Facing the Dictators* (1976)

Erikson, John *The Road to Stalingrad* (1975)

    The Road to Berlin (1983

Fanchev, Alex and Odoman, Daniel (eds) Field *Marshal Lord Alanbrooke War Diaries 1939-45* (2001)

Ford, ken *St Nazaire 1942. The Great Commando Raid o*(2002)

Gedye, G. E. R. *Fallen Bastions* (1939)

Gibson, Antony *Of Didcot and the Demon. The Cricketing Times of Alan Gibson* (2009)

Gilbert, Martin *A History of the Twentieth Century* Vol 2 (1985)

The Second World War 1995)

The Day The The War Ended (1995)

D-Day (2004)

    Kristalnacht. Prelude to Destruction (2005)

    The Routledge Atlas Of The Second *World War* (2008)

Churchill. The Power Of Words (2012)

Goebbels Joseph (ed. Fred Taylor) *The Goebbels Diaries1939-1941* (1976)

Gregory, Kenneth (ed.) *The First Cuckoo. Letters To The Times Since 1900* (1975)

Guderian, Hans *Panzer Leader* (1958)

Gunther, John *Inside Europe* (1936)

Halliday F. E., *A History of Cornwall* (1959)
Richard Carew's Survey of Cornwall 1602 (rev. ed. (1969)

Hamilton , Nigel *Monty* vol. 1 *The Making of a General 1887-1942* (1981)
vol 2 *Master of the Battlefiefield 1942-44* (1983)

Hartley, Ian *Goodnight Children Everywhere* (1968)

Hattersely , Roy *The Locust Years* (2007)

Henderson, Charles *Essays in Cornish History* edited A.L. Rowse & M. Henderson (1935)

A History of the Parish of Constantine in Cornwall (Truro 1937)
Old Cornish Bridges and Streams (1972, reprint of 1928 edition)

Hopkinson, Tom(ed.) *Picture Post 1938-59* (1970),

Horne, Alistair. *To Lose A Batte, France 1940* (1969)

Iremonger, F, A . *William Temple, Archbishop of Canterbury . His Life And Letters* (1948)

Jackson, Julian *De Gaulle* (1990)

Jacob, Valerie *Trgonissey to Trenarren – A.L. Rowse The Cornish Years* (St Austell 2001)

Johnson, David *V for Vengeance* (1988)

Kavanagh, Ted *Tommy Handley* (1949)

Kershaw, Ian *Hitler 1936-1945 Nemesis of Destruction* (1998

, Nazheda, *Memories Of Lenin* (? 1935)

Lacouture, Jean and O'Brien, Patrick *De Gaulle. The Rebel 1890-1944* (1990)

Lockhart, J. G. *Cosmo Gordon Lang* (1949)

Long, Christopher K. *Exmouth Through Time* (2010)

Lowles, Nick (ed.) I *From Cable Street to Oldham* (2007)

Macartney C.A. and Palmer A.W. *Independent Eastern Europe, A History* (1962)

McIntyre, Ian. *The Expense Of Glory, Sir John Reith* (1993)

Marder, A. J 'Winston's back', separate supplement *English Historical Review* (1972)

Moore, Charles *Margaret Thatcher, The Authorised Biography, vol. 1, Not For Turning* (2014)

Mosley, Leonard *Backs to the Wall* (1971)

Namier L.B. *Diplomatic Prelude* (1950),

Neillander, Robin *The Dieppe Raid, the Story of the Disastrous 1942 Mission* (2002)

Nicolson, Harold *King George V* (1950)

Nicolson, Nigel(ed.) *Harold Nicolson. Letters and Diaries, 1929-1939* (1966)

O'Brien, Terence *Civil Defence* (1958)

Ollard, Richard, *A Man of Contradictions. A Life Of A.L. Rowse*(1999)

Overty, Richard *The Battle of Britain . Myth and Reality* (2010)

Owen, Frank *The Fall of Singapore* (rev. Edmund. 2002)

Palmer, Alan *The Lands Between* (1970)

  The East End (rev. Ed. 2000)

  Northern Shores (2005)

  The Salient (2007)

Pelling, Henry *Britain in the Second World War* (1970)

Penrose, Roland *Picasso . His Life and Work* (3rd ed. 1992)

Peter II, King of Yugoslavia *A King's Heritage* (1955)

Pevsner, Nicholas (ed. Bridget Cherry & C. O'Bren) *The Buildings Of England. . London 5: Eas*(1994).

Pitt , Barrie *Zeebrugge, St George's Day 1918* (1954)

Pope-Hennessy, James, *Queen Mary* (1959)

Priestley, J.B. *Postscripts* (1940)

Quilley, Denis *Happiness Indeed. An Actor's Life* (2007)

Reith, John *Into The Wind* (1949)

Rhodes James, Robert *'Chips', The Diaries Of Sir Henry Channon* (1967)

Roberts, Andrew, *The holy Fox, A Life of Lord Halifax* (1991)
    Eminent Churchillians (1994)

Roche, T. W. E. *The Withered Arm* (Bracknell, 1967)

Rose, Kenneth. *King George V* (1995)

Rowse A, L., *Tudor Cornwall* (1941)
    A Cornish Childhood (1943)

Salisbury, E. Harrison *The Siege of Leningrad* (1969)

Schussnigg, Kurt von *Austrian Eequiem* (1946)

Sebag Montefiore, Hugh *Dunkirk. Fight To The Last* (2006)

Self, Robert *Neville Chamberlain* (2006)

Shirer, William L *Berlin Diary 1934-1941* (1941)

Sisman, Adam, *A.J.P. Taylor. A Life* (1994)
    Hugh Trevor-Roper . The Life (2010)

Smith, D. Mack *Mussolini* (1994)

Stacey C. P. *The Canadian Army 1939-45* (Ottawa 1948)

Synge, Allen and Cooper, Leo *Tales From Far Pavilions* (1984)

Taylor A.J.P. *English History 1914-1945* (1965)
    A Personal History (1982)

Thompson, Peter, *the Battle for Singapore .* (2006)

Thwaite, Ann (ed.) *My Oxford* (1975)

Titmus,, Richard *Problems of Social Policy* (1950)

Trevelyan G. M. *An Autobigraphy, and Other Essays* (1949)

Trevor-Roper, Hugh *The Last Days of Hitler* (1949)

Trotter,W. R. *The Winter War* (2003)

Waddell, Dan *Field of Shadow* (2014)

Watson, David R. *Georges Clemenceau. A Political Biography* (1974)

Watt, Donald Cameron *How War Came* (2001)

Weiss, Rene *Criminal Justice* (1988)

Werth, Alexander *The Last Days of Paris, A Journalist's Diay* (2940)
    Russia at War 1941-45 (1964)

Weygand, Maxime *Memoires. Rapelle Au Service (Paris,1949)*

Wheeler-Bennett, J.W. *King George VI. His Life and Reign* (1966)

Williams, Charles *Petain* (2005)

Wing, Kevin *Bancroft's School 1737-1987* (1987)

Wiskemann, Elizabeth. *Czechs and Germans* (1938)

Wykes, Alan *The Siege of Leningrad* (1968)

Ziegler, Philip *Edward VIII* (1990)
    London at War(1995)